Beau Smith

WYNONNA EARP

THE YETI WARS

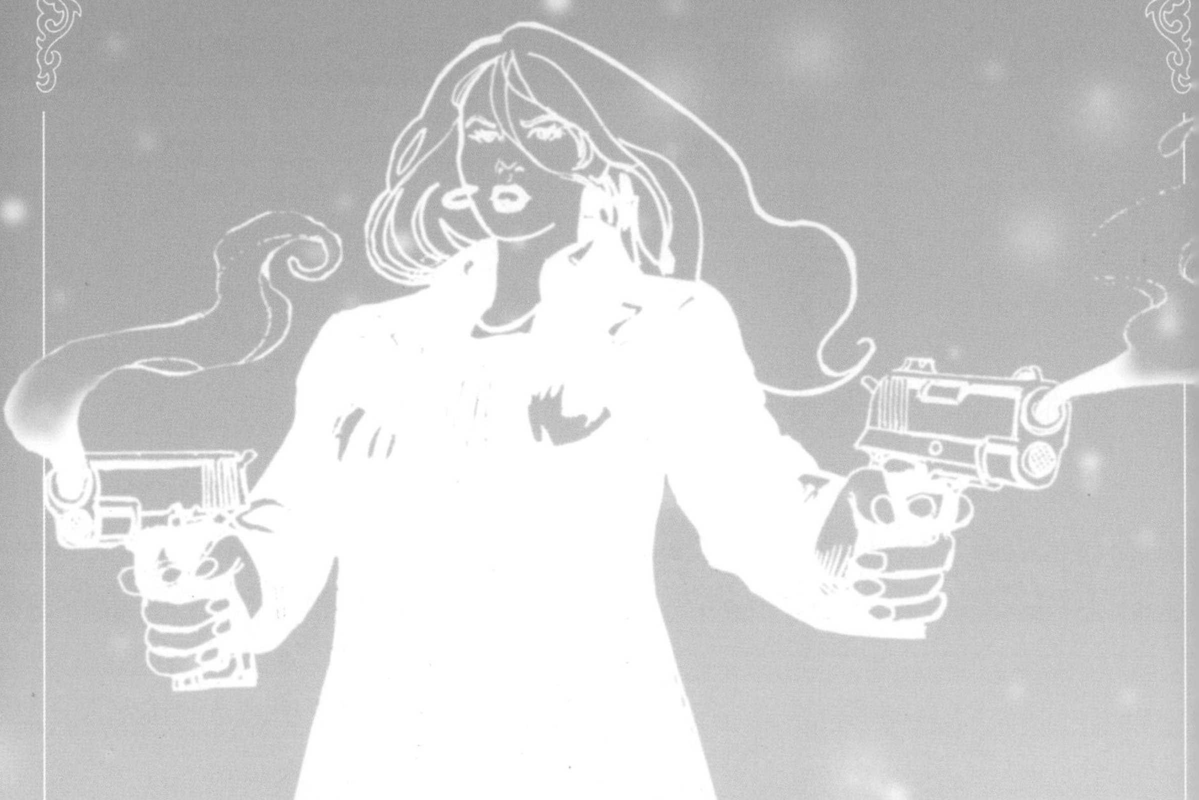

WYNONNA EARP: THE YETI WARS

WRITTEN AND CREATED BY **BEAU SMITH**
ART BY **ENRIQUE VILLAGRAN**
COLORS BY **KRIS CARTER**

WYNONNA EARP: BLOOD IS THE HARVEST

WRITTEN AND CREATED BY **BEAU SMITH**
ART BY **MANUEL VIDAL**
COLORS BY **ADRIANO HONORATO LUCAS**

COVER BY **ENRIQUE VILLIGRAN**
COVER COLOR ASSIST BY **LUCIANA GARCIA ARANGO**
EDITS BY **DENTON J. TIPTON**
DESIGN BY **SHAWN LEE**

www.**IDWPUBLISHING**.com

ISBN: 978-1-60010-807-5 13 12 11 10 1 2 3 4

IDW Publishing is: Operations: Ted Adams, CEO & Publisher • Greg Goldstein, Chief Operating Officer • Matthew Ruzicka, CPA, Chief Financial Officer • Alan Payne, VP of Sales • Lorelei Bunjes, Director of Digital Services • Jeff Webber, Director of ePublishing • AnnaMaria White, Dir., Marketing and Public Relations • Dirk Wood, Dir., Retail Marketing • Marci Hubbard, Executive Assistant • Alonzo Simon, Shipping Manager • Angela Loggins, Staff Accountant • Cherrie Go, Assistant Web Designer • Editorial: Chris Ryall, Chief Creative Officer, Editor-In-Chief • Scott Dunbier, Senior Editor, Special Projects • Andy Schmidt, Senior Editor • Justin Eisinger, Senior Editor, Books • Kris Oprisko, Editor/Foreign Lic. • Denton J. Tipton, Editor • Tom Waltz, Editor • Mariah Huehner, Editor • Carlos Guzman, Assistant Editor • Bobby Curnow, Assistant Editor • Design: Robbie Robbins, EVP/Sr. Graphic Artist • Neil Uyetake, Senior Art Director • Chris Mowry, Senior Graphic Artist • Amauri Osorio, Graphic Artist • Gilberto Lazcano, Production Assistant • Shawn Lee, Graphic Artist

INTRODUCTION
BY CHRISTOPHER FARNSWORTH

This was one of the real highlights of publishing a book for me. Out of nowhere, I got an e-mail from a guy who told me how much he liked it.

It was signed "Beau Smith, The Flying Fist Ranch."

I was sure this couldn't be the same guy who wrote *Guy Gardner: Warrior*, which took a second-string Green Lantern with a bowl cut and made him a badass. The same guy who took the Black Terror out of the '40s and set him down in a noir underworld a decade or so before anyone else thought of it.

But it was, in fact, the legendary Beau Smith.

If "legendary" strikes you as too strong a word, you don't know Beau.

How manly is Beau Smith?

Other people bite the caps off beer bottles; Beau Smith chews them like bubblegum.

You know what Beau Smith eats for breakfast? Anything he wants, pal.

Beau Smith is so manly his Rice Krispies don't say anything except, "Shhhh, here he comes."

Bullets don't bounce off Beau's chest; they hide in the gun, whimpering.

Mrs. Smith irons Beau's shirts—while Beau is wearing them.

Chuck Norris grew a beard to be more like Beau Smith.*

I should be clear: when I say "manly," I don't mean the wrecked, low-grade brand of testosterone that passes for manhood among too many frat-rats and "Jersey Shore" candidates. I'm talking about the possibly antique notion that being a man should include ideals like honor, honesty, courtesy, and courage. Other people have forgotten what it means. Beau hasn't.

In addition to his grueling schedule of manliness, Beau somehow finds time to write dozens of books, correspond with hundreds of friends and well-wishers, read thousands of pages, clean his guns, walk his dogs, and spread the word about classic comics and new works to the greater world. Beau is one of those rare and valuable people whose interests are as far-ranging as his energy and endurance.

That's what's most impressive to me about Beau. In our current excuse for a culture, the dominant pose is that of the been-there, done-that, too-cool-to-care hipster. Way too many of us—including myself—stand behind a protective sneeze-guard of irony, afraid to commit to anything for fear of the withering snark that's sure to follow in the comments section. Too many of us are embarrassed by our enthusiasms. (Hence the term "comics geek.")

Beau's not ashamed to love comics, and he's not afraid to stand up and cheer for them, even when other people might roll their eyes. The proof is all over the pages of *Wynonna Earp: The Yeti Wars*.

Wynonna Earp, a descendant of the famous lawman, is one of the few characters as manly as Beau, although wrapped in a much more attractive package. As an agent with the U.S. Marshal Service's Black Badge Division, she handles the crimes that involve things too dark for the general public to handle.

This time out, she faces truly abominable snowmen, deadly immortals, vampires, high-tech weapons, massive explosions, mad scientists, and Bigfoot.

Even if you don't hear the same echoes I did—from "Bigfoot and Wildboy," from *Jonny Quest*, from old westerns and classic horror flicks—you'll find something you love in here. Because at some point, you probably got into comics for the chance to see federal agents blow up monsters and a hot woman wield a sword made of metal scavenged from the Roswell crash. In other words, for the sheer, insane fun of it.

Beau delivers. He gives us a chance to stop being that hipster douchebag and simply enjoy ourselves again.

Beau Smith is so manly he's willing to show the whole world how much he loves everything strange and fantastic in comics. We could all learn something from him.

Enjoy.

Christopher Farnsworth
Los Angeles, CA, October 8, 2010

*Some of these jokes were shamelessly lifted from the comedian George Smilovici's routine, "I'm Tuff." I suspect it was actually about Beau, though I have no proof of that.

Christopher Farnsworth is the author of *Blood Oath*, a novel about Nathaniel Cade, a vampire sworn to serve the President of the United States. His next novel, *The President's Vampire*, will be out in April 2011.

ART BY ENRIQUE VILLAGRAN
COLOR ASSIST BY LUCIANA GARCIA ARANGO

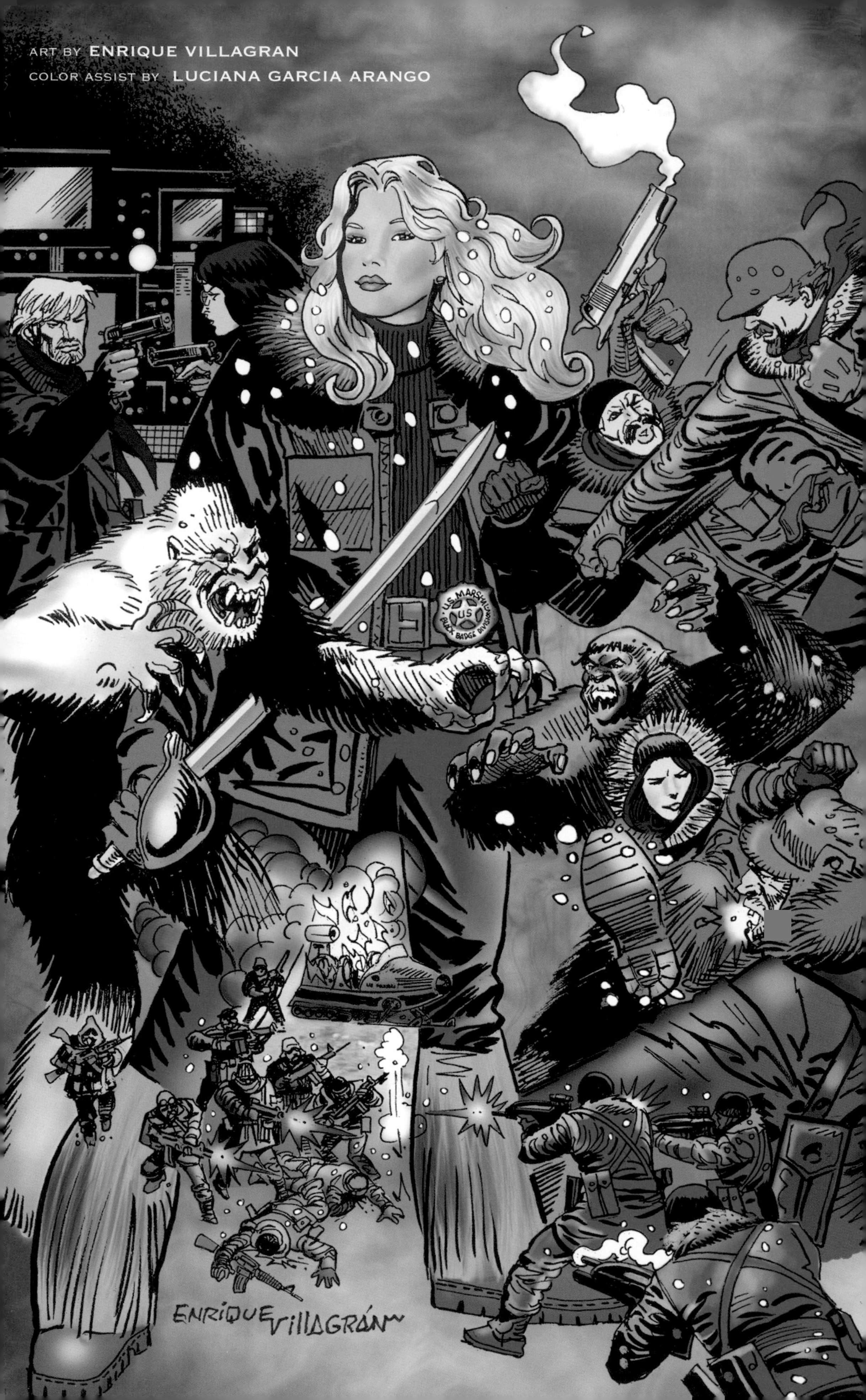
U.S. MARSHAL
US
BLACK BADGE DIVISION
ENRIQUE VILLAGRÁN

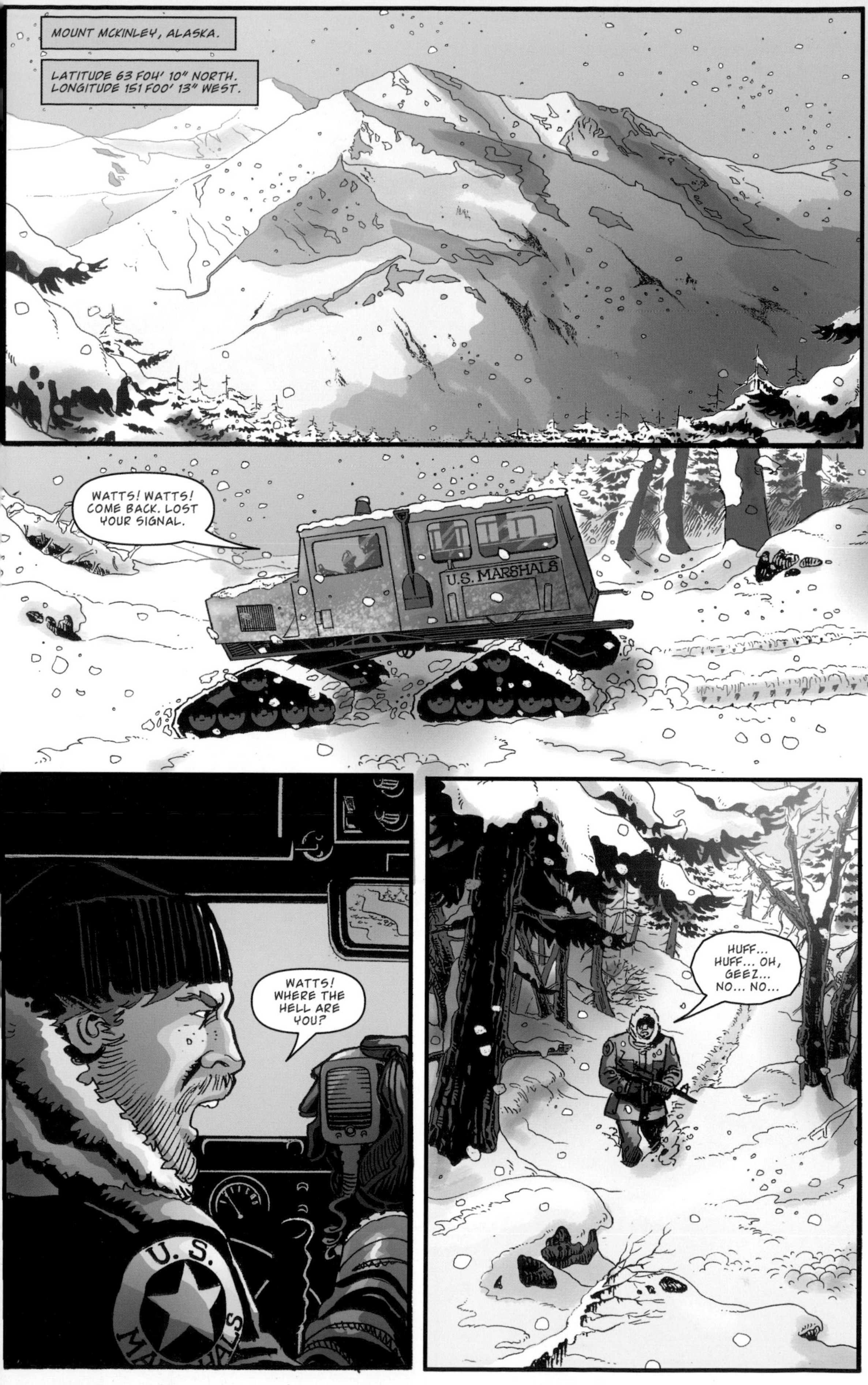
MOUNT MCKINLEY, ALASKA.
LATITUDE 63 FO4' 10" NORTH. LONGITUDE 151 FOO' 13" WEST.
WATTS! WATTS! COME BACK. LOST YOUR SIGNAL.
U.S. MARSHALS
WATTS! WHERE THE HELL ARE YOU?
U.S. MARSHALS
HUFF... HUFF... OH, GEEZ... NO... NO...

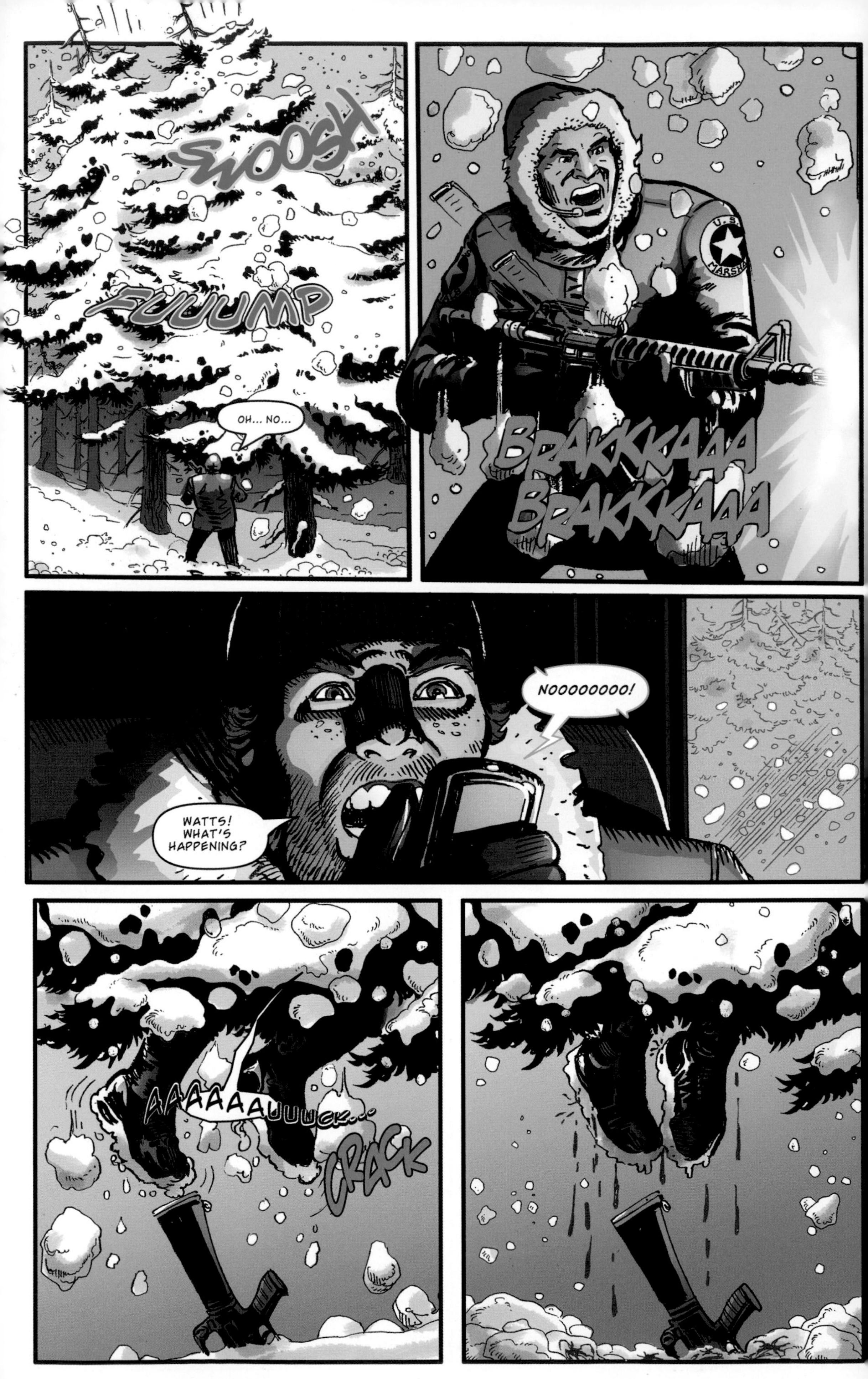
SWOOSH
FUUUMP
OH... NO...
BRAKKKAAA
BRAKKKAAA
NOOOOOOOO!
WATTS! WHAT'S HAPPENING?
AAAAAAUUUCK...
CRACK

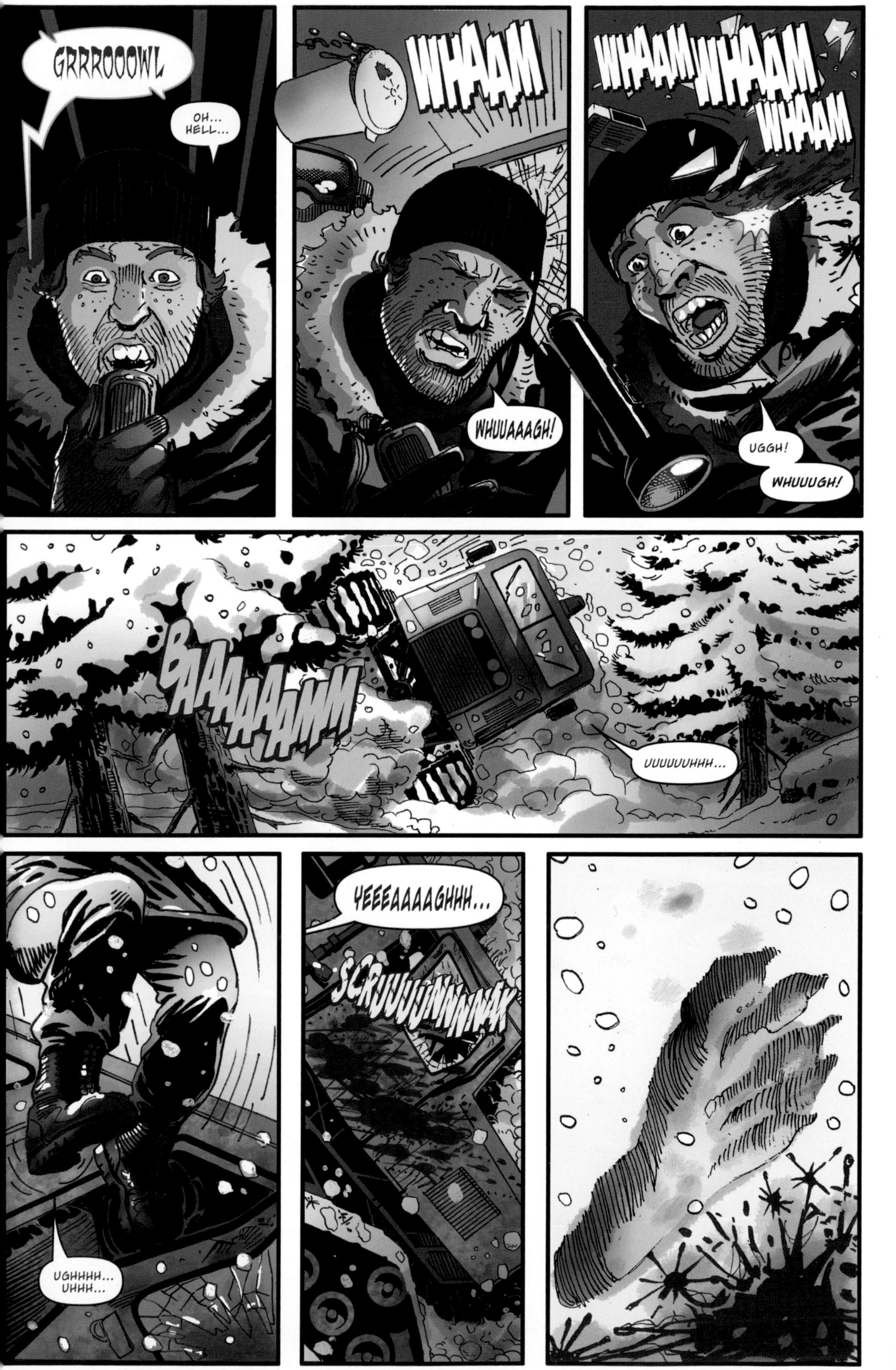
GRRROOOWL
OH... HELL...
WHAAM
WHUUAAAGH!
WHAAM WHAAM WHAAM
UGGH!
WHUUUGH!
BAAAAAAMM
UUUUUUHHH...
UGHHHH... UHHH...
YEEEAAAAGHHH...
SCRUUUUNNNNK

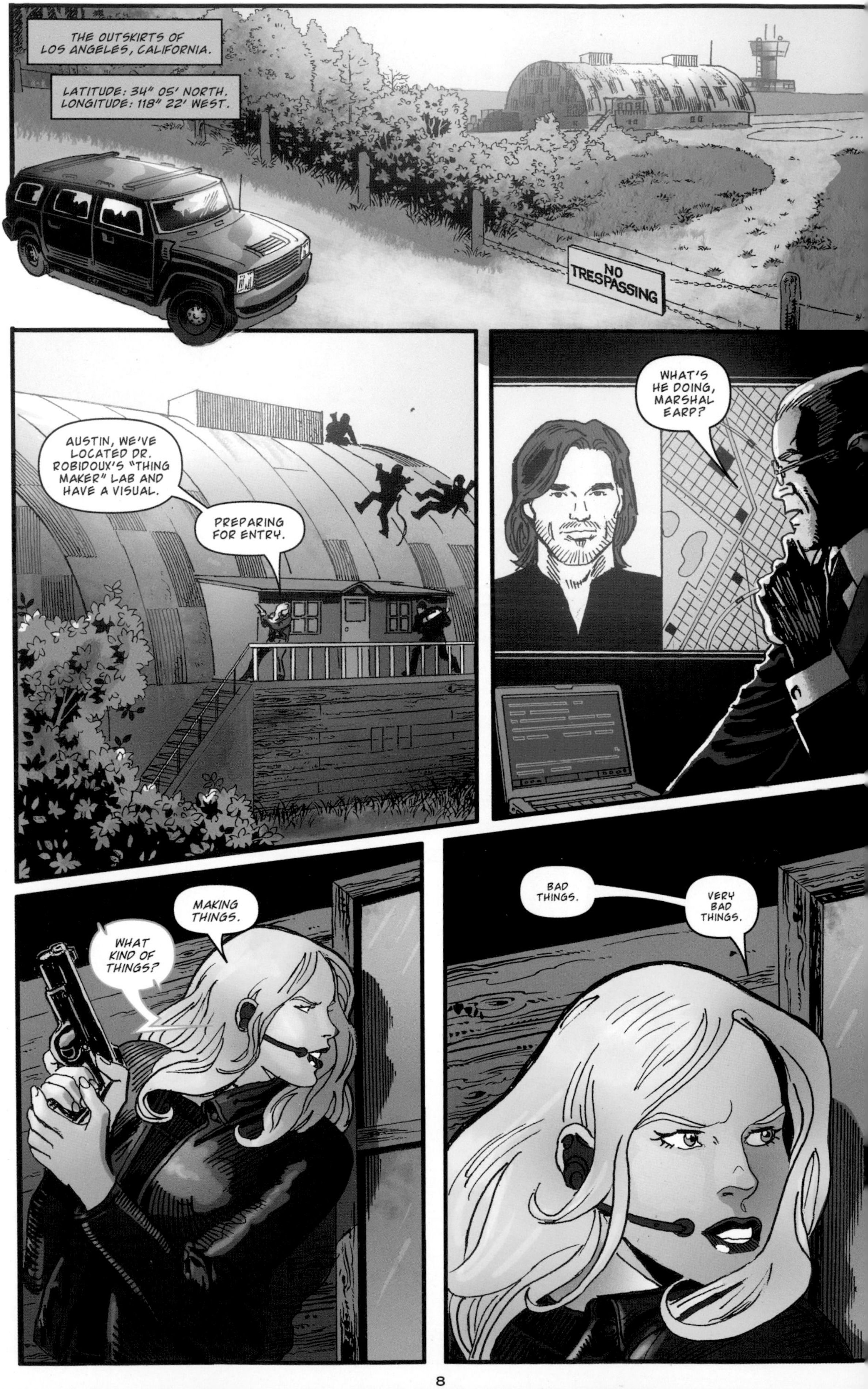
THE OUTSKIRTS OF LOS ANGELES, CALIFORNIA.
LATITUDE: 34" 05' NORTH. LONGITUDE: 118" 22' WEST.
NO TRESPASSING
AUSTIN, WE'VE LOCATED DR. ROBIDOUX'S "THING MAKER" LAB AND HAVE A VISUAL.
PREPARING FOR ENTRY.
WHAT'S HE DOING, MARSHAL EARP?
MAKING THINGS.
WHAT KIND OF THINGS?
BAD THINGS.
VERY BAD THINGS.

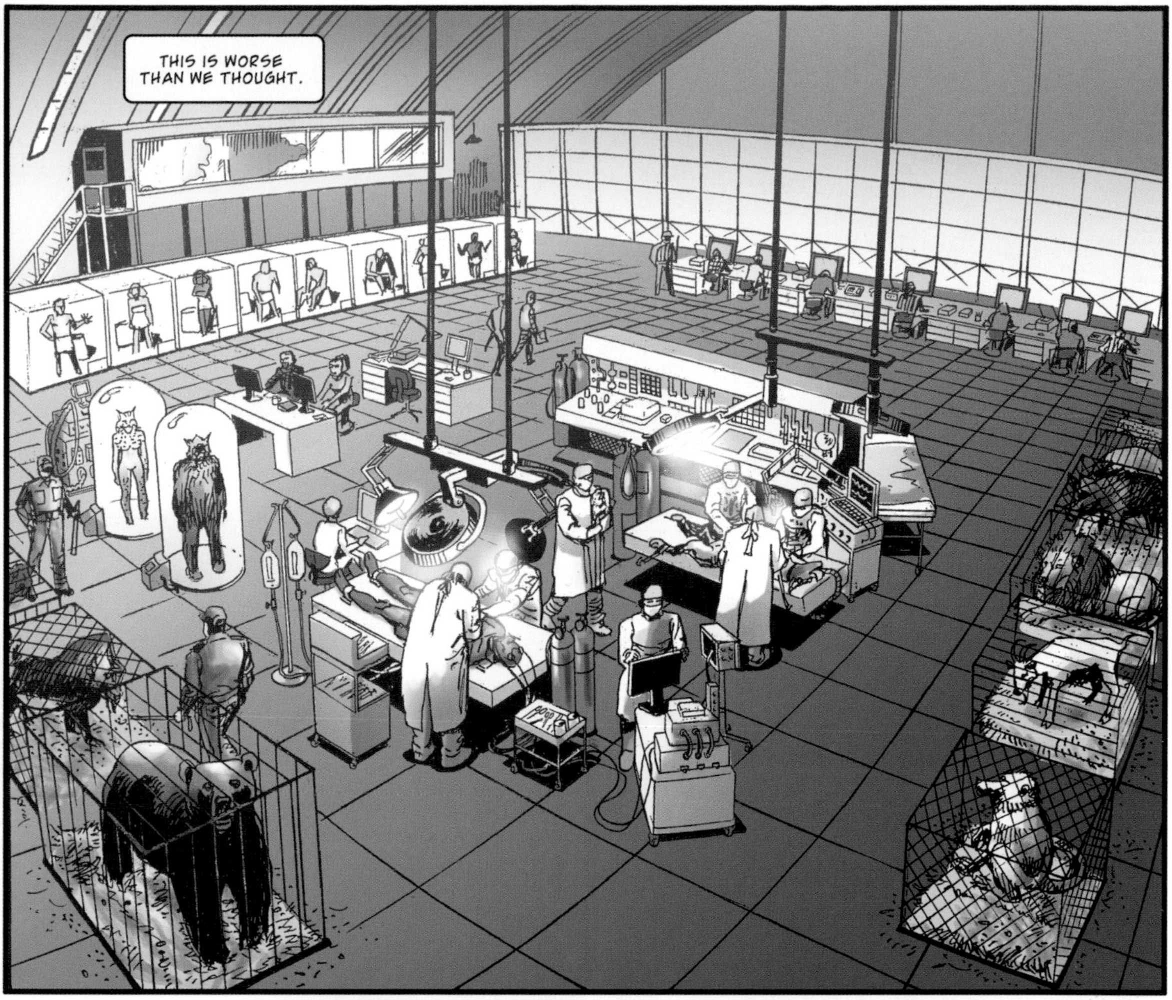
THIS IS WORSE THAN WE THOUGHT.

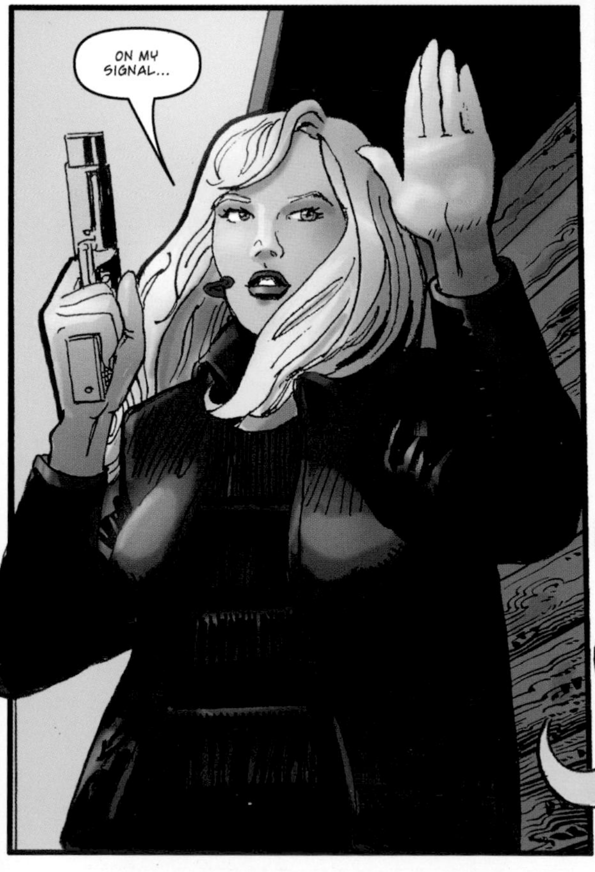
ON MY SIGNAL...

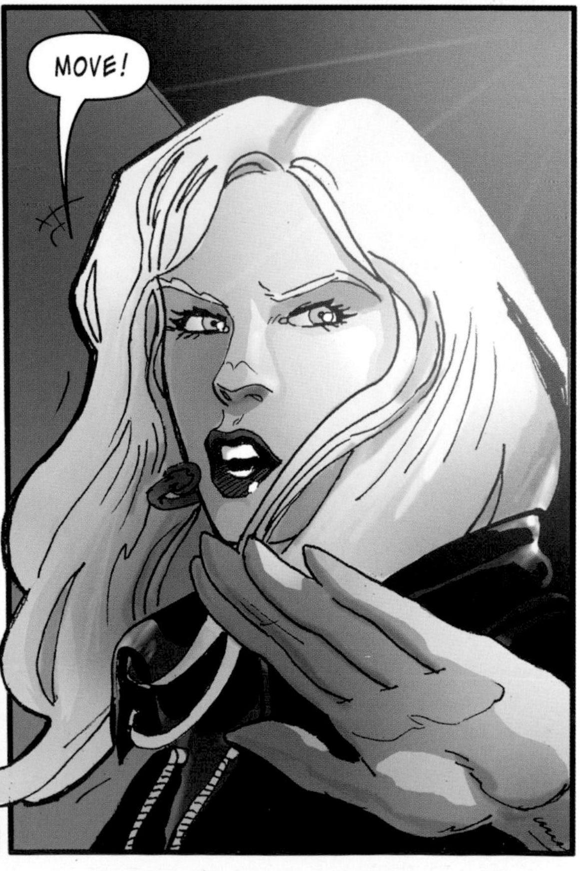
MOVE!

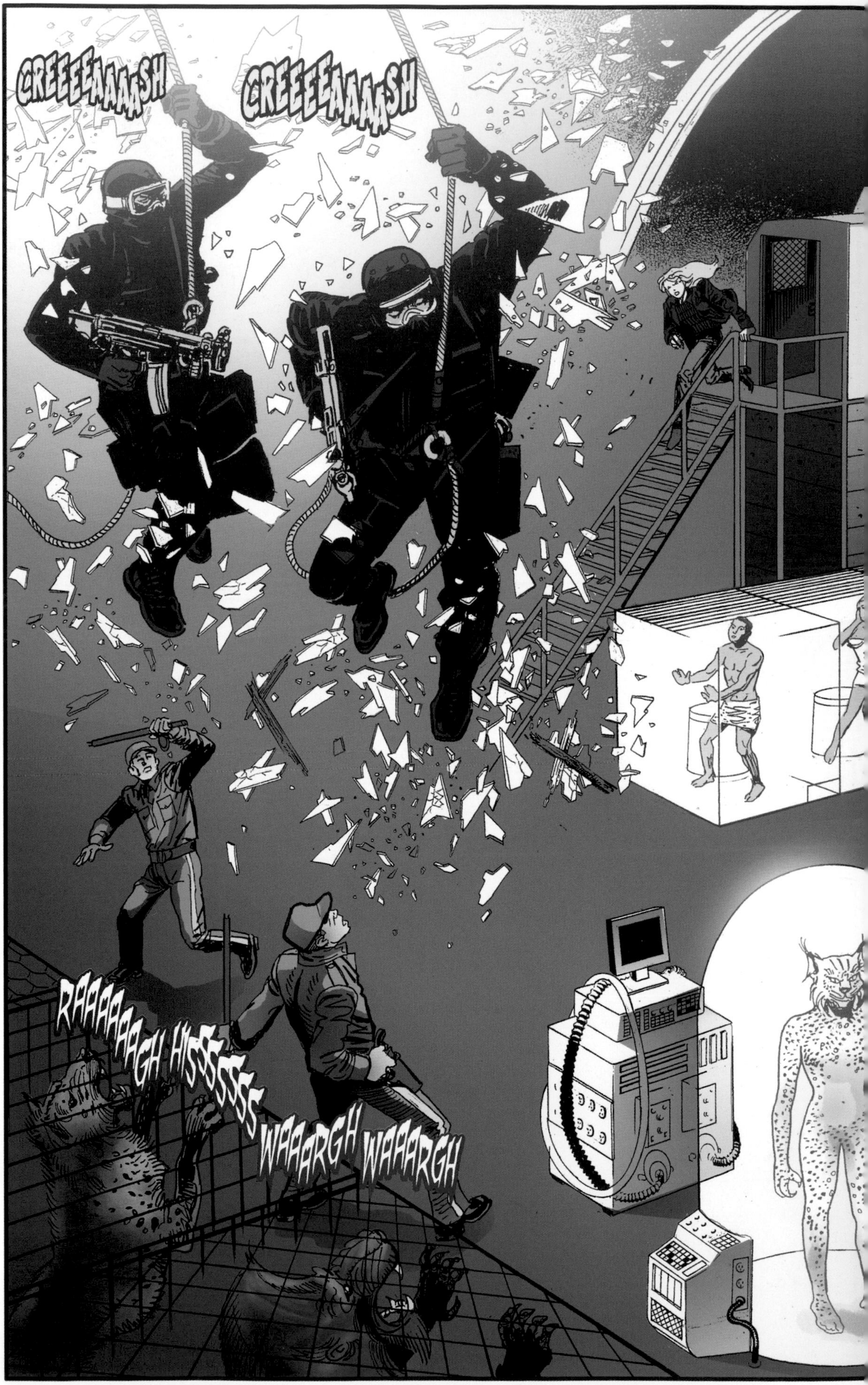
CREEEEAAAASH
CREEEEAAAASH
RAAAAAAGH HISSSSSS
WAAARGH WAAARGH

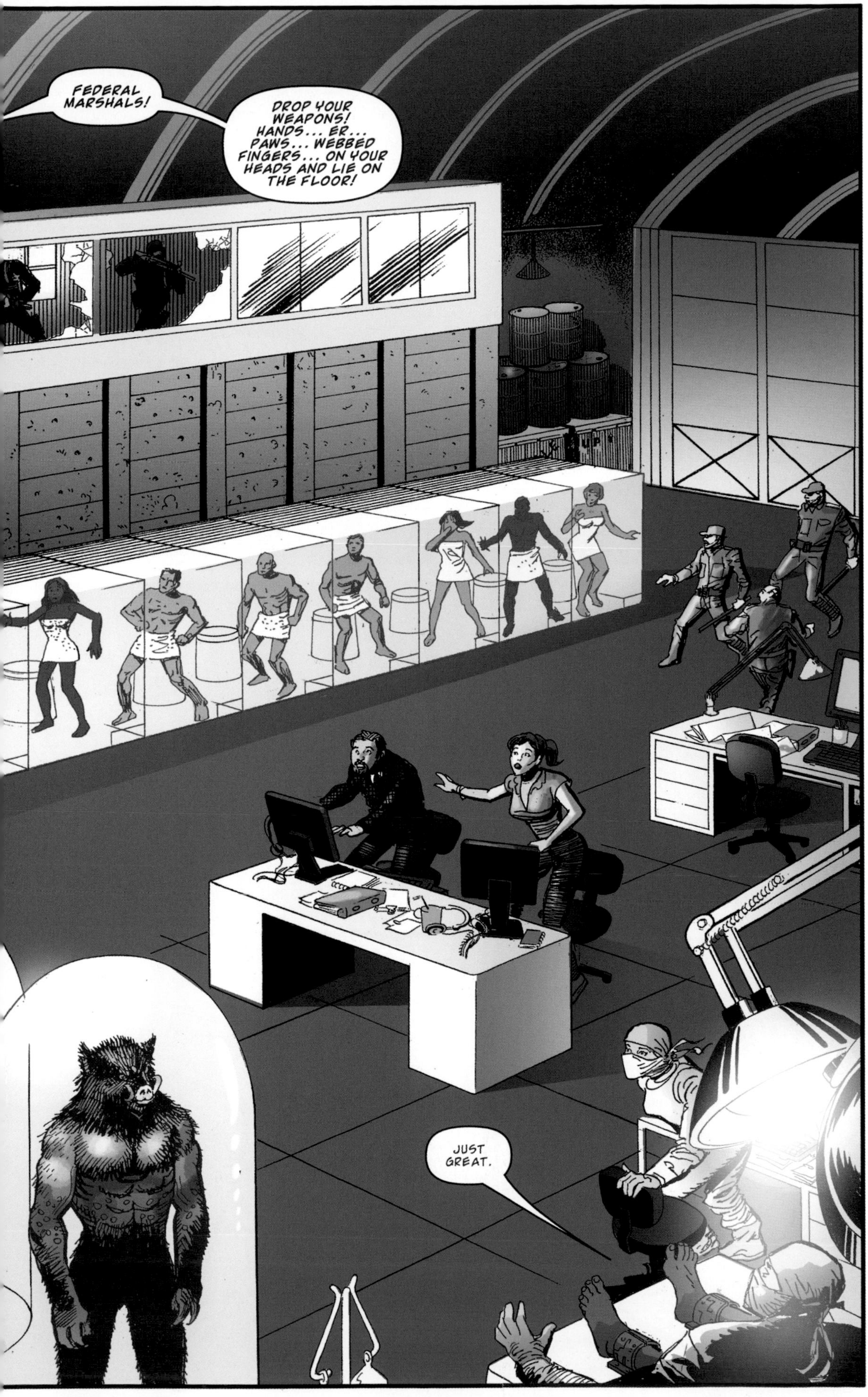
FEDERAL MARSHALS!
DROP YOUR WEAPONS! HANDS... ER... PAWS... WEBBED FINGERS... ON YOUR HEADS AND LIE ON THE FLOOR!
JUST GREAT.

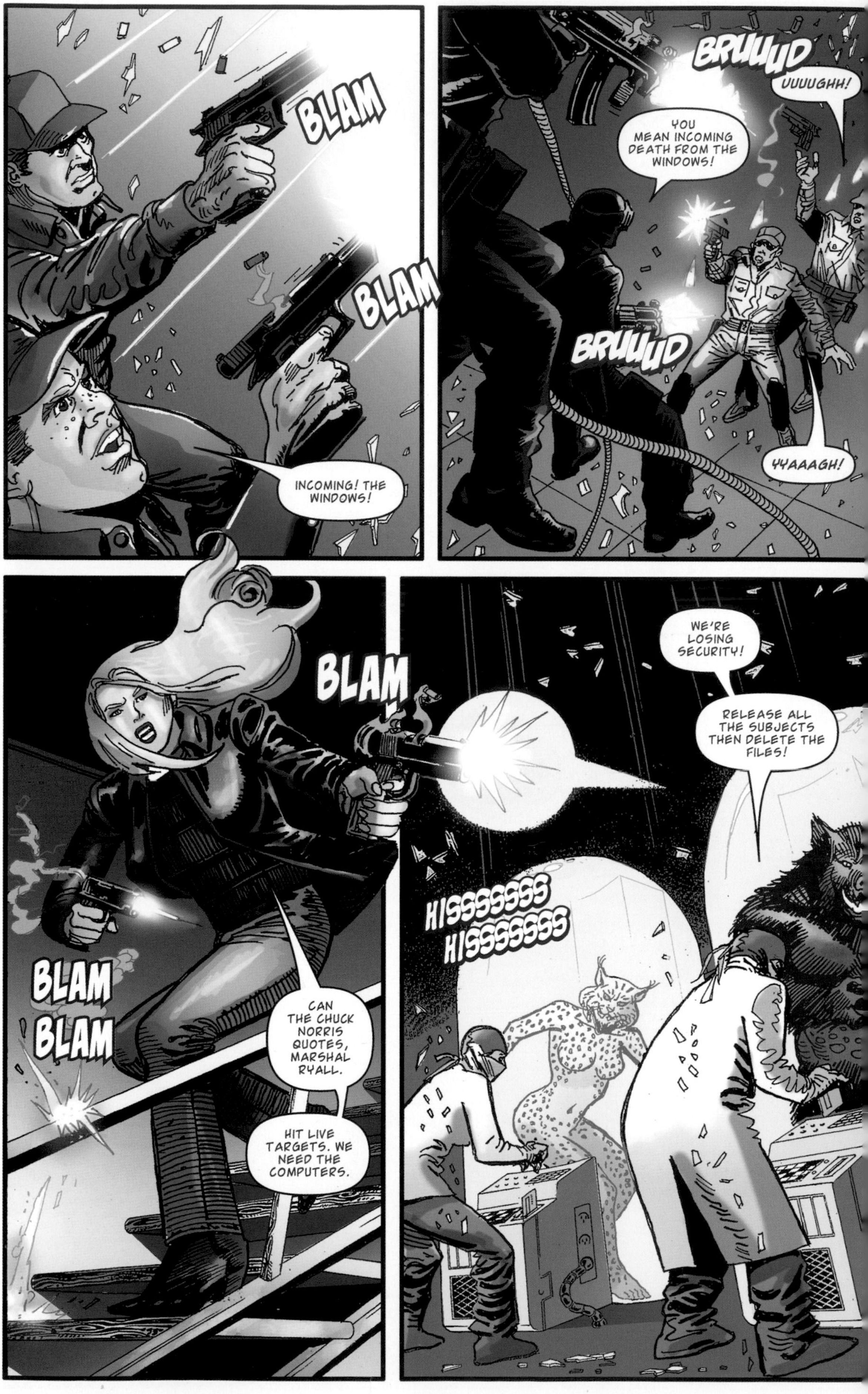

BLAM
BLAM
INCOMING! THE WINDOWS!
BRUUUD
UUUUGHH!
YOU MEAN INCOMING DEATH FROM THE WINDOWS!
BRUUUD
YYAAAGH!
BLAM
BLAM
BLAM
CAN THE CHUCK NORRIS QUOTES, MARSHAL RYALL.
HIT LIVE TARGETS. WE NEED THE COMPUTERS.
WE'RE LOSING SECURITY!
RELEASE ALL THE SUBJECTS THEN DELETE THE FILES!
HISSSSSSS
HISSSSSSS

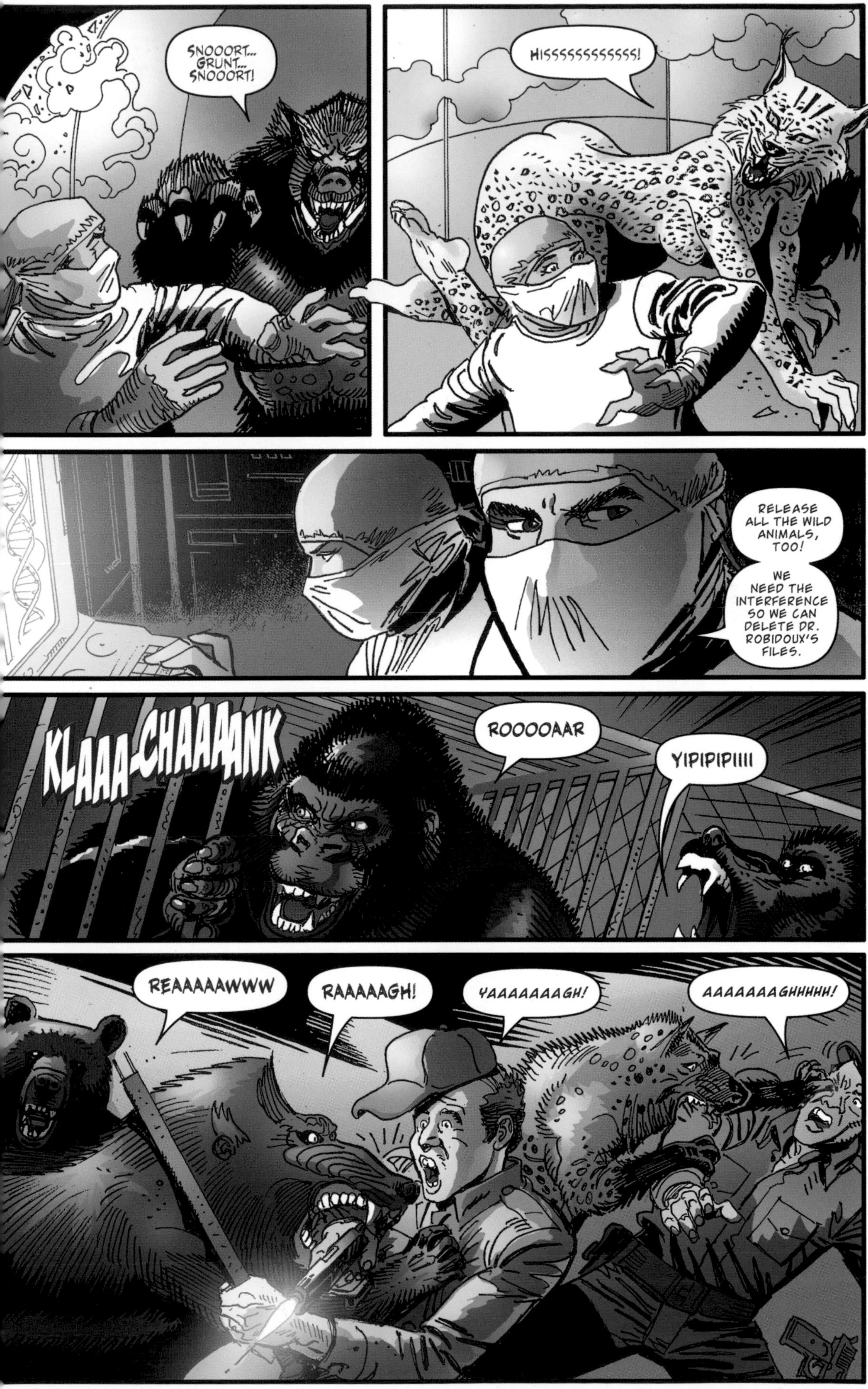
SNOOORT... GRUNT... SNOOORT!
HISSSSSSSSSSSS!
RELEASE ALL THE WILD ANIMALS, TOO!
WE NEED THE INTERFERENCE SO WE CAN DELETE DR. ROBIDOUX'S FILES.
KLAAA-CHAAAANK
ROOOOAAR
YIPIPIPIIII
REAAAAAWWW
RAAAAAGH!
YAAAAAAAGH!
AAAAAAAGHHHHH!

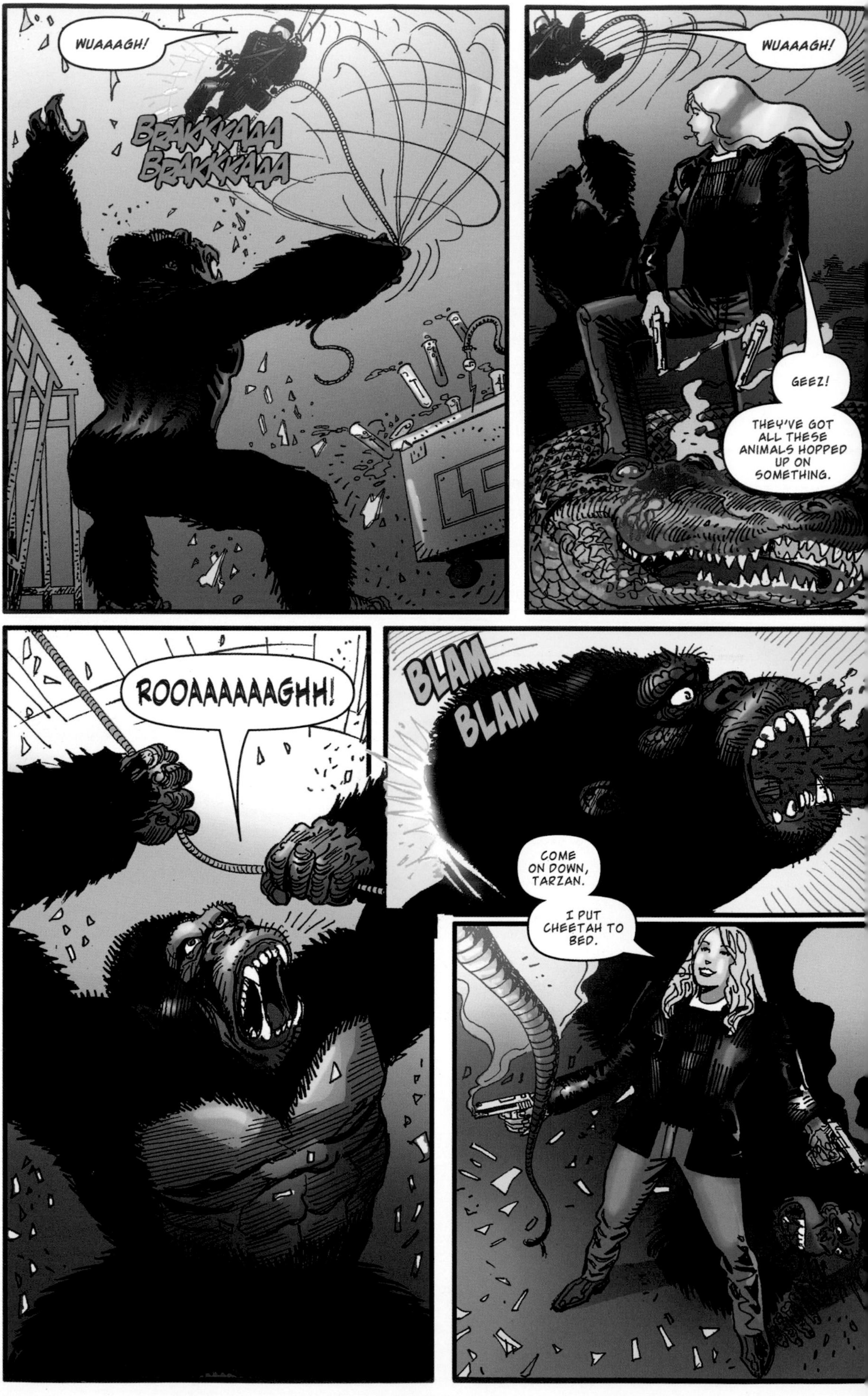
WUAAAGH!
BRAKKKAAA BRAKKKAAA
WUAAAGH!
GEEZ!
THEY'VE GOT ALL THESE ANIMALS HOPPED UP ON SOMETHING.
ROOAAAAAAGHH!
BLAM BLAM
COME ON DOWN, TARZAN.
I PUT CHEETAH TO BED.

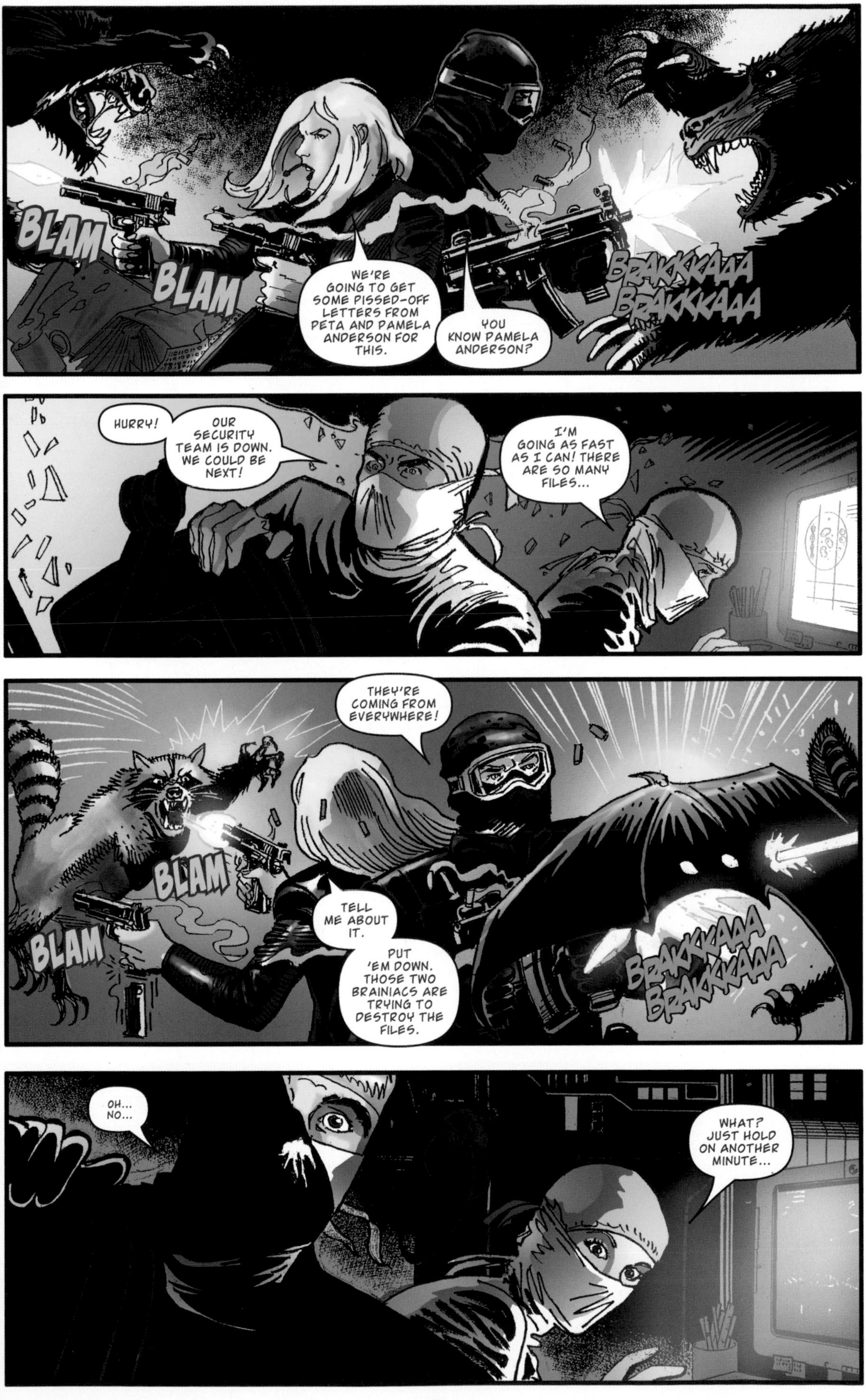
BLAM
BLAM
WE'RE GOING TO GET SOME PISSED-OFF LETTERS FROM PETA AND PAMELA ANDERSON FOR THIS.
YOU KNOW PAMELA ANDERSON?
BRAKKKAAA
BRAKKKAAA
HURRY!
OUR SECURITY TEAM IS DOWN. WE COULD BE NEXT!
I'M GOING AS FAST AS I CAN! THERE ARE SO MANY FILES...
THEY'RE COMING FROM EVERYWHERE!
BLAM
BLAM
TELL ME ABOUT IT.
PUT 'EM DOWN. THOSE TWO BRAINIACS ARE TRYING TO DESTROY THE FILES.
BRAKKKAAA
BRAKKKAAA
OH... NO...
WHAT? JUST HOLD ON ANOTHER MINUTE...

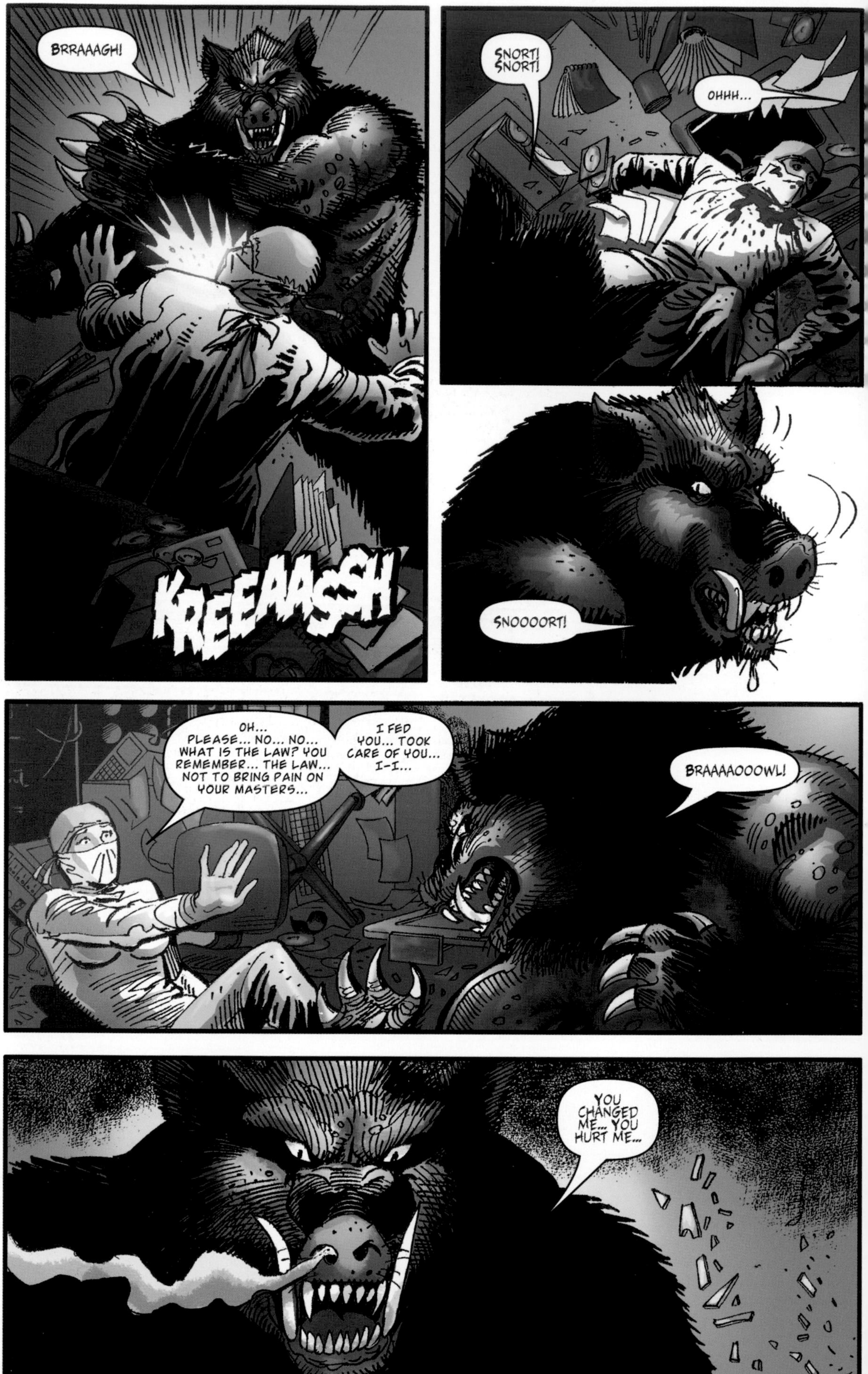
BRRAAAGH!
KREEAASSH
SNORT! SNORT!
OHHH...
SNOOOORT!
OH... PLEASE... NO... NO... WHAT IS THE LAW? YOU REMEMBER... THE LAW... NOT TO BRING PAIN ON YOUR MASTERS...
I FED YOU... TOOK CARE OF YOU... I-I...
BRAAAAOOOWL!
YOU CHANGED ME... YOU HURT ME...

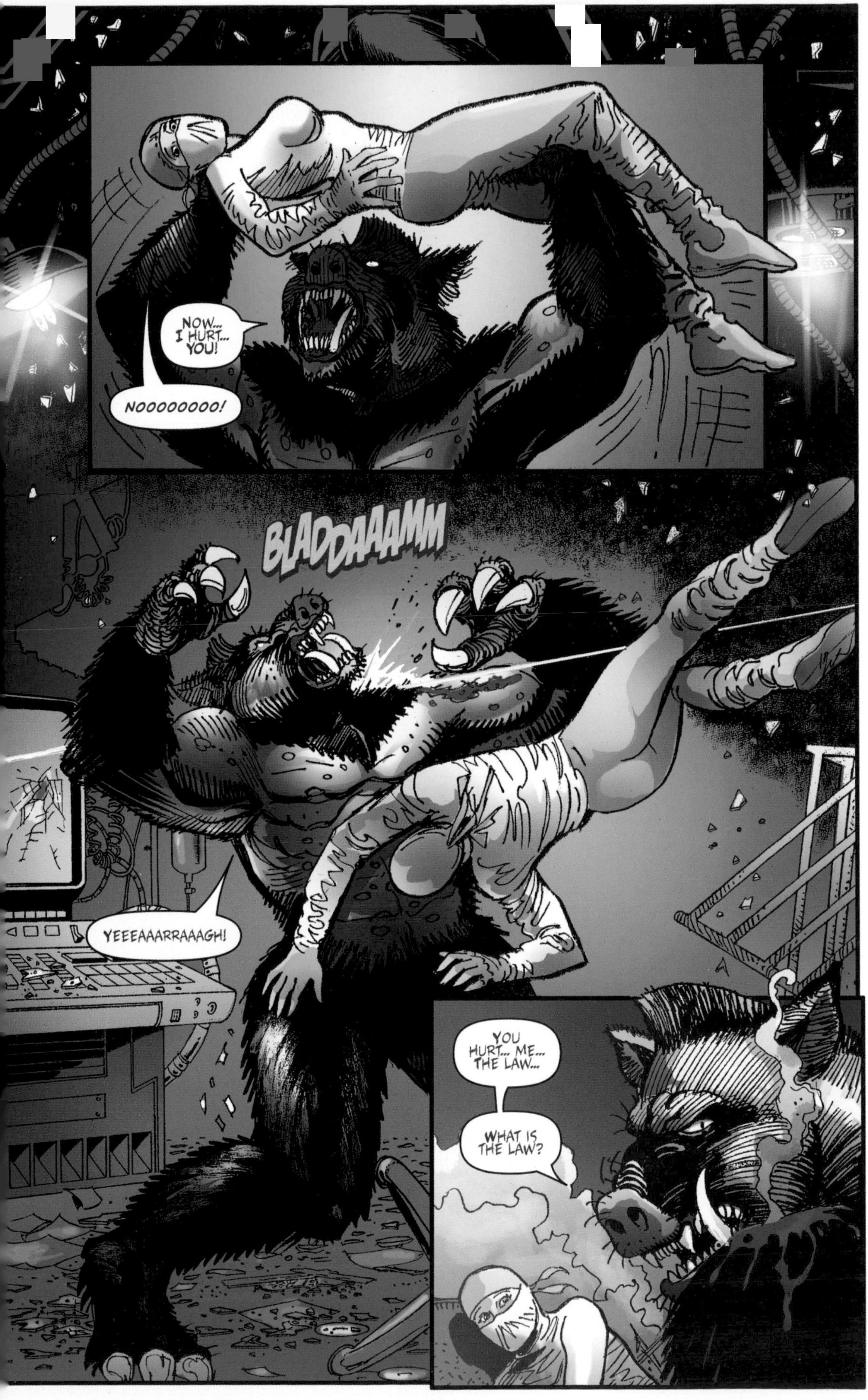
NOW... I HURT... YOU!
NOOOOOOOO!
BLADDAAAMM
YEEEAAARRAAAGH!
YOU HURT... ME... THE LAW...
WHAT IS THE LAW?

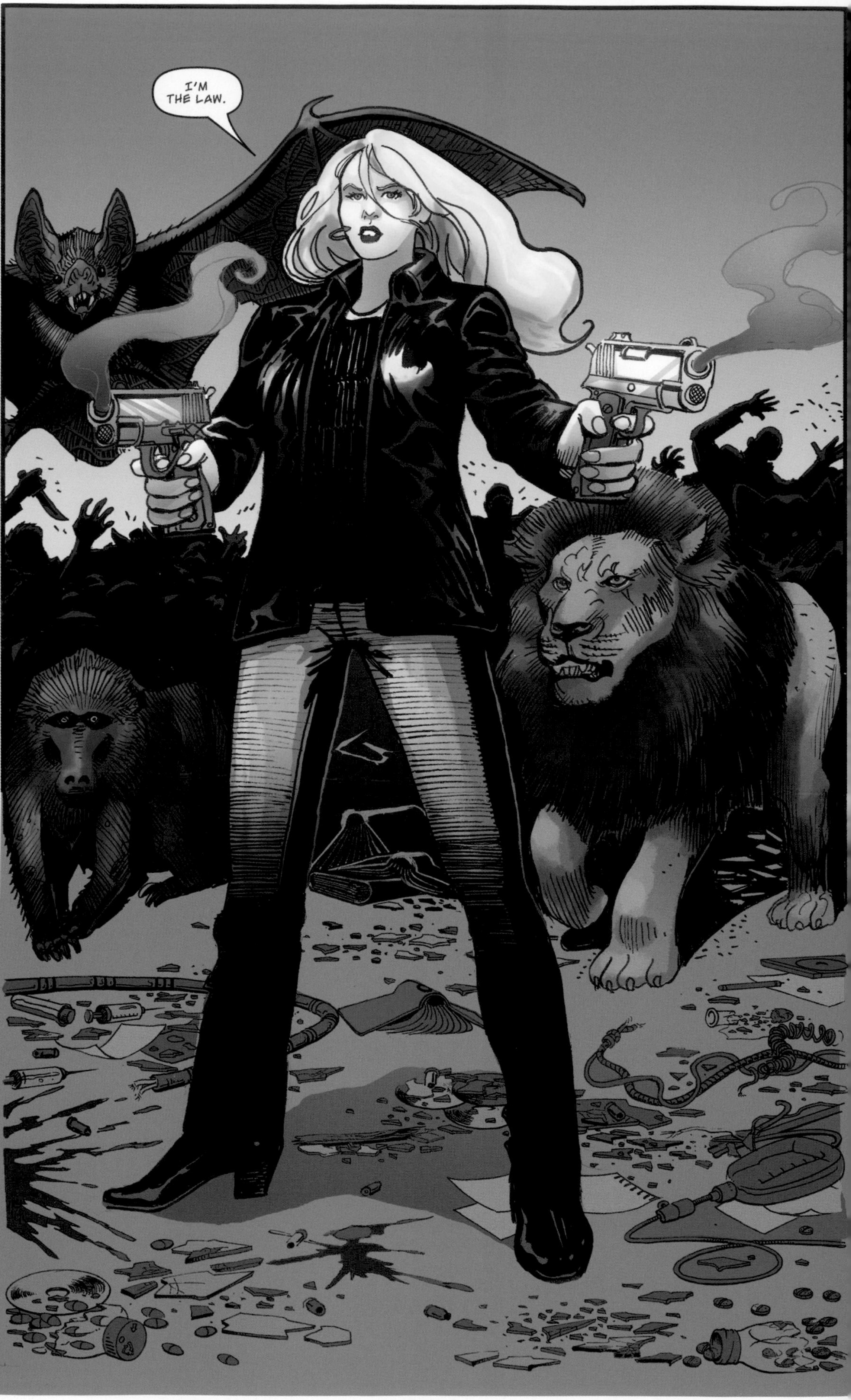
I'M THE LAW.

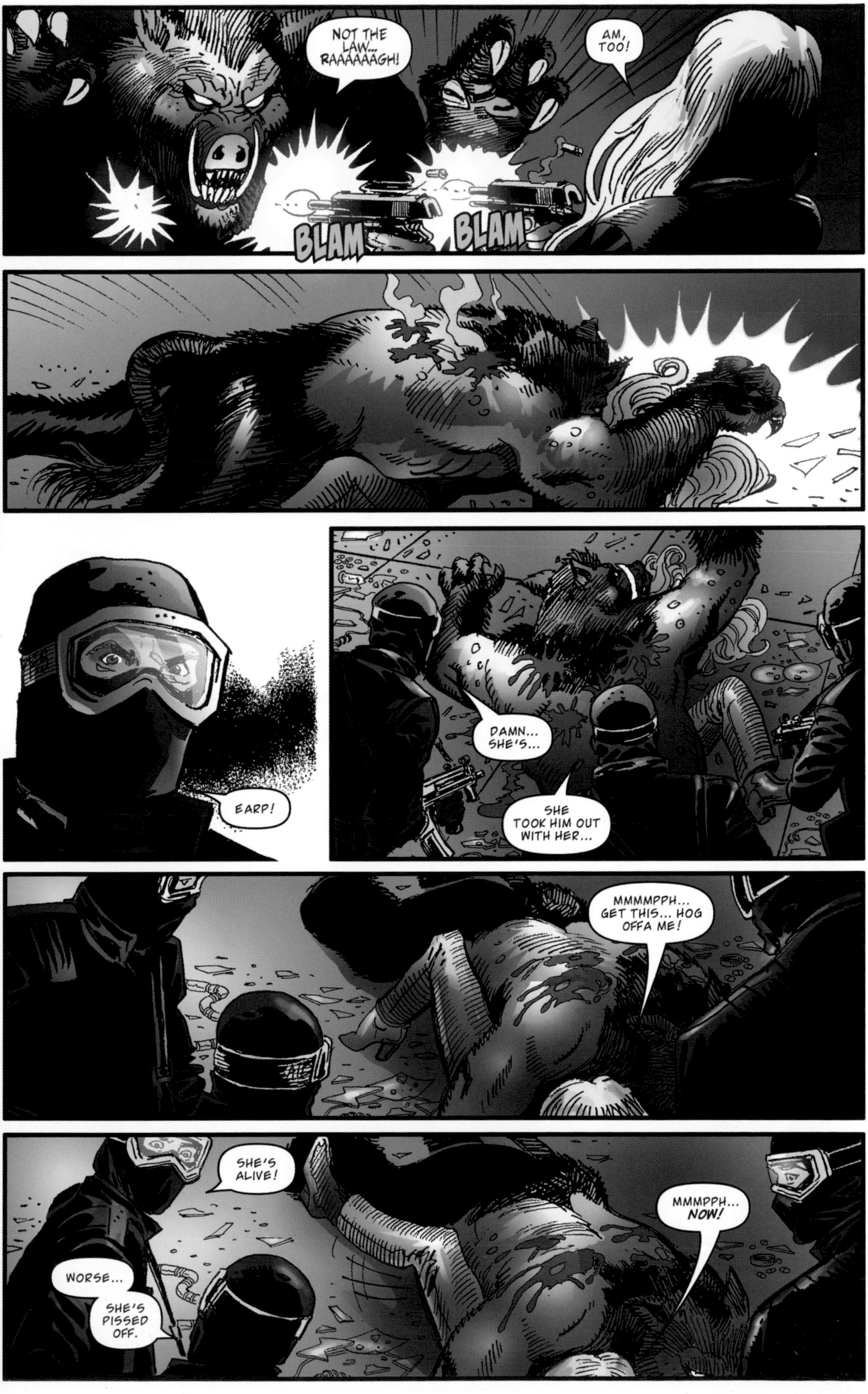
NOT THE LAW... RAAAAAAGH!
AM, TOO!
BLAM
BLAM
EARP!
DAMN... SHE'S...
SHE TOOK HIM OUT WITH HER...
MMMMPPH... GET THIS... HOG OFFA ME!
SHE'S ALIVE!
WORSE...
SHE'S PISSED OFF.
MMMPPH... NOW!

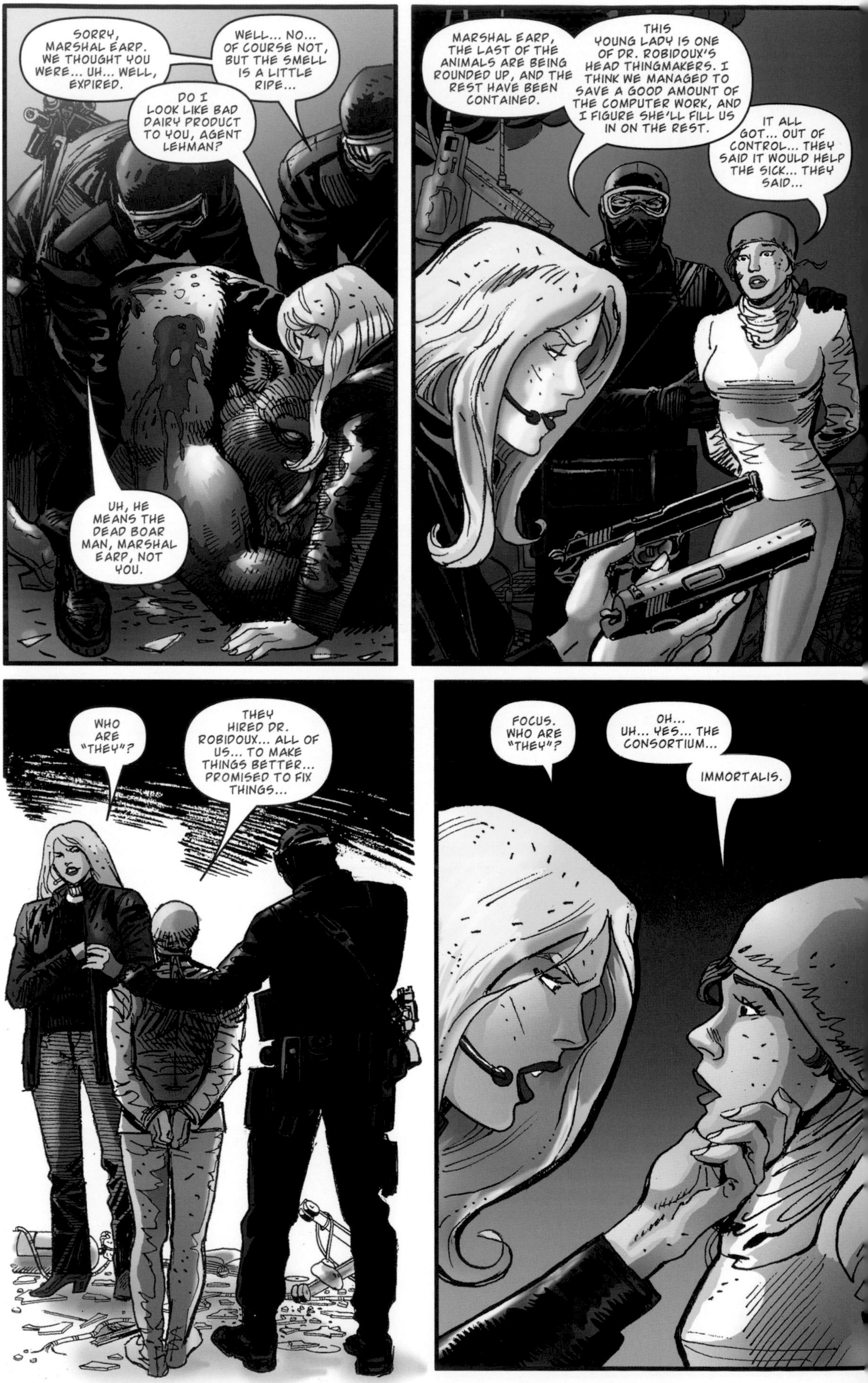

SORRY, MARSHAL EARP. WE THOUGHT YOU WERE... UH... WELL, EXPIRED.
WELL... NO... OF COURSE NOT, BUT THE SMELL IS A LITTLE RIPE...
DO I LOOK LIKE BAD DAIRY PRODUCT TO YOU, AGENT LEHMAN?
UH, HE MEANS THE DEAD BOAR MAN, MARSHAL EARP, NOT YOU.
MARSHAL EARP, THE LAST OF THE ANIMALS ARE BEING ROUNDED UP, AND THE REST HAVE BEEN CONTAINED.
THIS YOUNG LADY IS ONE OF DR. ROBIDOUX'S HEAD THINGMAKERS. I THINK WE MANAGED TO SAVE A GOOD AMOUNT OF THE COMPUTER WORK, AND I FIGURE SHE'LL FILL US IN ON THE REST.
IT ALL GOT... OUT OF CONTROL... THEY SAID IT WOULD HELP THE SICK... THEY SAID...
WHO ARE "THEY"?
THEY HIRED DR. ROBIDOUX... ALL OF US... TO MAKE THINGS BETTER... PROMISED TO FIX THINGS...
FOCUS. WHO ARE "THEY"?
OH... UH... YES... THE CONSORTIUM...
IMMORTALIS.

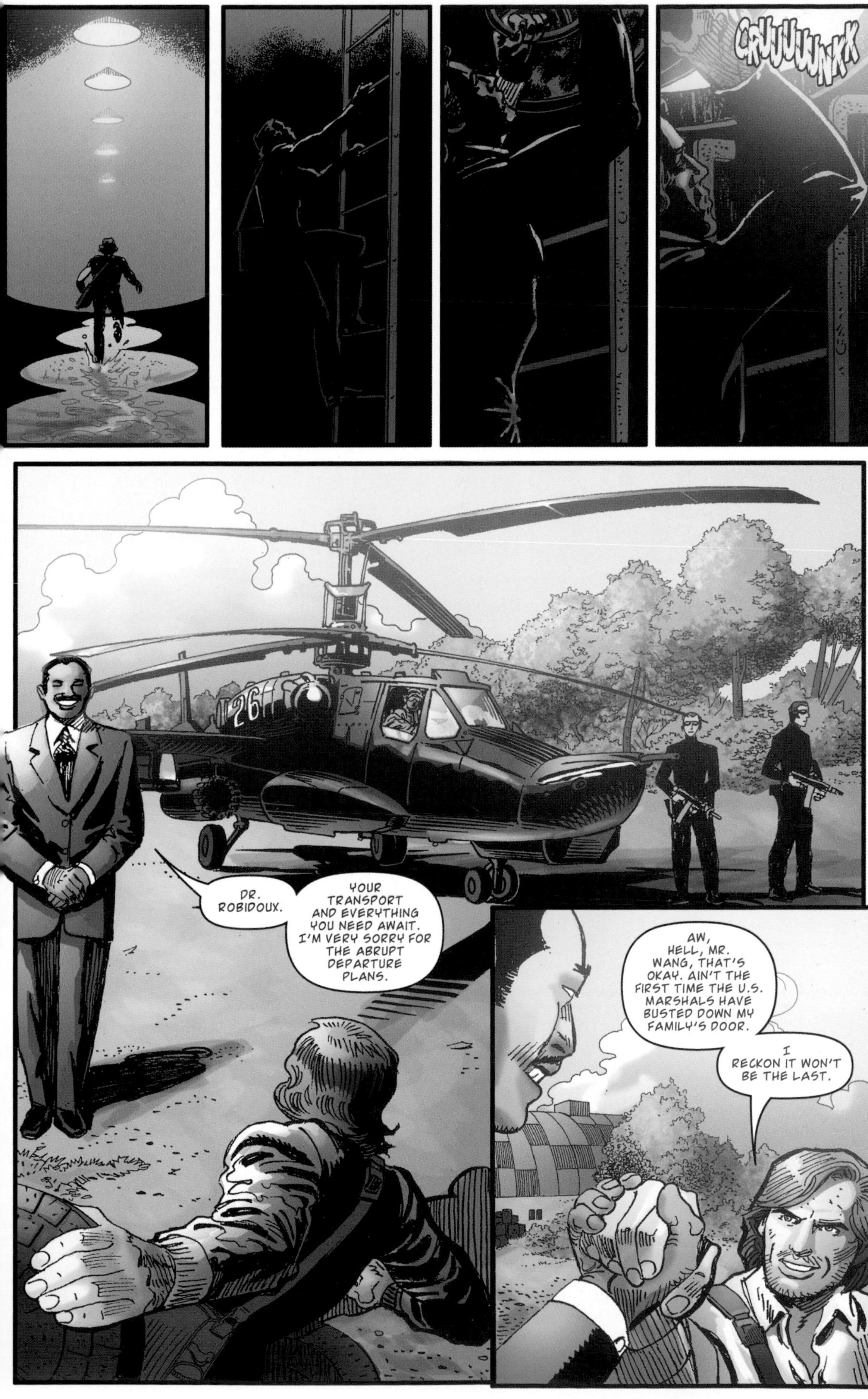
CRUUUUNKK
DR. ROBIDOUX.
YOUR TRANSPORT AND EVERYTHING YOU NEED AWAIT. I'M VERY SORRY FOR THE ABRUPT DEPARTURE PLANS.
AW, HELL, MR. WANG, THAT'S OKAY. AIN'T THE FIRST TIME THE U.S. MARSHALS HAVE BUSTED DOWN MY FAMILY'S DOOR.
I RECKON IT WON'T BE THE LAST.

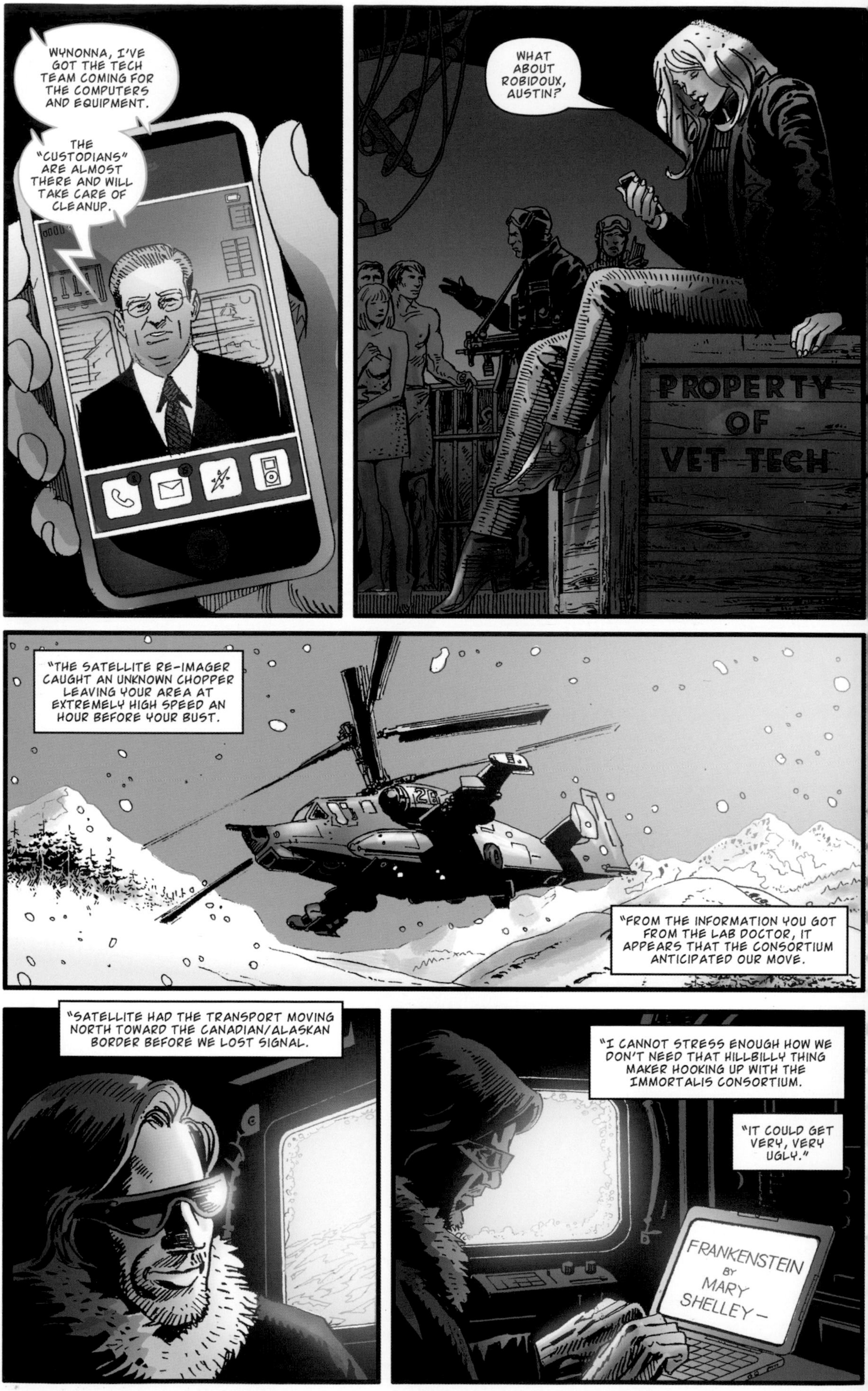
WYNONNA, I'VE GOT THE TECH TEAM COMING FOR THE COMPUTERS AND EQUIPMENT.
THE "CUSTODIANS" ARE ALMOST THERE AND WILL TAKE CARE OF CLEANUP.
WHAT ABOUT ROBIDOUX, AUSTIN?
PROPERTY OF VET TECH
"THE SATELLITE RE-IMAGER CAUGHT AN UNKNOWN CHOPPER LEAVING YOUR AREA AT EXTREMELY HIGH SPEED AN HOUR BEFORE YOUR BUST.
"FROM THE INFORMATION YOU GOT FROM THE LAB DOCTOR, IT APPEARS THAT THE CONSORTIUM ANTICIPATED OUR MOVE.
"SATELLITE HAD THE TRANSPORT MOVING NORTH TOWARD THE CANADIAN/ALASKAN BORDER BEFORE WE LOST SIGNAL.
"I CANNOT STRESS ENOUGH HOW WE DON'T NEED THAT HILLBILLY THING MAKER HOOKING UP WITH THE IMMORTALIS CONSORTIUM.
"IT COULD GET VERY, VERY UGLY."
FRANKENSTEIN BY MARY SHELLEY–

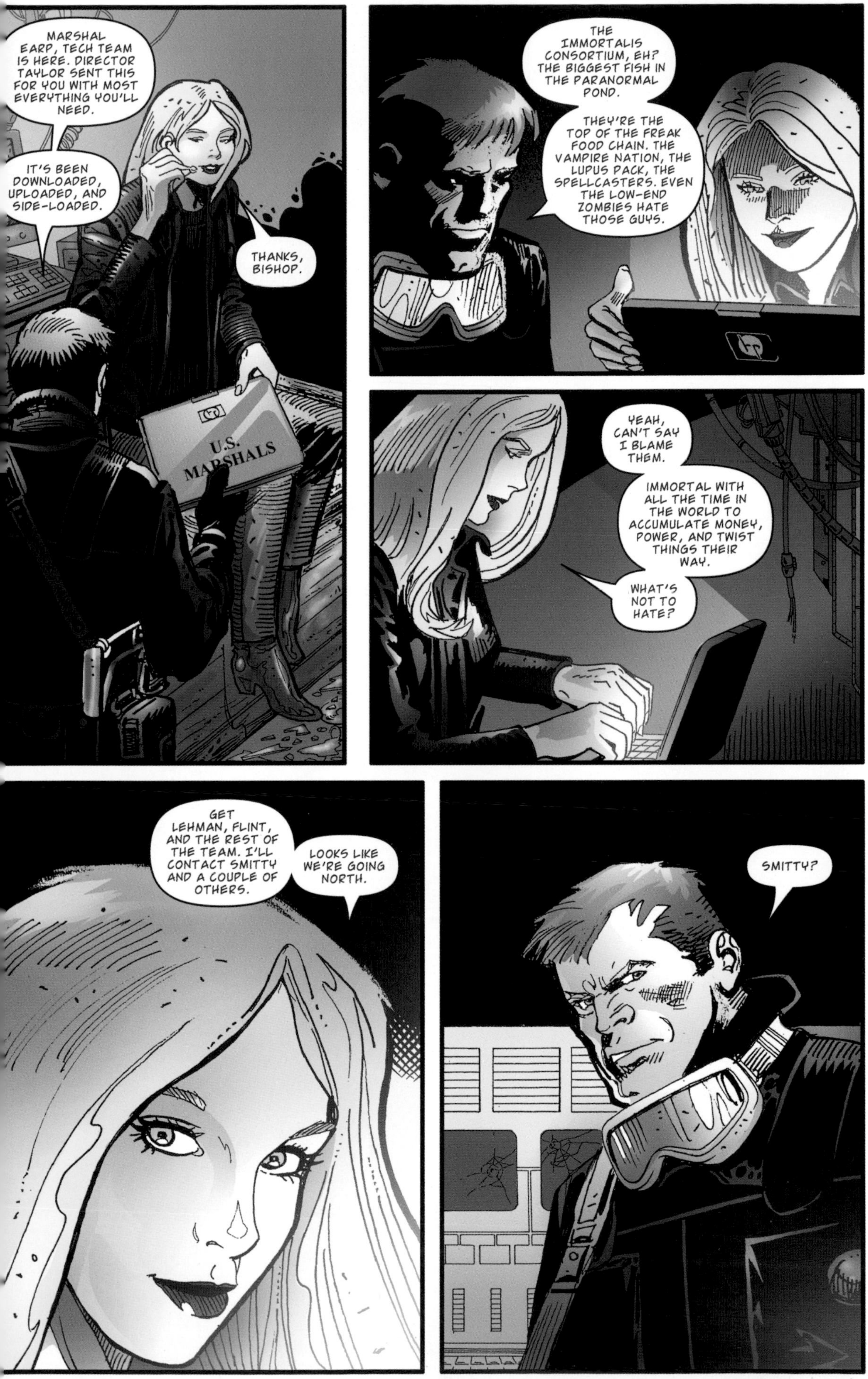
MARSHAL EARP, TECH TEAM IS HERE. DIRECTOR TAYLOR SENT THIS FOR YOU WITH MOST EVERYTHING YOU'LL NEED.
IT'S BEEN DOWNLOADED, UPLOADED, AND SIDE-LOADED.
THANKS, BISHOP.
U.S. MARSHALS
THE IMMORTALIS CONSORTIUM, EH? THE BIGGEST FISH IN THE PARANORMAL POND.
THEY'RE THE TOP OF THE FREAK FOOD CHAIN. THE VAMPIRE NATION, THE LUPUS PACK, THE SPELLCASTERS. EVEN THE LOW-END ZOMBIES HATE THOSE GUYS.
YEAH, CAN'T SAY I BLAME THEM.
IMMORTAL WITH ALL THE TIME IN THE WORLD TO ACCUMULATE MONEY, POWER, AND TWIST THINGS THEIR WAY.
WHAT'S NOT TO HATE?
GET LEHMAN, FLINT, AND THE REST OF THE TEAM. I'LL CONTACT SMITTY AND A COUPLE OF OTHERS.
LOOKS LIKE WE'RE GOING NORTH.
SMITTY?

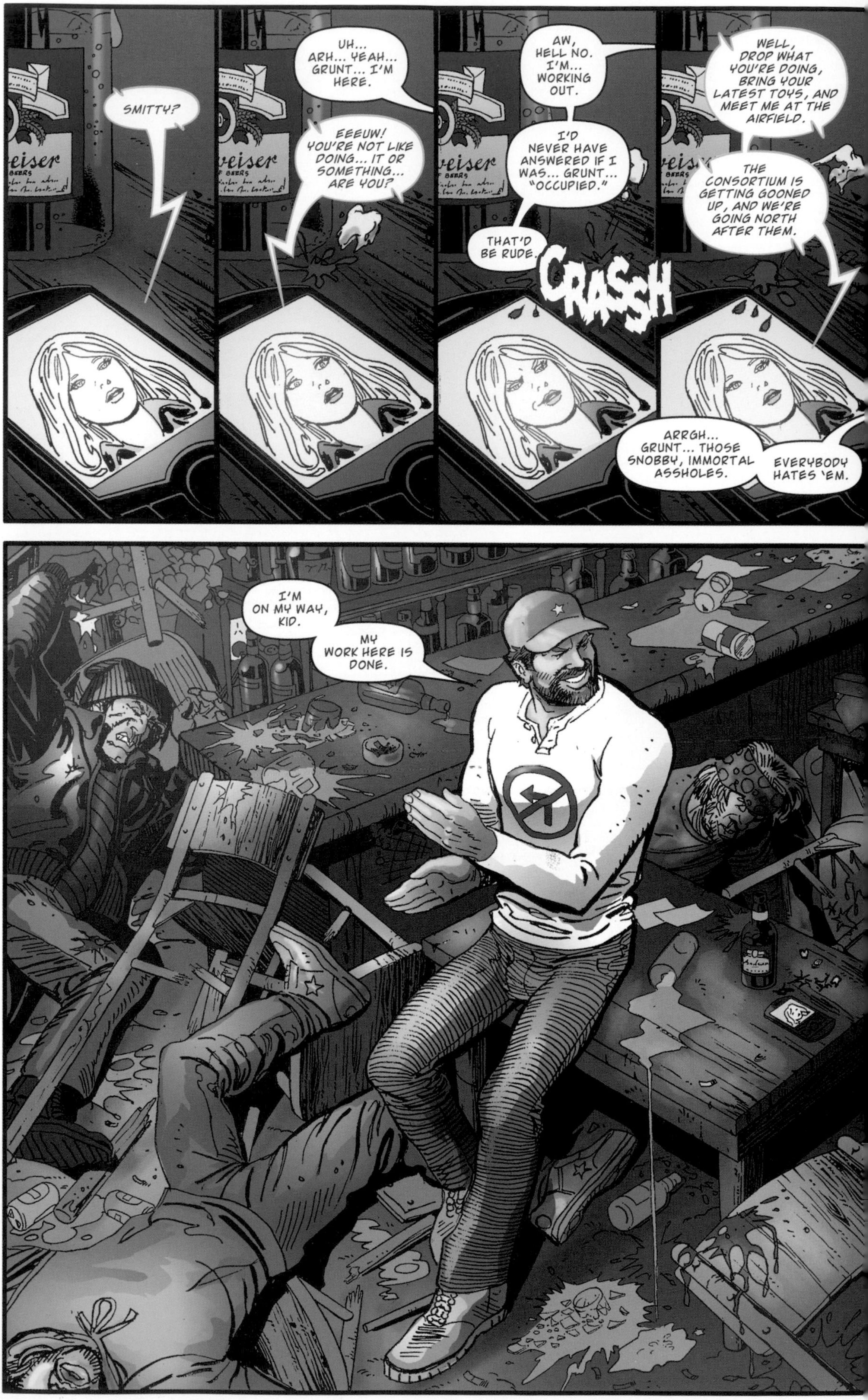
SMITTY?
UH... ARH... YEAH... GRUNT... I'M HERE.
EEEUW! YOU'RE NOT LIKE DOING... IT OR SOMETHING... ARE YOU?
AW, HELL NO. I'M... WORKING OUT.
I'D NEVER HAVE ANSWERED IF I WAS... GRUNT... "OCCUPIED."
THAT'D BE RUDE.
CRASSH
WELL, DROP WHAT YOU'RE DOING, BRING YOUR LATEST TOYS, AND MEET ME AT THE AIRFIELD.
THE CONSORTIUM IS GETTING GOONED UP, AND WE'RE GOING NORTH AFTER THEM.
ARRGH... GRUNT... THOSE SNOBBY, IMMORTAL ASSHOLES.
EVERYBODY HATES 'EM.
I'M ON MY WAY, KID.
MY WORK HERE IS DONE.

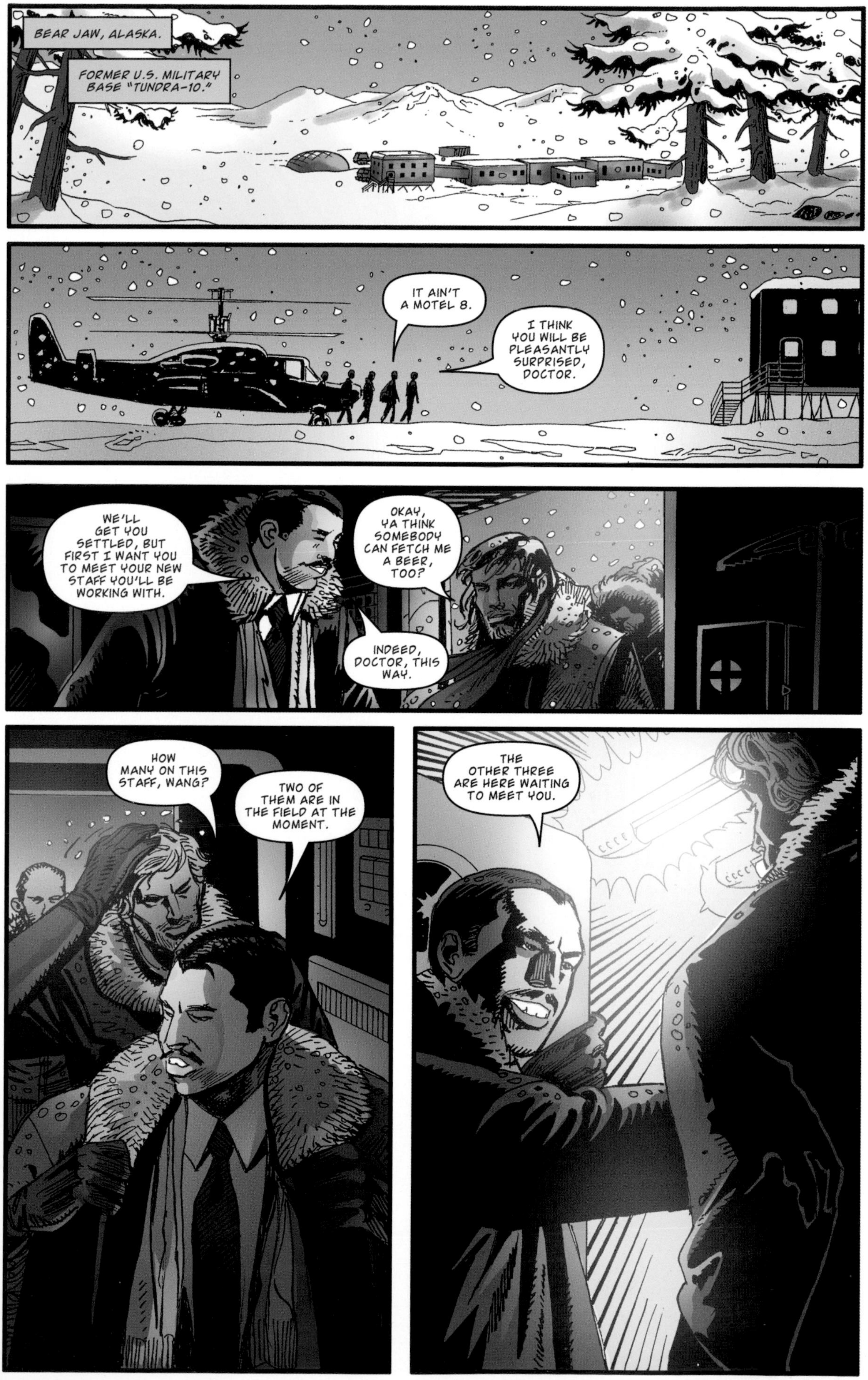
BEAR JAW, ALASKA.
FORMER U.S. MILITARY BASE "TUNDRA-10."
IT AIN'T A MOTEL 8.
I THINK YOU WILL BE PLEASANTLY SURPRISED, DOCTOR.
WE'LL GET YOU SETTLED, BUT FIRST I WANT YOU TO MEET YOUR NEW STAFF YOU'LL BE WORKING WITH.
OKAY, YA THINK SOMEBODY CAN FETCH ME A BEER, TOO?
INDEED, DOCTOR, THIS WAY.
HOW MANY ON THIS STAFF, WANG?
TWO OF THEM ARE IN THE FIELD AT THE MOMENT.
THE OTHER THREE ARE HERE WAITING TO MEET YOU.

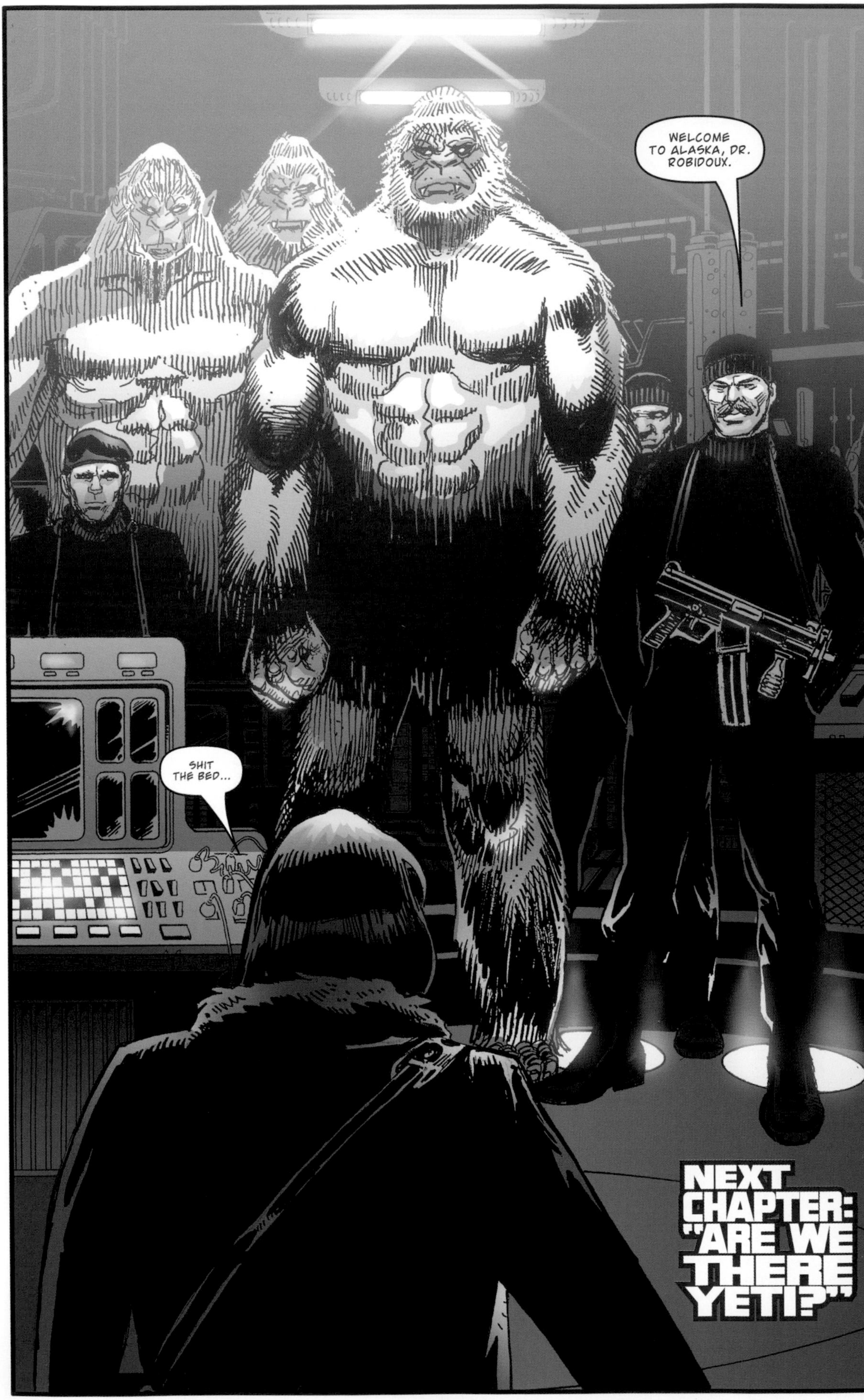
WELCOME TO ALASKA, DR. ROBIDOUX.
SHIT THE BED...
NEXT CHAPTER: "ARE WE THERE YETI?"

ART BY **ENRIQUE VILLAGRAN**

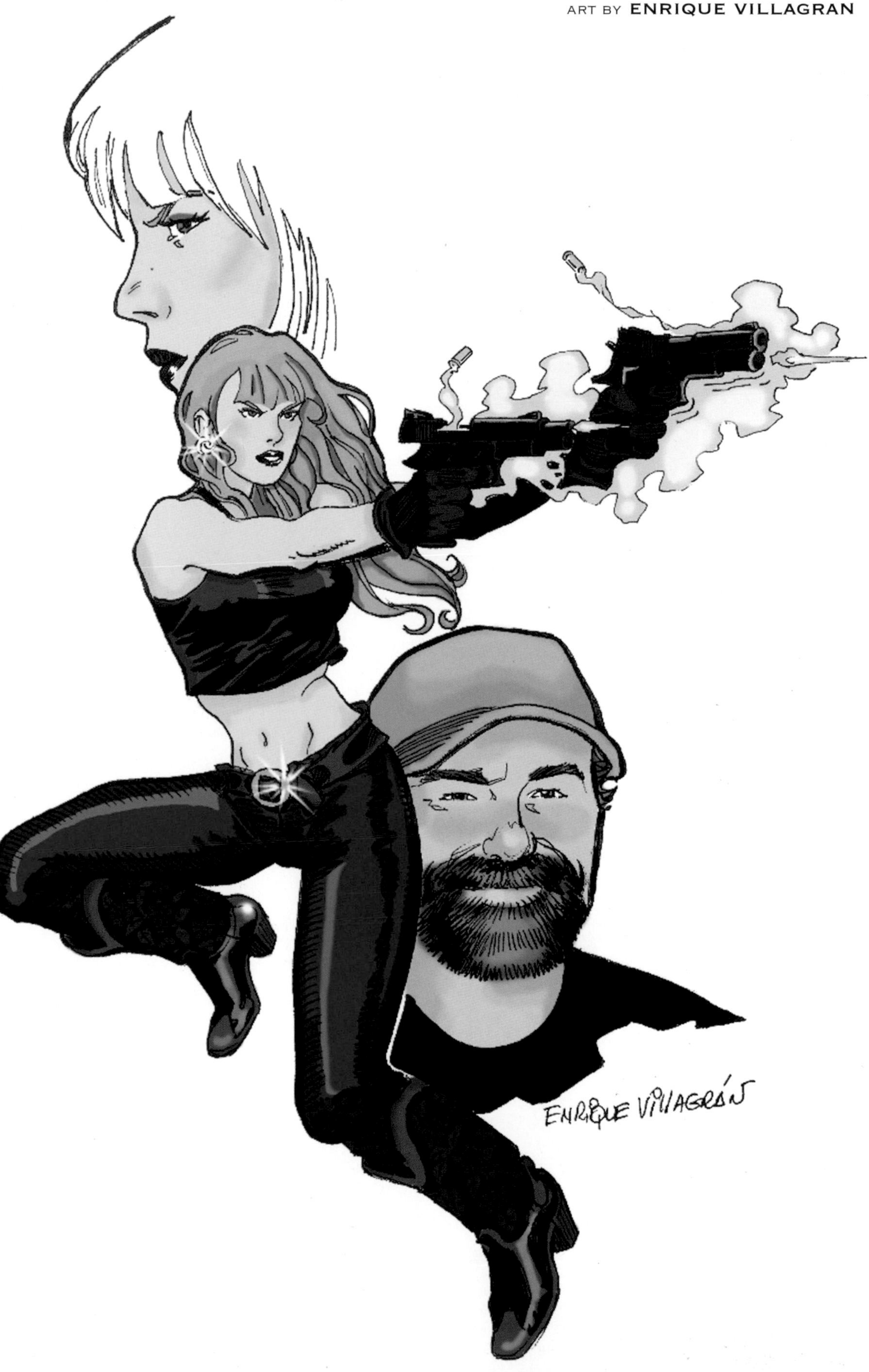
ENRIQUE VILLAGRÁN

ART BY ENRIQUE VILLAGRAN

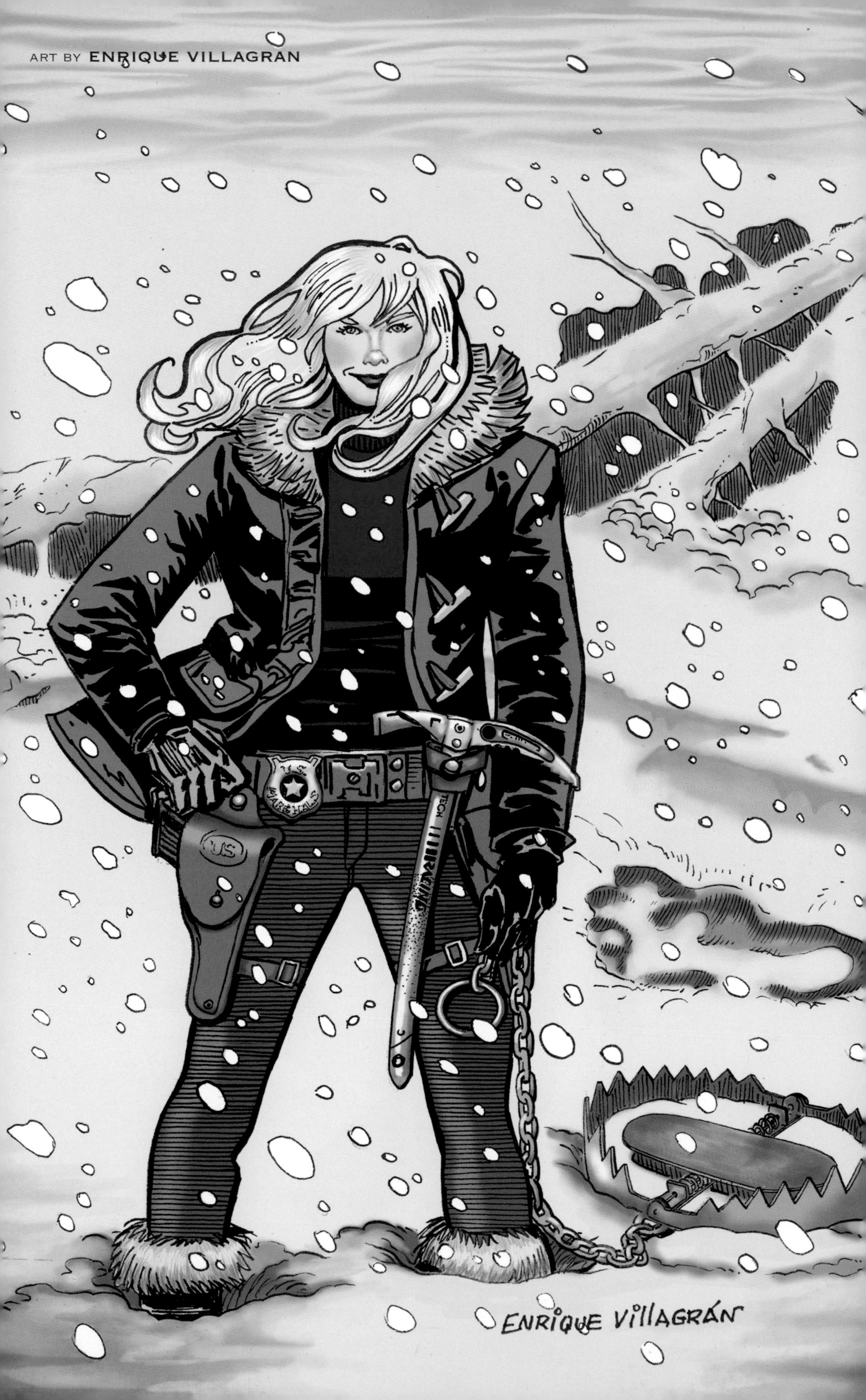

U.S. MARSHALS
US
TECH
ENRIQUE VILLAGRÁN

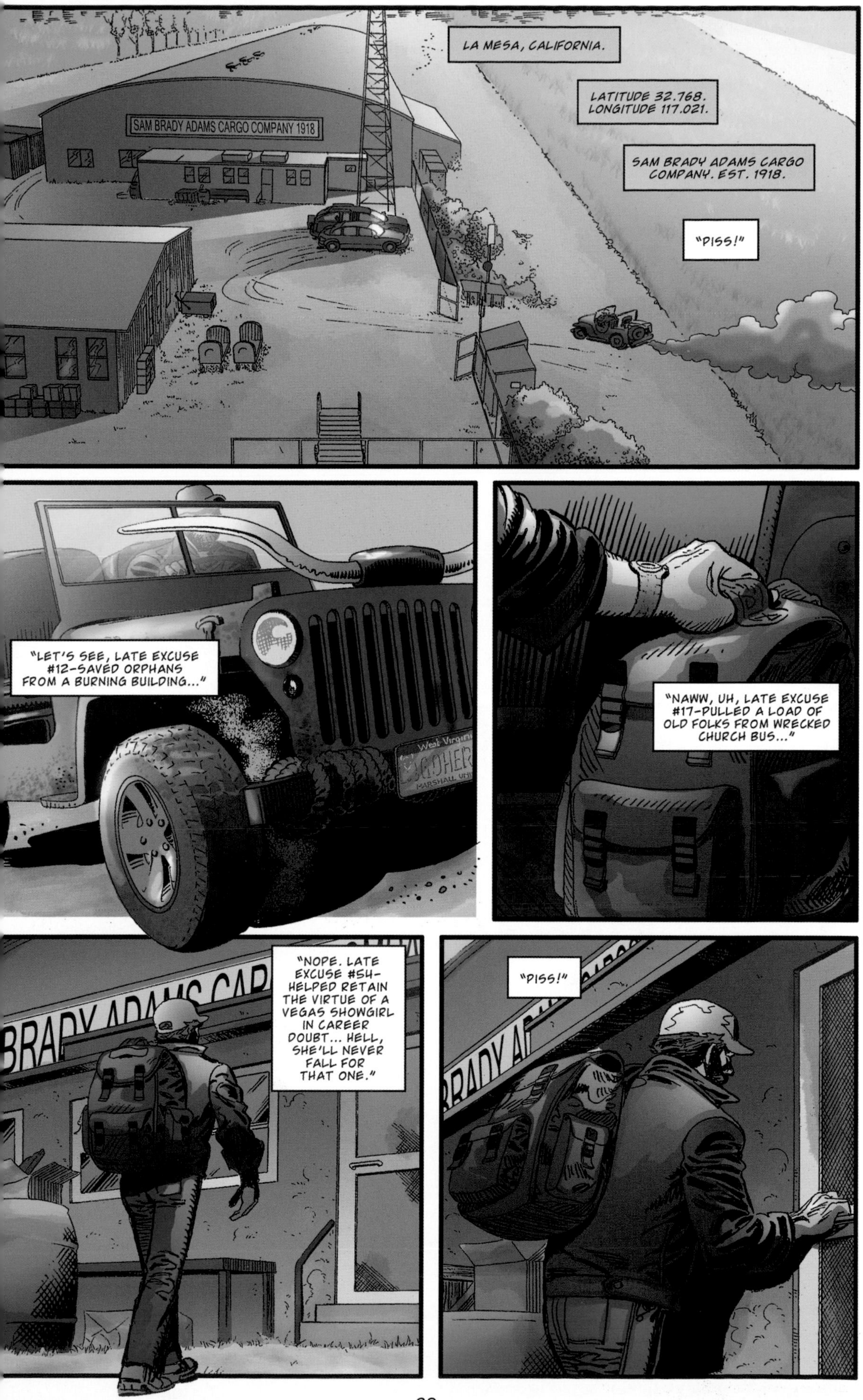
SAM BRADY ADAMS CARGO COMPANY 1918
LA MESA, CALIFORNIA.
LATITUDE 32.768. LONGITUDE 117.021.
SAM BRADY ADAMS CARGO COMPANY. EST. 1918.
"PISS!"
"LET'S SEE, LATE EXCUSE #12–SAVED ORPHANS FROM A BURNING BUILDING..."
"NAWW, UH, LATE EXCUSE #17–PULLED A LOAD OF OLD FOLKS FROM WRECKED CHURCH BUS..."
"NOPE. LATE EXCUSE #54–HELPED RETAIN THE VIRTUE OF A VEGAS SHOWGIRL IN CAREER DOUBT... HELL, SHE'LL NEVER FALL FOR THAT ONE."
"PISS!"

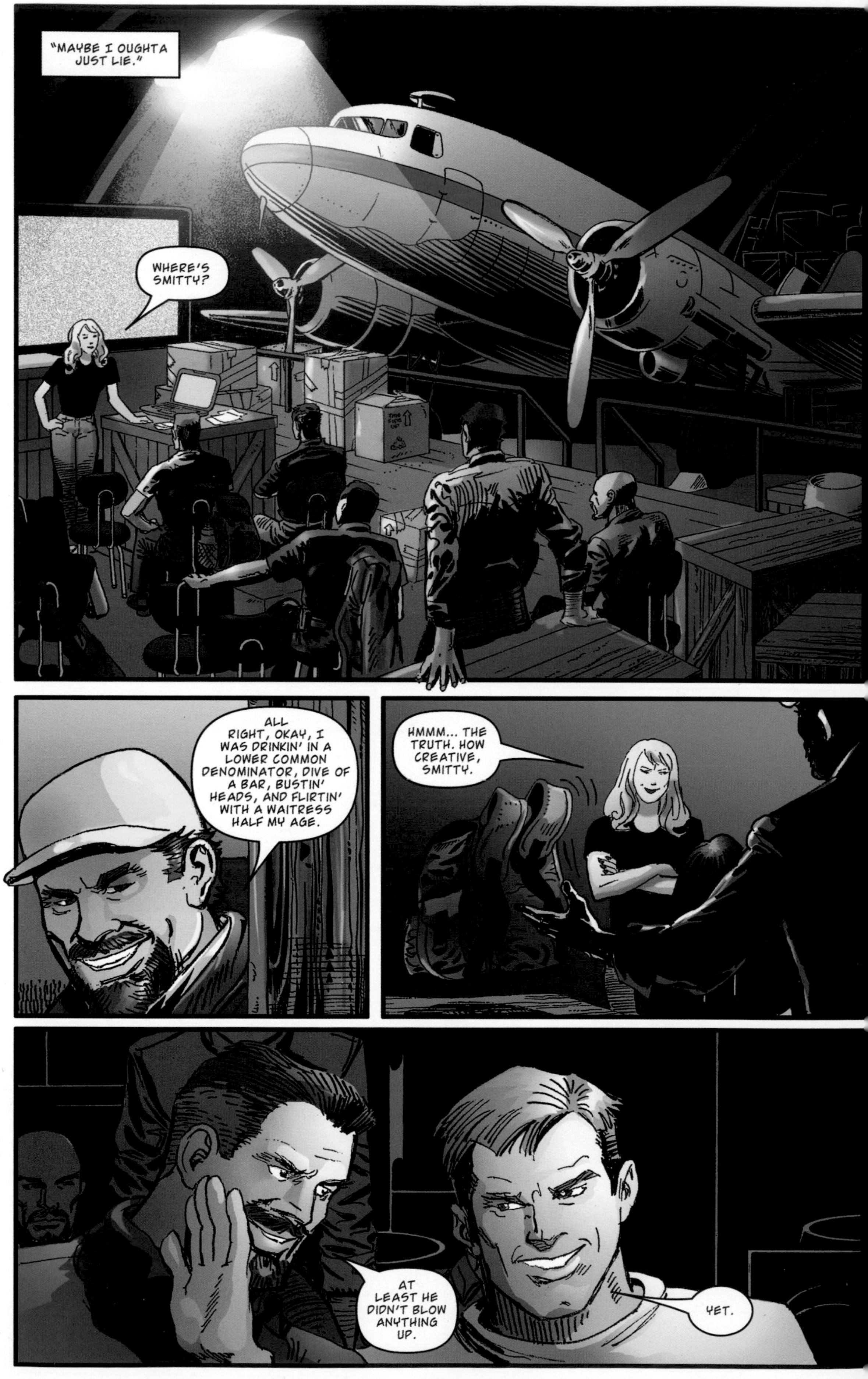
"MAYBE I OUGHTA JUST LIE."
WHERE'S SMITTY?
ALL RIGHT, OKAY, I WAS DRINKIN' IN A LOWER COMMON DENOMINATOR, DIVE OF A BAR, BUSTIN' HEADS, AND FLIRTIN' WITH A WAITRESS HALF MY AGE.
HMMM... THE TRUTH. HOW CREATIVE, SMITTY.
AT LEAST HE DIDN'T BLOW ANYTHING UP.
YET.

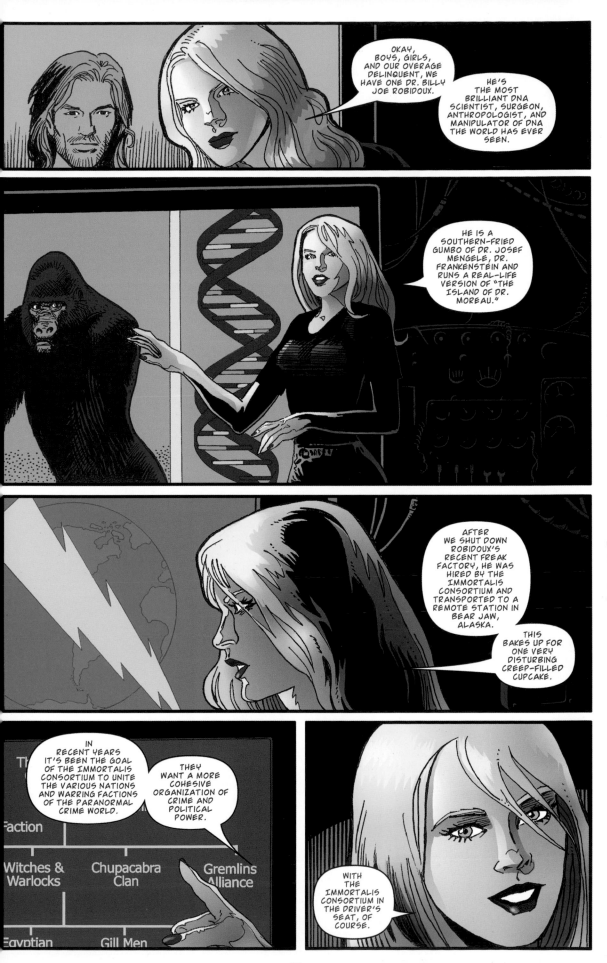

OKAY, BOYS, GIRLS, AND OUR OVERAGE DELINQUENT, WE HAVE ONE DR. BILLY JOE ROBIDOUX.

HE'S THE MOST BRILLIANT DNA SCIENTIST, SURGEON, ANTHROPOLOGIST, AND MANIPULATOR OF DNA THE WORLD HAS EVER SEEN.

HE IS A SOUTHERN-FRIED GUMBO OF DR. JOSEF MENGELE, DR. FRANKENSTEIN AND RUNS A REAL-LIFE VERSION OF "THE ISLAND OF DR. MOREAU."

AFTER WE SHUT DOWN ROBIDOUX'S RECENT FREAK FACTORY, HE WAS HIRED BY THE IMMORTALIS CONSORTIUM AND TRANSPORTED TO A REMOTE STATION IN BEAR JAW, ALASKA.

THIS BAKES UP FOR ONE VERY DISTURBING CREEP-FILLED CUPCAKE.

IN RECENT YEARS IT'S BEEN THE GOAL OF THE IMMORTALIS CONSORTIUM TO UNITE THE VARIOUS NATIONS AND WARRING FACTIONS OF THE PARANORMAL CRIME WORLD.

THEY WANT A MORE COHESIVE ORGANIZATION OF CRIME AND POLITICAL POWER.

Faction

Witches & Warlocks

Chupacabra Clan

Gremlins Alliance

Egyptian

Gill Men

WITH THE IMMORTALIS CONSORTIUM IN THE DRIVER'S SEAT, OF COURSE.

31

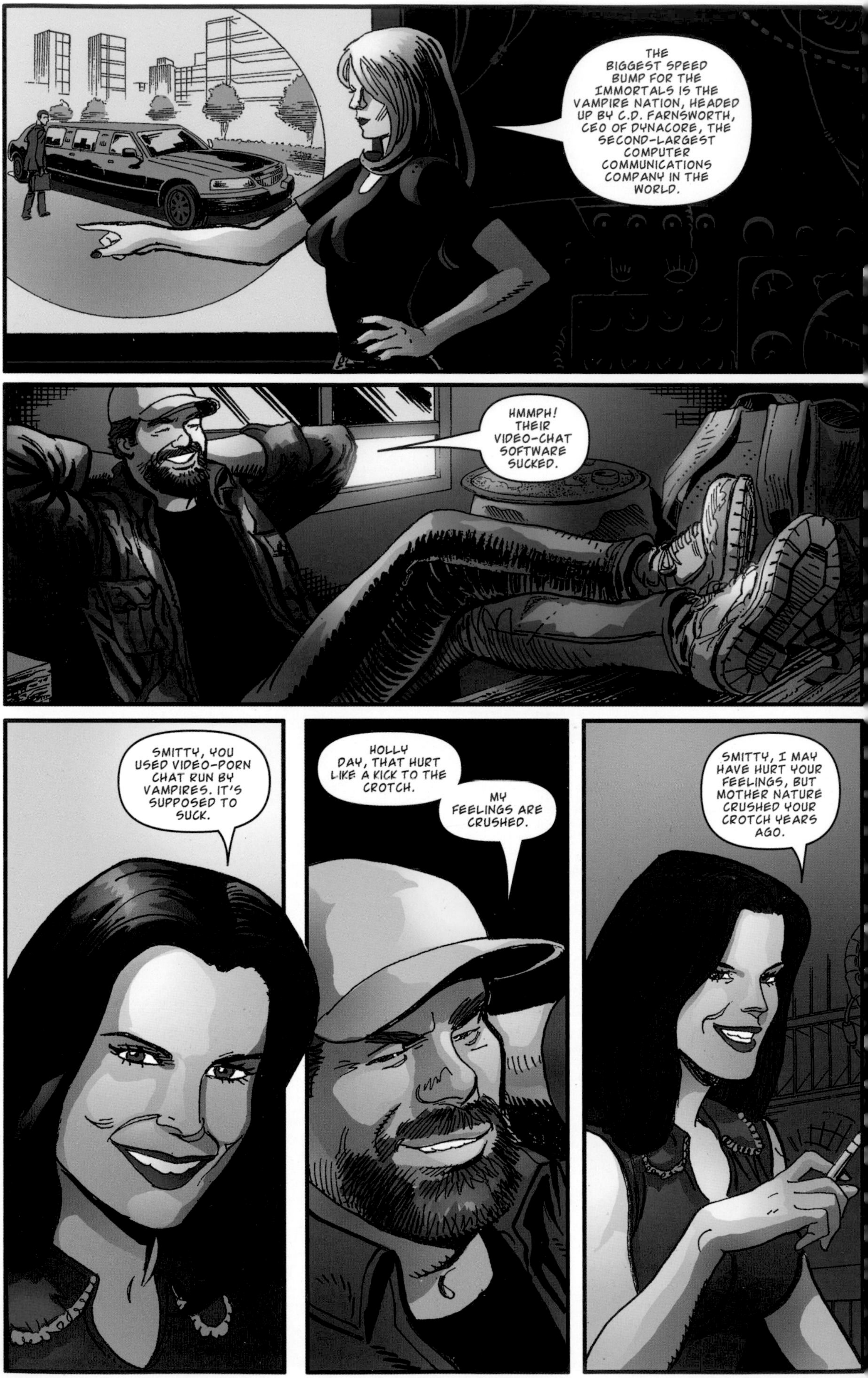
THE BIGGEST SPEED BUMP FOR THE IMMORTALS IS THE VAMPIRE NATION, HEADED UP BY C.D. FARNSWORTH, CEO OF DYNACORE, THE SECOND-LARGEST COMPUTER COMMUNICATIONS COMPANY IN THE WORLD.
HMMPH! THEIR VIDEO-CHAT SOFTWARE SUCKED.
SMITTY, YOU USED VIDEO-PORN CHAT RUN BY VAMPIRES. IT'S SUPPOSED TO SUCK.
HOLLY DAY, THAT HURT LIKE A KICK TO THE CROTCH.
MY FEELINGS ARE CRUSHED.
SMITTY, I MAY HAVE HURT YOUR FEELINGS, BUT MOTHER NATURE CRUSHED YOUR CROTCH YEARS AGO.

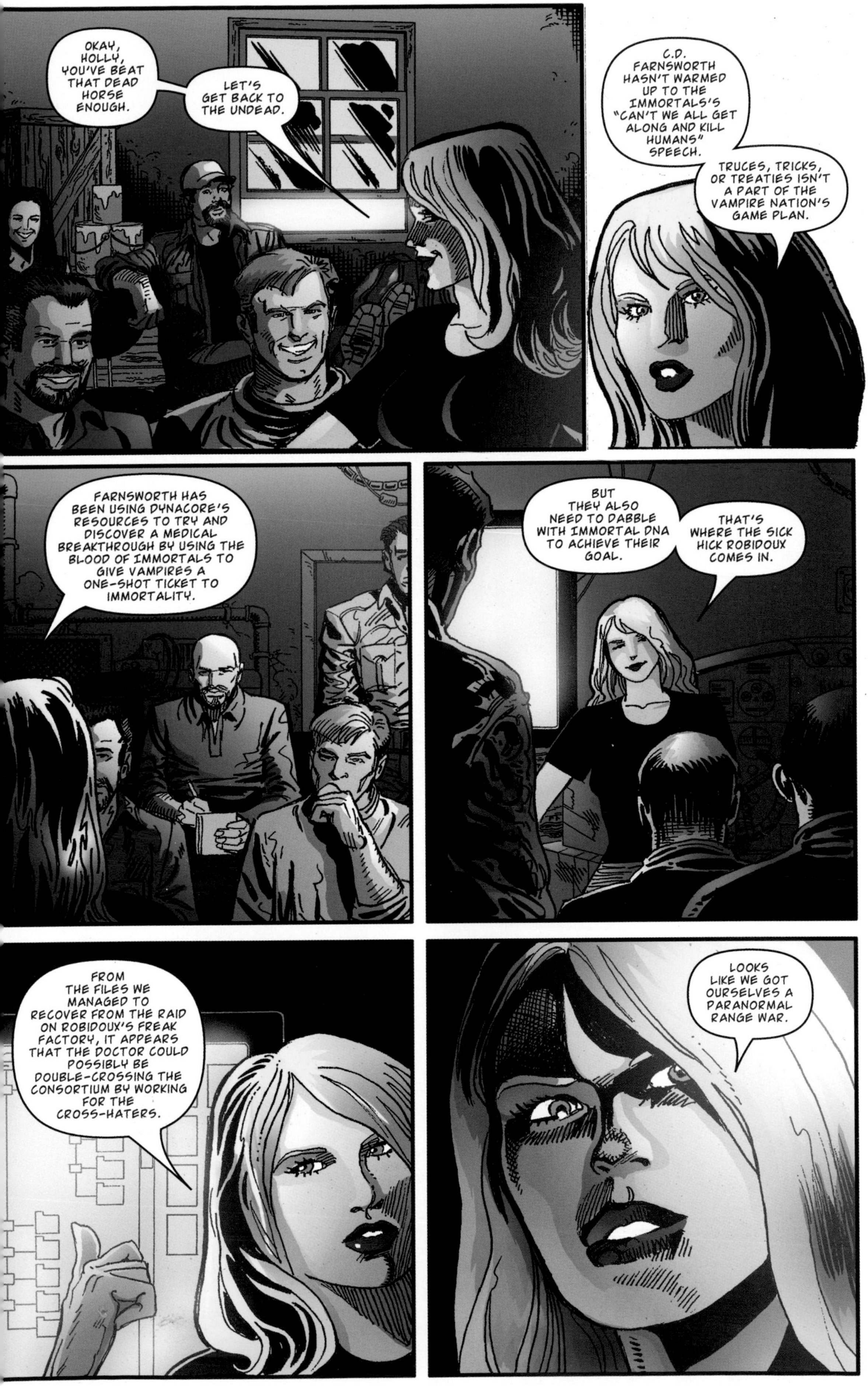
OKAY, HOLLY, YOU'VE BEAT THAT DEAD HORSE ENOUGH.
LET'S GET BACK TO THE UNDEAD.
C.D. FARNSWORTH HASN'T WARMED UP TO THE IMMORTALS'S "CAN'T WE ALL GET ALONG AND KILL HUMANS" SPEECH.
TRUCES, TRICKS, OR TREATIES ISN'T A PART OF THE VAMPIRE NATION'S GAME PLAN.
FARNSWORTH HAS BEEN USING DYNACORE'S RESOURCES TO TRY AND DISCOVER A MEDICAL BREAKTHROUGH BY USING THE BLOOD OF IMMORTALS TO GIVE VAMPIRES A ONE-SHOT TICKET TO IMMORTALITY.
BUT THEY ALSO NEED TO DABBLE WITH IMMORTAL DNA TO ACHIEVE THEIR GOAL.
THAT'S WHERE THE SICK HICK ROBIDOUX COMES IN.
FROM THE FILES WE MANAGED TO RECOVER FROM THE RAID ON ROBIDOUX'S FREAK FACTORY, IT APPEARS THAT THE DOCTOR COULD POSSIBLY BE DOUBLE-CROSSING THE CONSORTIUM BY WORKING FOR THE CROSS-HATERS.
LOOKS LIKE WE GOT OURSELVES A PARANORMAL RANGE WAR.

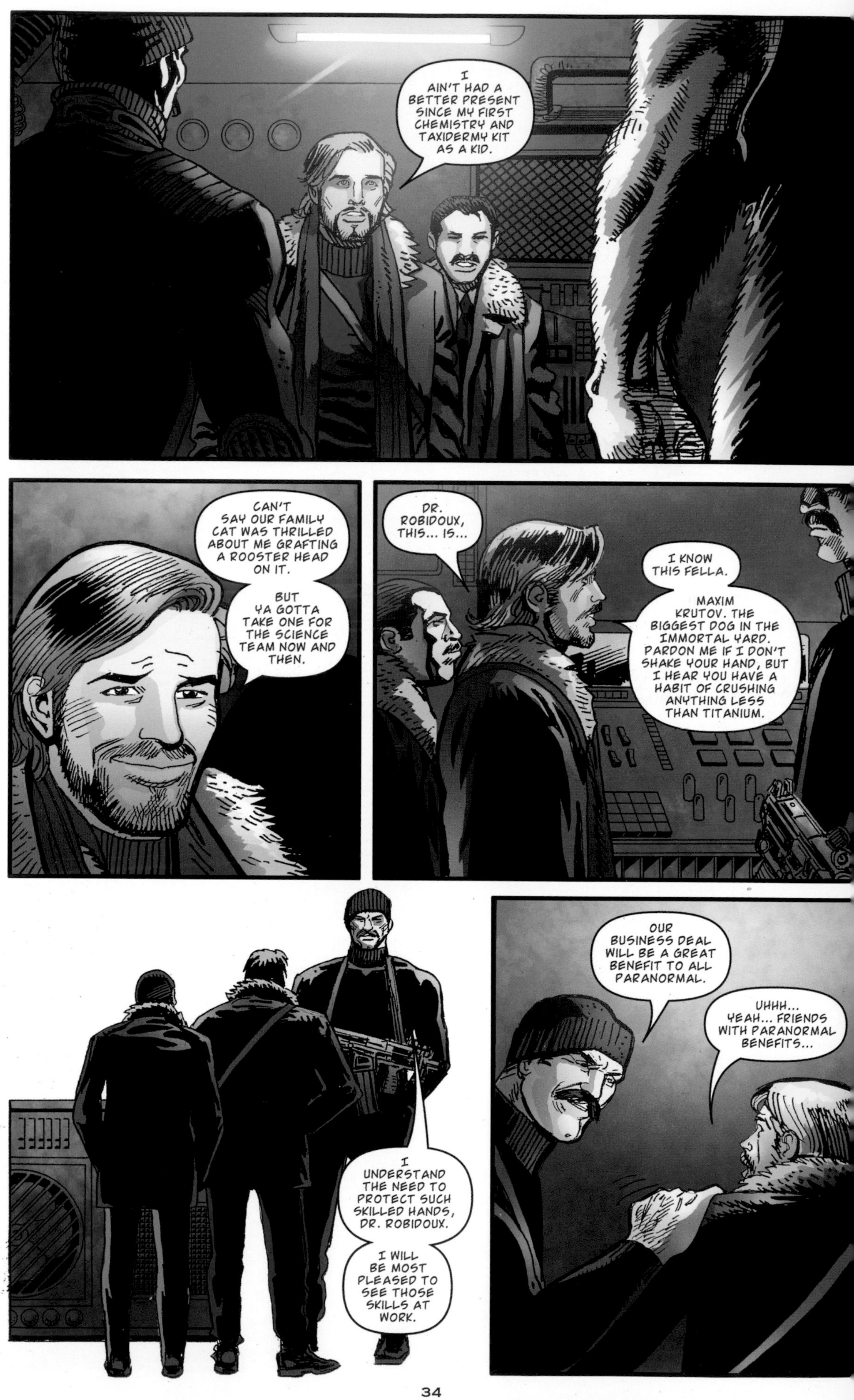
I AIN'T HAD A BETTER PRESENT SINCE MY FIRST CHEMISTRY AND TAXIDERMY KIT AS A KID.
CAN'T SAY OUR FAMILY CAT WAS THRILLED ABOUT ME GRAFTING A ROOSTER HEAD ON IT.
BUT YA GOTTA TAKE ONE FOR THE SCIENCE TEAM NOW AND THEN.
DR. ROBIDOUX, THIS... IS...
I KNOW THIS FELLA.
MAXIM KRUTOV. THE BIGGEST DOG IN THE IMMORTAL YARD. PARDON ME IF I DON'T SHAKE YOUR HAND, BUT I HEAR YOU HAVE A HABIT OF CRUSHING ANYTHING LESS THAN TITANIUM.
I UNDERSTAND THE NEED TO PROTECT SUCH SKILLED HANDS, DR. ROBIDOUX.
I WILL BE MOST PLEASED TO SEE THOSE SKILLS AT WORK.
OUR BUSINESS DEAL WILL BE A GREAT BENEFIT TO ALL PARANORMAL.
UHHH... YEAH... FRIENDS WITH PARANORMAL BENEFITS...

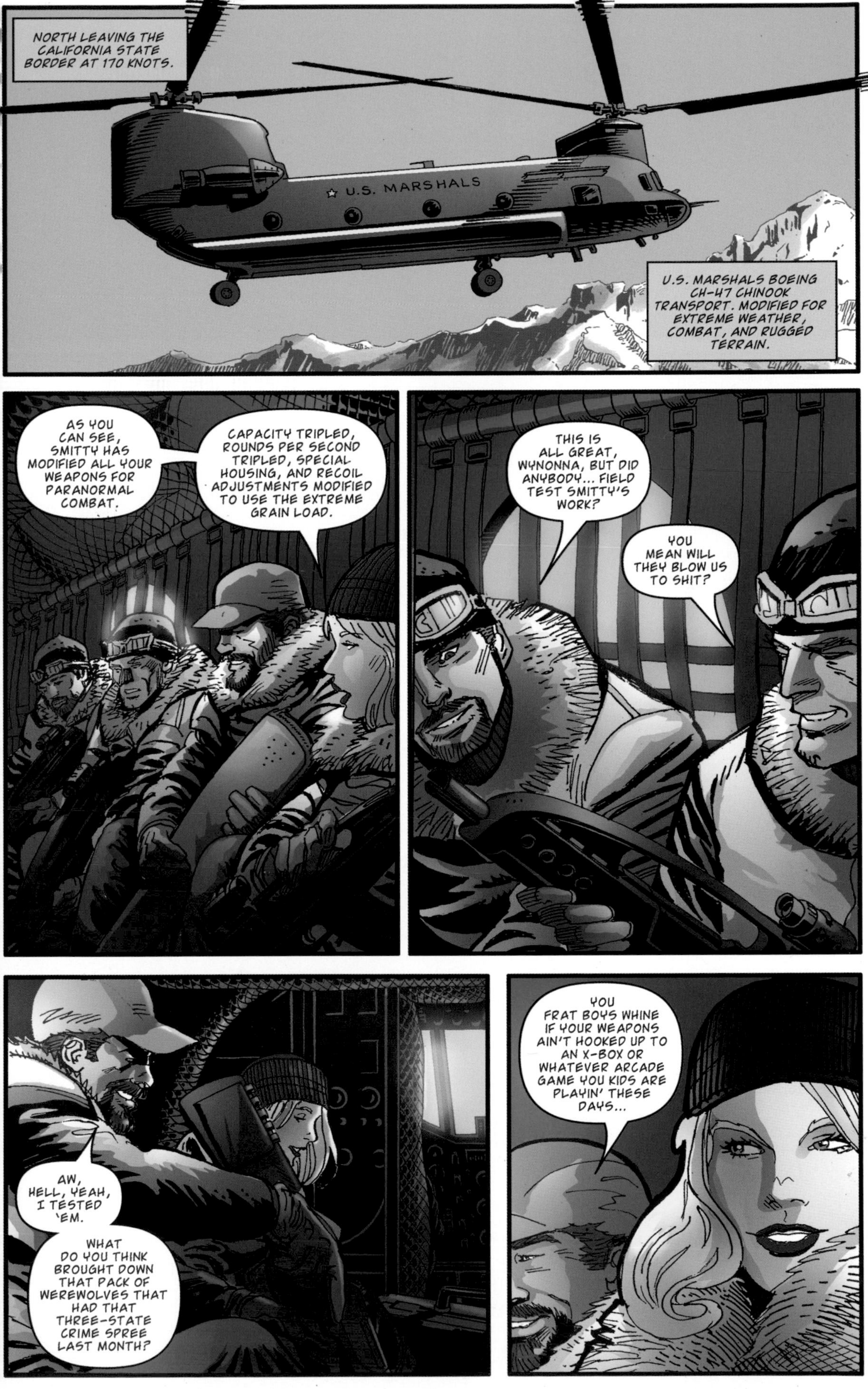
NORTH LEAVING THE CALIFORNIA STATE BORDER AT 170 KNOTS.
U.S. MARSHALS
U.S. MARSHALS BOEING CH-47 CHINOOK TRANSPORT. MODIFIED FOR EXTREME WEATHER, COMBAT, AND RUGGED TERRAIN.
AS YOU CAN SEE, SMITTY HAS MODIFIED ALL YOUR WEAPONS FOR PARANORMAL COMBAT.
CAPACITY TRIPLED, ROUNDS PER SECOND TRIPLED, SPECIAL HOUSING, AND RECOIL ADJUSTMENTS MODIFIED TO USE THE EXTREME GRAIN LOAD.
THIS IS ALL GREAT, WYNONNA, BUT DID ANYBODY... FIELD TEST SMITTY'S WORK?
YOU MEAN WILL THEY BLOW US TO SHIT?
AW, HELL, YEAH, I TESTED 'EM.
WHAT DO YOU THINK BROUGHT DOWN THAT PACK OF WEREWOLVES THAT HAD THAT THREE-STATE CRIME SPREE LAST MONTH?
YOU FRAT BOYS WHINE IF YOUR WEAPONS AIN'T HOOKED UP TO AN X-BOX OR WHATEVER ARCADE GAME YOU KIDS ARE PLAYIN' THESE DAYS...

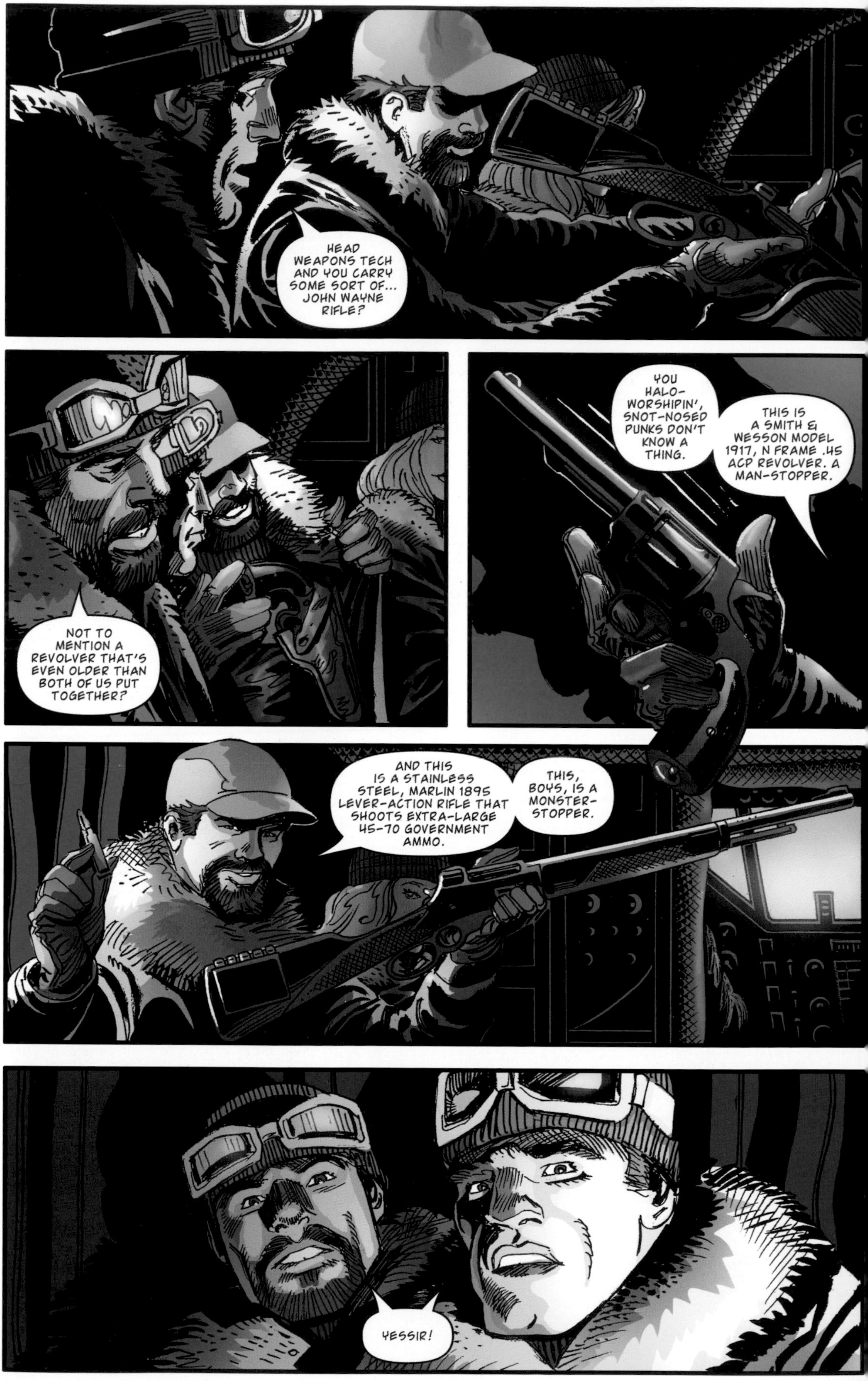
HEAD WEAPONS TECH AND YOU CARRY SOME SORT OF... JOHN WAYNE RIFLE?
NOT TO MENTION A REVOLVER THAT'S EVEN OLDER THAN BOTH OF US PUT TOGETHER?
YOU HALO-WORSHIPIN', SNOT-NOSED PUNKS DON'T KNOW A THING.
THIS IS A SMITH & WESSON MODEL 1917, N FRAME .45 ACP REVOLVER. A MAN-STOPPER.
AND THIS IS A STAINLESS STEEL, MARLIN 1895 LEVER-ACTION RIFLE THAT SHOOTS EXTRA-LARGE 45-70 GOVERNMENT AMMO.
THIS, BOYS, IS A MONSTER-STOPPER.
YESSIR!

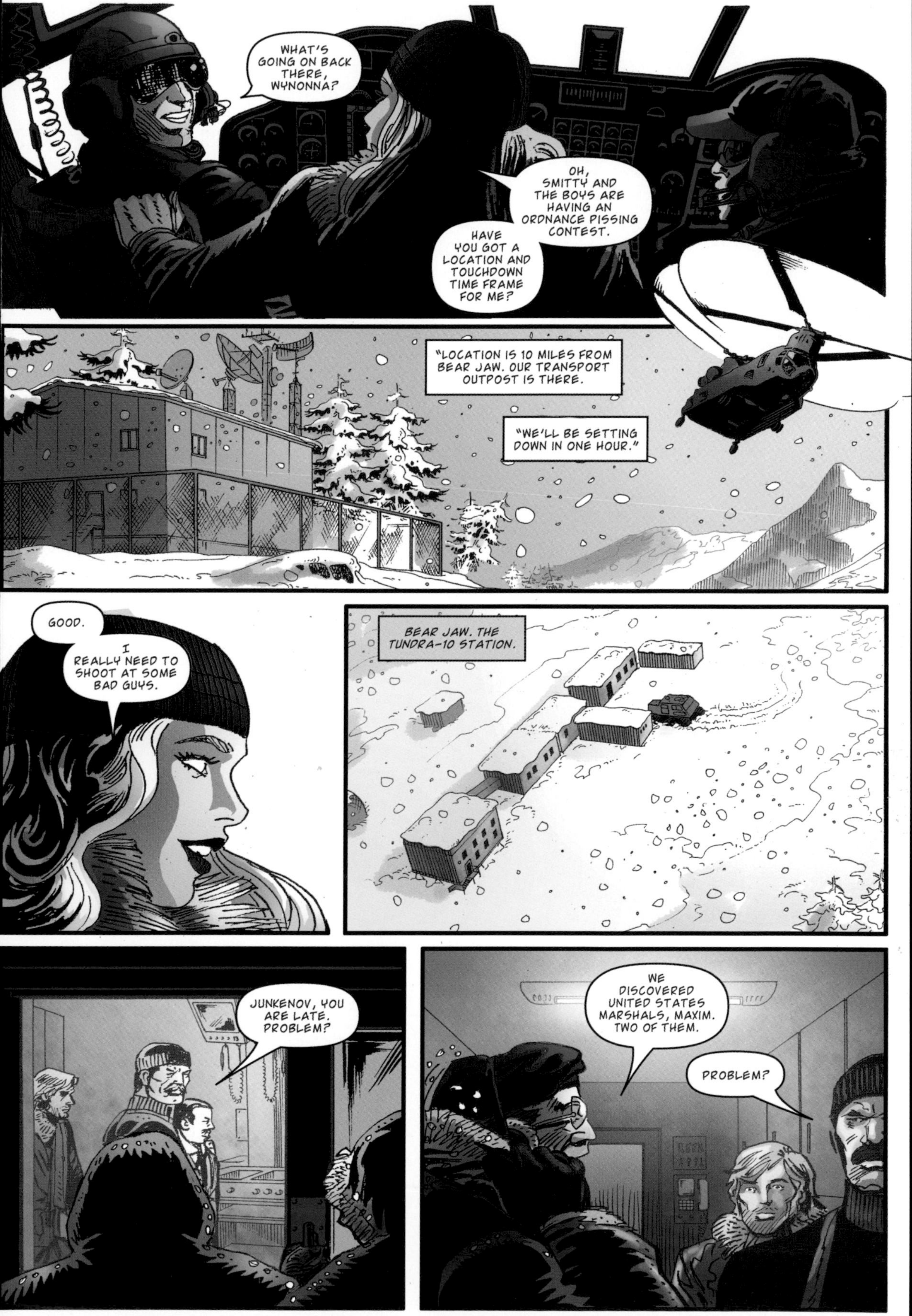

WHAT'S GOING ON BACK THERE, WYNONNA?
OH, SMITTY AND THE BOYS ARE HAVING AN ORDNANCE PISSING CONTEST.
HAVE YOU GOT A LOCATION AND TOUCHDOWN TIME FRAME FOR ME?
"LOCATION IS 10 MILES FROM BEAR JAW. OUR TRANSPORT OUTPOST IS THERE.
"WE'LL BE SETTING DOWN IN ONE HOUR."
GOOD.
I REALLY NEED TO SHOOT AT SOME BAD GUYS.
BEAR JAW. THE TUNDRA-10 STATION.
JUNKENOV, YOU ARE LATE. PROBLEM?
WE DISCOVERED UNITED STATES MARSHALS, MAXIM. TWO OF THEM.
PROBLEM?

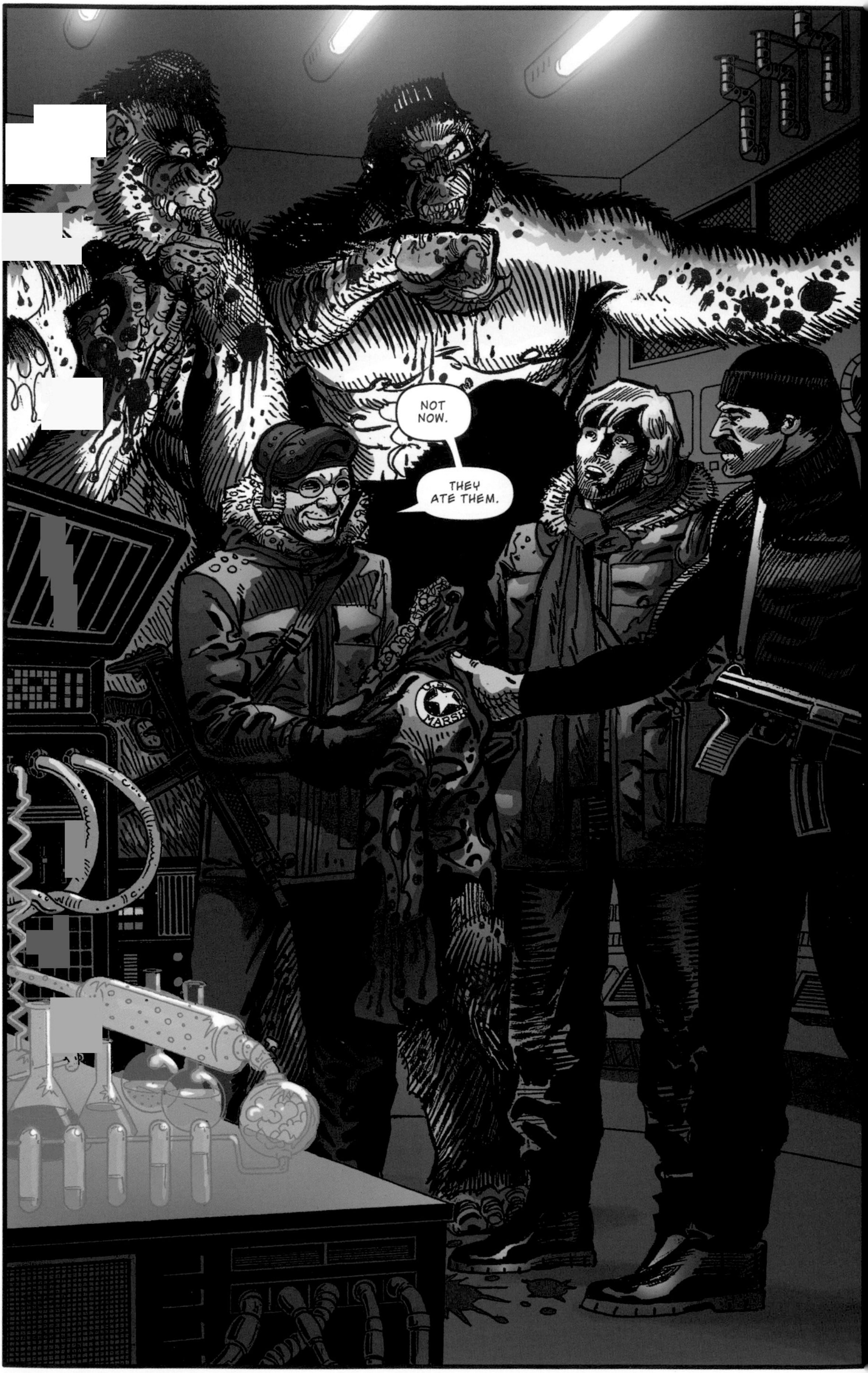
NOT NOW.
THEY ATE THEM.
U.S. MARSH

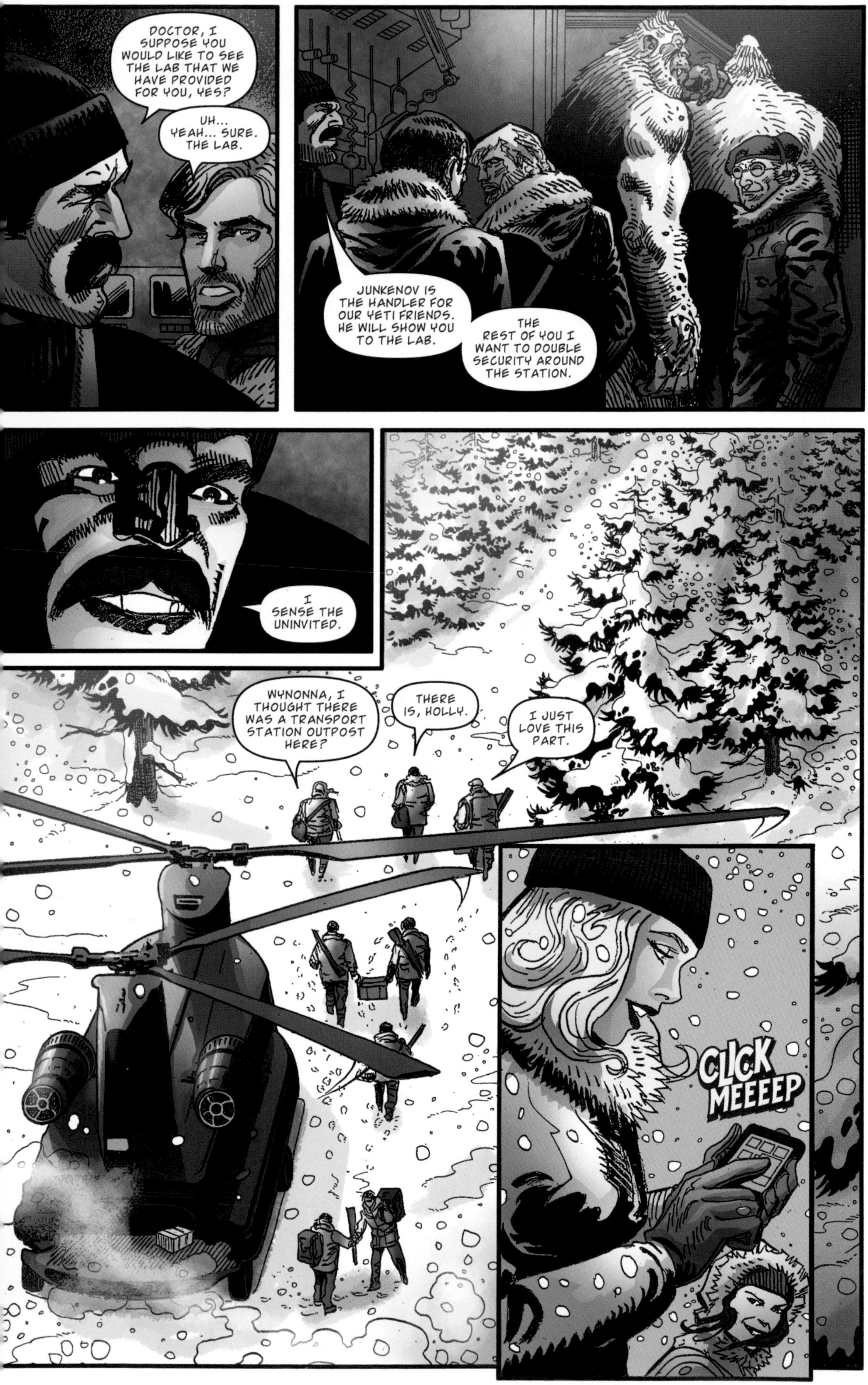
DOCTOR, I SUPPOSE YOU WOULD LIKE TO SEE THE LAB THAT WE HAVE PROVIDED FOR YOU, YES?
UH... YEAH... SURE. THE LAB.
JUNKENOV IS THE HANDLER FOR OUR YETI FRIENDS. HE WILL SHOW YOU TO THE LAB.
THE REST OF YOU I WANT TO DOUBLE SECURITY AROUND THE STATION.
I SENSE THE UNINVITED.
WYNONNA, I THOUGHT THERE WAS A TRANSPORT STATION OUTPOST HERE?
THERE IS, HOLLY.
I JUST LOVE THIS PART.
CLICK
MEEEEP

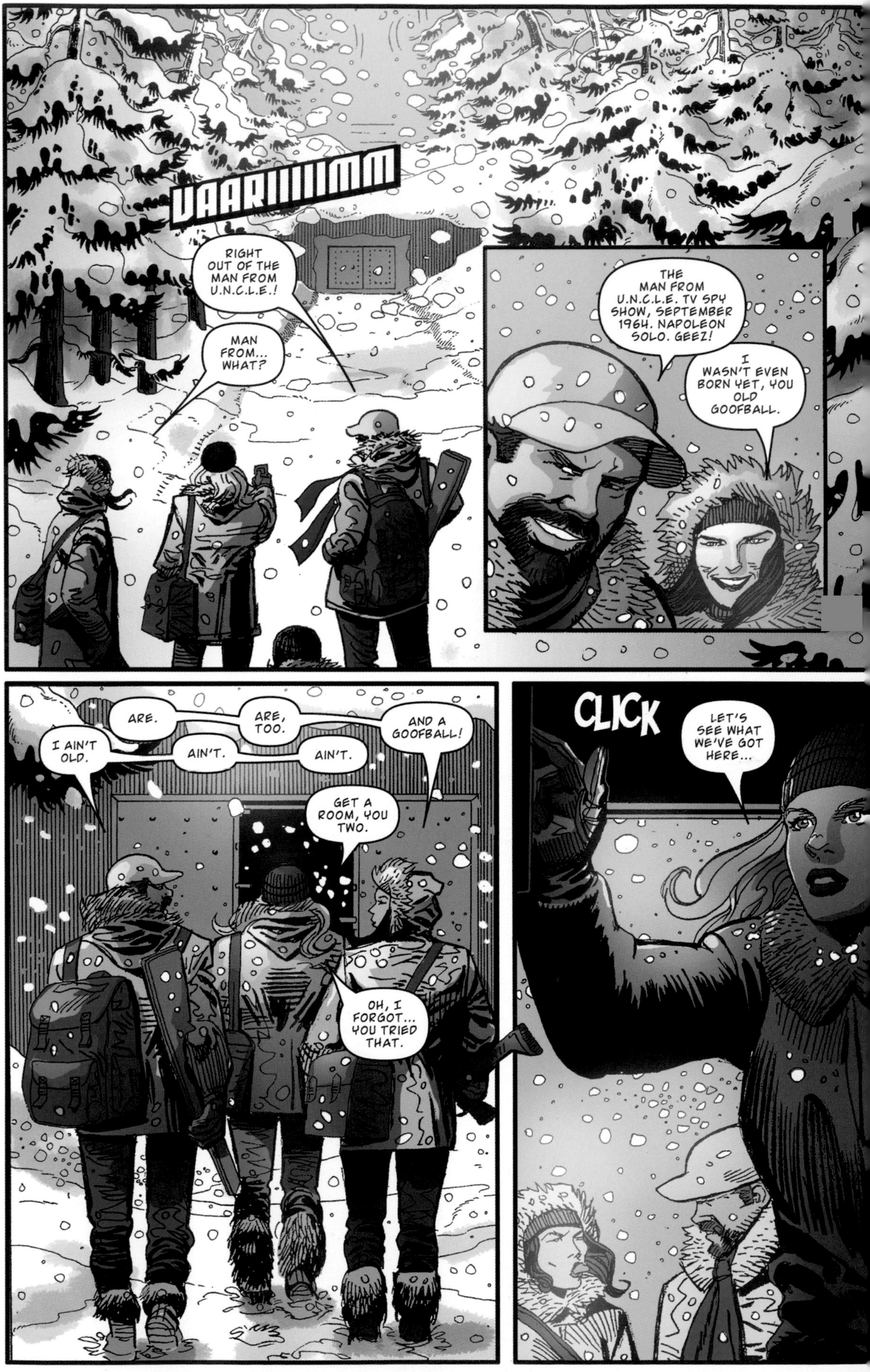
VAARIIIIIMM
RIGHT OUT OF THE MAN FROM U.N.C.L.E.!
MAN FROM... WHAT?
THE MAN FROM U.N.C.L.E. TV SPY SHOW, SEPTEMBER 1964. NAPOLEON SOLO. GEEZ!
I WASN'T EVEN BORN YET, YOU OLD GOOFBALL.
I AIN'T OLD.
ARE.
AIN'T.
ARE, TOO.
AIN'T.
AND A GOOFBALL!
GET A ROOM, YOU TWO.
OH, I FORGOT... YOU TRIED THAT.
CLICK
LET'S SEE WHAT WE'VE GOT HERE...

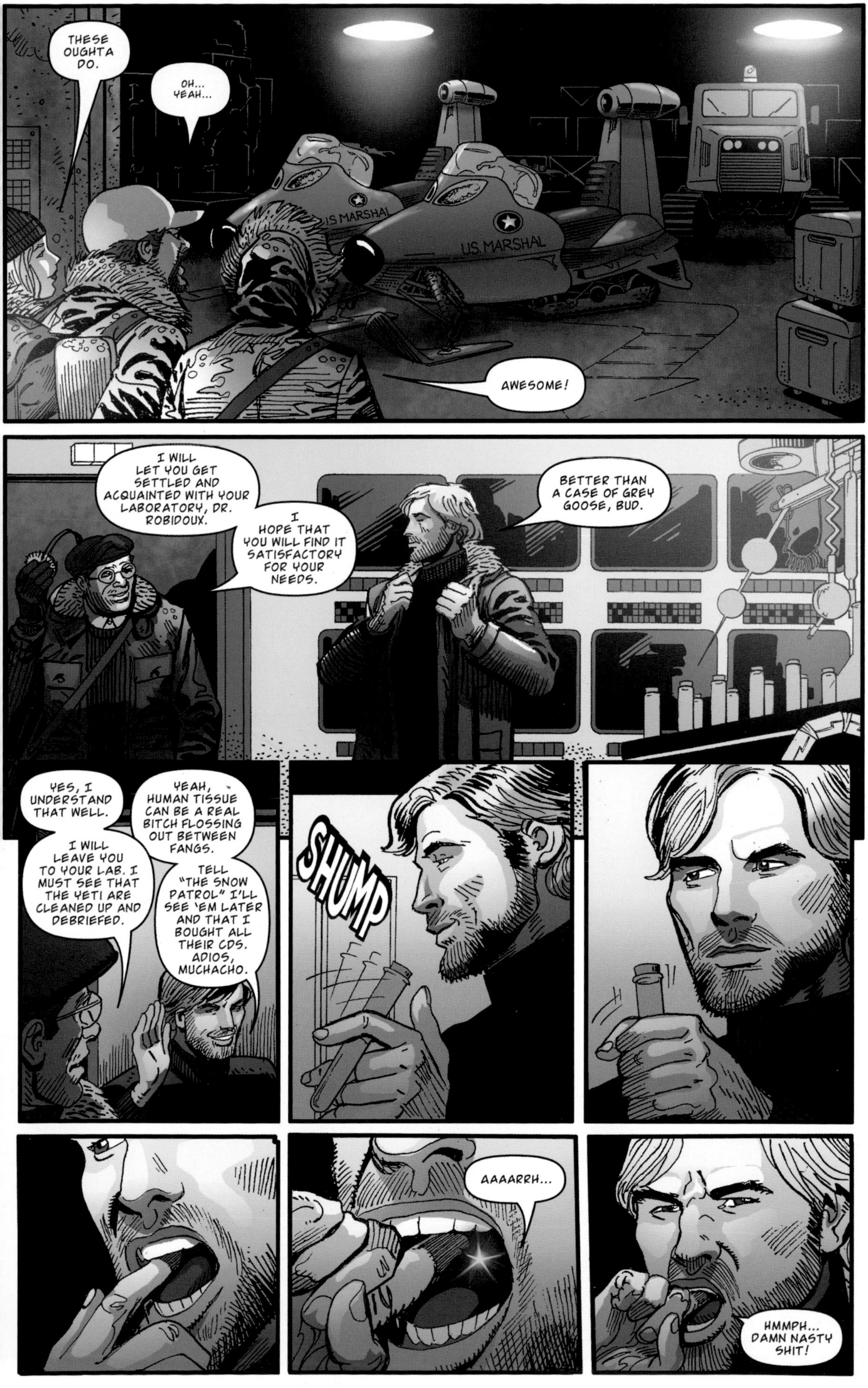
THESE OUGHTA DO.
OH... YEAH...
AWESOME!
I WILL LET YOU GET SETTLED AND ACQUAINTED WITH YOUR LABORATORY, DR. ROBIDOUX.
I HOPE THAT YOU WILL FIND IT SATISFACTORY FOR YOUR NEEDS.
BETTER THAN A CASE OF GREY GOOSE, BUD.
YES, I UNDERSTAND THAT WELL.
YEAH, HUMAN TISSUE CAN BE A REAL BITCH FLOSSING OUT BETWEEN FANGS.
I WILL LEAVE YOU TO YOUR LAB. I MUST SEE THAT THE YETI ARE CLEANED UP AND DEBRIEFED.
TELL "THE SNOW PATROL" I'LL SEE 'EM LATER AND THAT I BOUGHT ALL THEIR CDS. ADIOS, MUCHACHO.
SHUMP
AAAARRH...
HMMPH... DAMN NASTY SHIT!

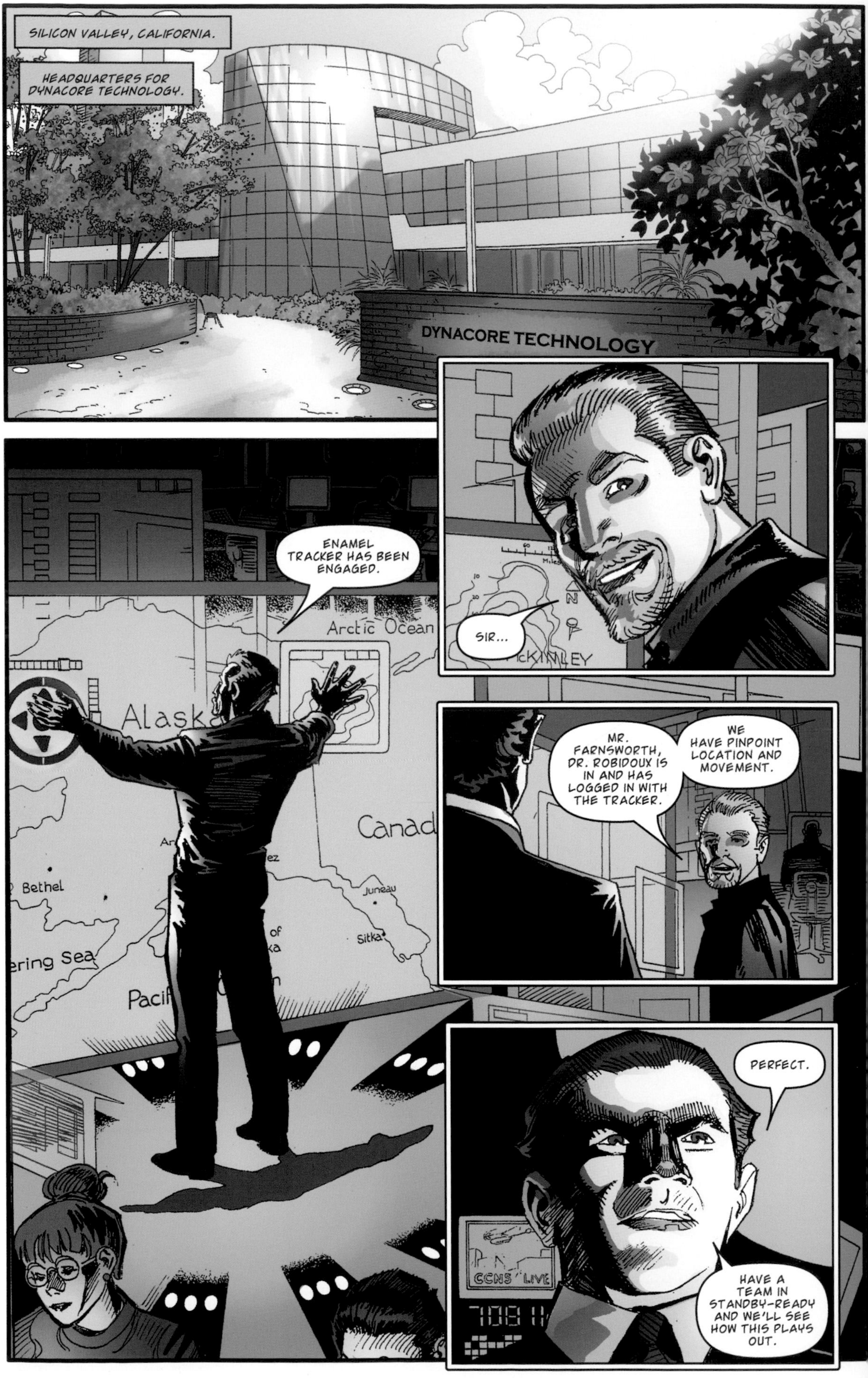
SILICON VALLEY, CALIFORNIA.
HEADQUARTERS FOR DYNACORE TECHNOLOGY.
DYNACORE TECHNOLOGY
SIR...
ENAMEL TRACKER HAS BEEN ENGAGED.
Arctic Ocean
Alaska
Bethel
Juneau
Sitka
MR. FARNSWORTH, DR. ROBIDOUX IS IN AND HAS LOGGED IN WITH THE TRACKER.
WE HAVE PINPOINT LOCATION AND MOVEMENT.
PERFECT.
HAVE A TEAM IN STANDBY-READY AND WE'LL SEE HOW THIS PLAYS OUT.

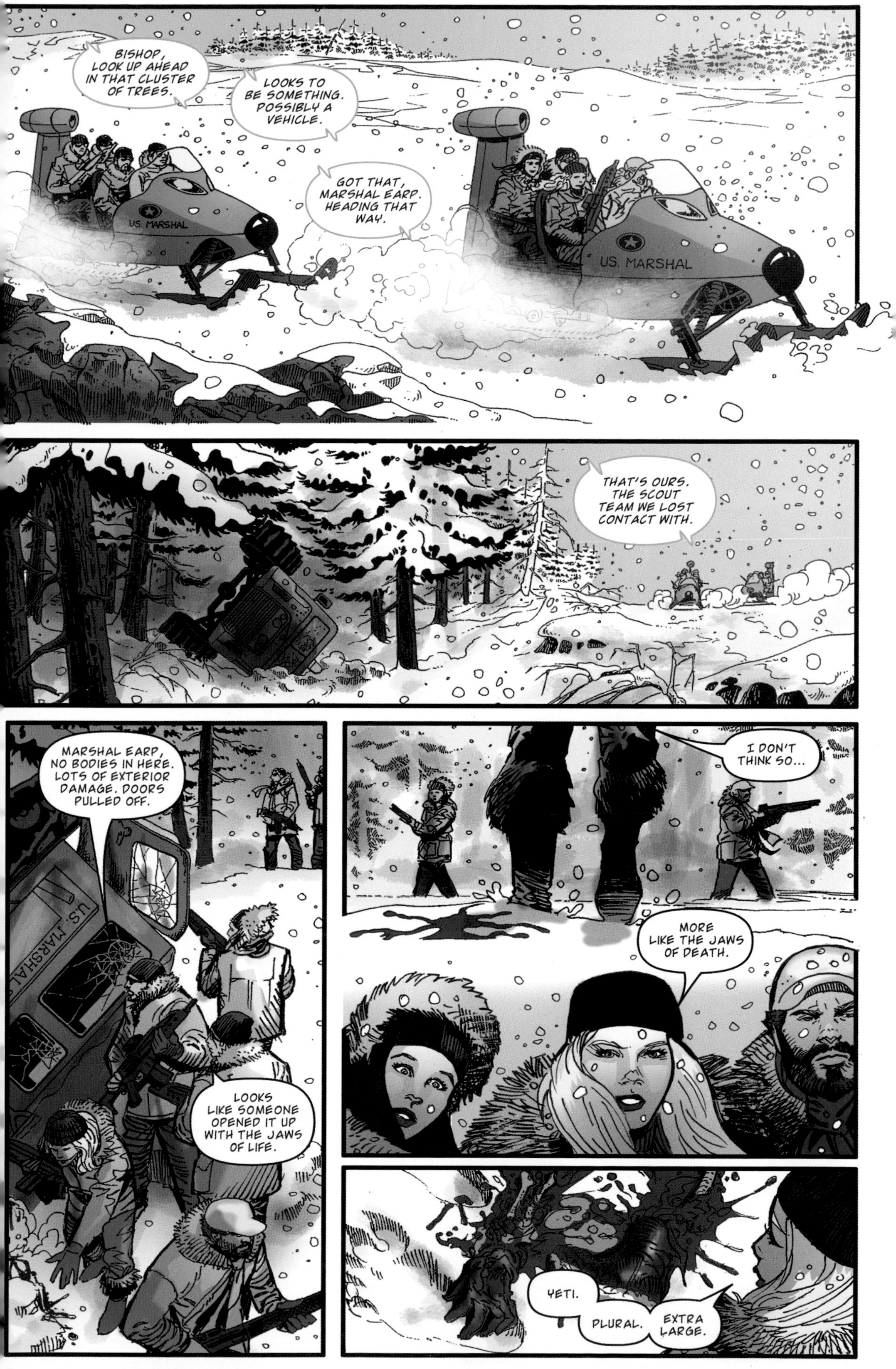
BISHOP, LOOK UP AHEAD IN THAT CLUSTER OF TREES.
LOOKS TO BE SOMETHING. POSSIBLY A VEHICLE.
GOT THAT, MARSHAL EARP. HEADING THAT WAY.
U.S. MARSHAL
U.S. MARSHAL
THAT'S OURS. THE SCOUT TEAM WE LOST CONTACT WITH.
MARSHAL EARP, NO BODIES IN HERE. LOTS OF EXTERIOR DAMAGE. DOORS PULLED OFF.
U.S. MARSHAL
LOOKS LIKE SOMEONE OPENED IT UP WITH THE JAWS OF LIFE.
I DON'T THINK SO...
MORE LIKE THE JAWS OF DEATH.
YETI.
PLURAL.
EXTRA LARGE.

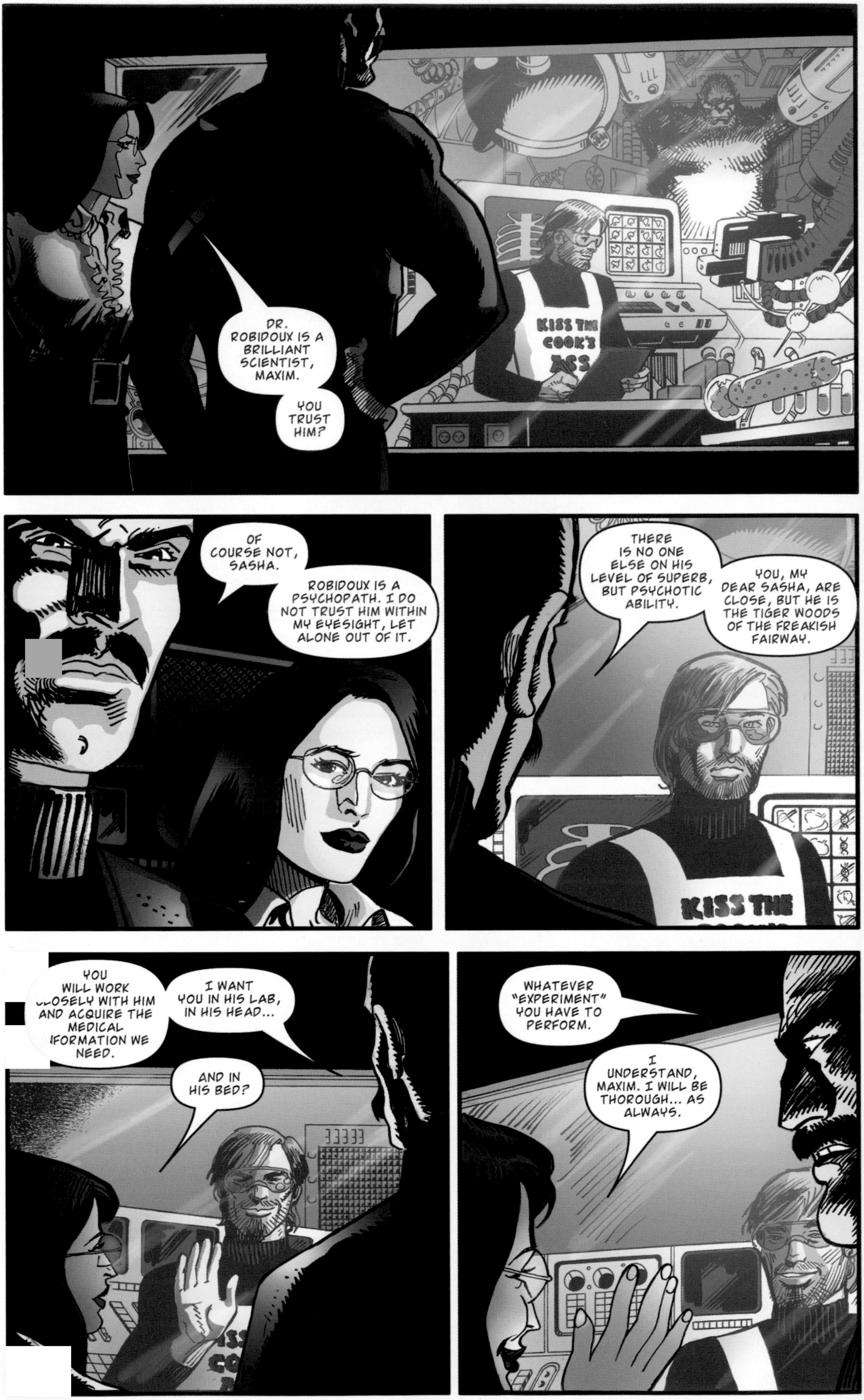
KISS THE COOK'S ASS
DR. ROBIDOUX IS A BRILLIANT SCIENTIST, MAXIM.
YOU TRUST HIM?
OF COURSE NOT, SASHA.
ROBIDOUX IS A PSYCHOPATH. I DO NOT TRUST HIM WITHIN MY EYESIGHT, LET ALONE OUT OF IT.
THERE IS NO ONE ELSE ON HIS LEVEL OF SUPERB, BUT PSYCHOTIC ABILITY.
YOU, MY DEAR SASHA, ARE CLOSE, BUT HE IS THE TIGER WOODS OF THE FREAKISH FAIRWAY.
KISS THE
YOU WILL WORK OSELY WITH HIM AND ACQUIRE THE MEDICAL FORMATION WE NEED.
I WANT YOU IN HIS LAB, IN HIS HEAD...
AND IN HIS BED?
WHATEVER "EXPERIMENT" YOU HAVE TO PERFORM.
I UNDERSTAND, MAXIM. I WILL BE THOROUGH... AS ALWAYS.

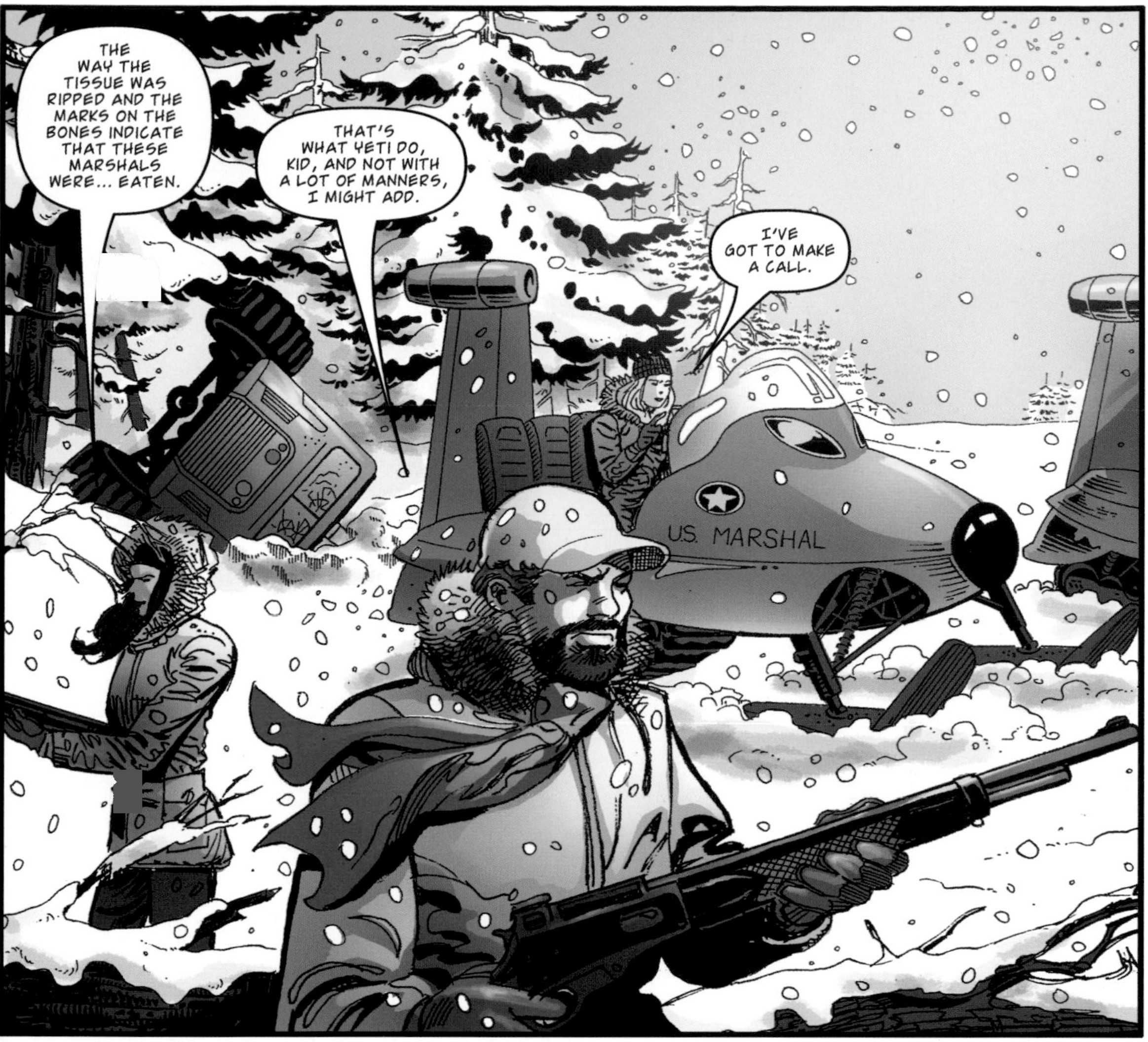
THE WAY THE TISSUE WAS RIPPED AND THE MARKS ON THE BONES INDICATE THAT THESE MARSHALS WERE... EATEN.
THAT'S WHAT YETI DO, KID, AND NOT WITH A LOT OF MANNERS, I MIGHT ADD.
I'VE GOT TO MAKE A CALL.
U.S. MARSHAL

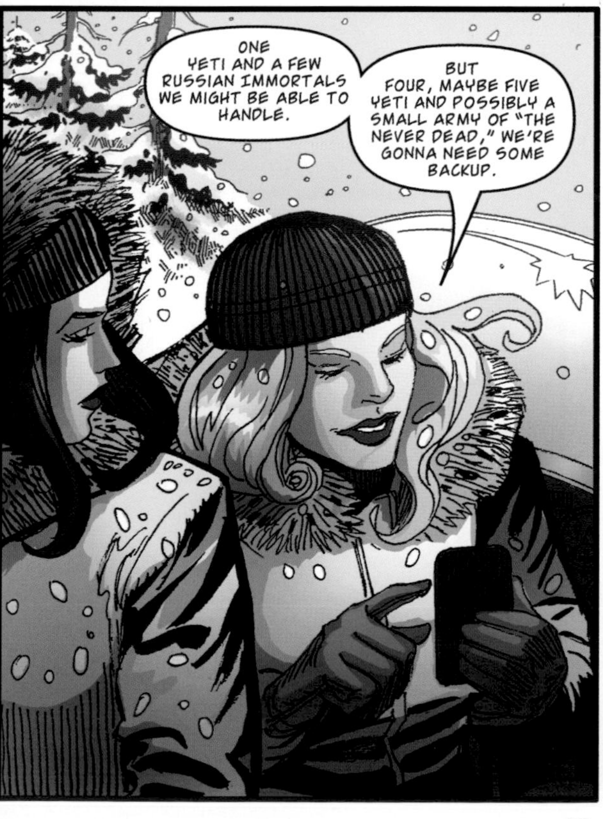
ONE YETI AND A FEW RUSSIAN IMMORTALS WE MIGHT BE ABLE TO HANDLE.
BUT FOUR, MAYBE FIVE YETI AND POSSIBLY A SMALL ARMY OF "THE NEVER DEAD," WE'RE GONNA NEED SOME BACKUP.

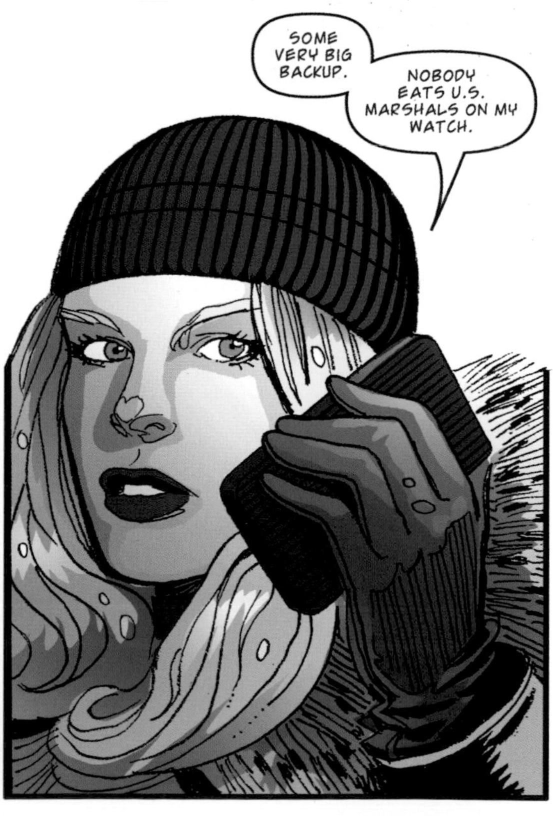
SOME VERY BIG BACKUP.
NOBODY EATS U.S. MARSHALS ON MY WATCH.

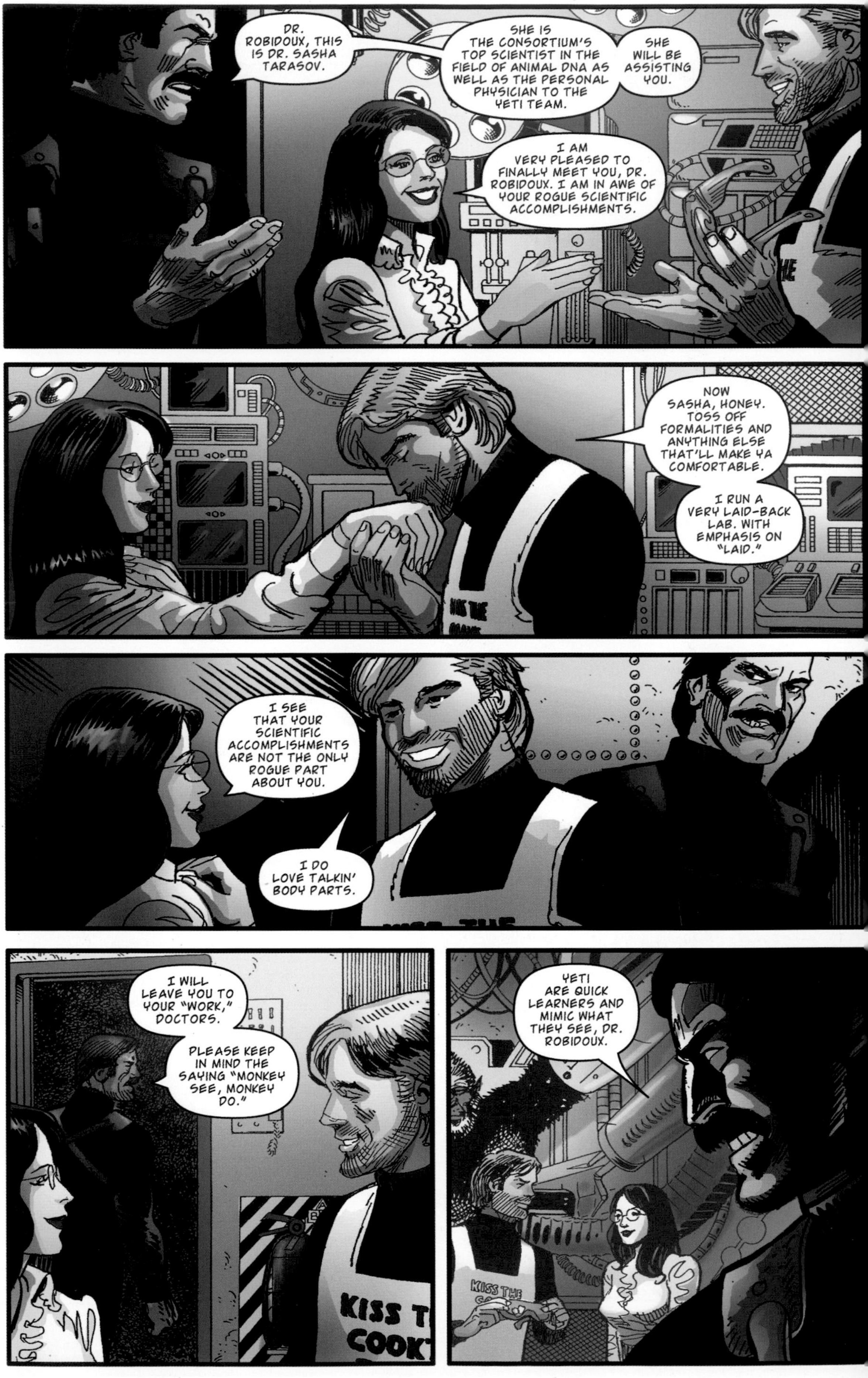
DR. ROBIDOUX, THIS IS DR. SASHA TARASOV.
SHE IS THE CONSORTIUM'S TOP SCIENTIST IN THE FIELD OF ANIMAL DNA AS WELL AS THE PERSONAL PHYSICIAN TO THE YETI TEAM.
SHE WILL BE ASSISTING YOU.
I AM VERY PLEASED TO FINALLY MEET YOU, DR. ROBIDOUX. I AM IN AWE OF YOUR ROGUE SCIENTIFIC ACCOMPLISHMENTS.
NOW SASHA, HONEY. TOSS OFF FORMALITIES AND ANYTHING ELSE THAT'LL MAKE YA COMFORTABLE.
I RUN A VERY LAID-BACK LAB. WITH EMPHASIS ON "LAID."
I SEE THAT YOUR SCIENTIFIC ACCOMPLISHMENTS ARE NOT THE ONLY ROGUE PART ABOUT YOU.
I DO LOVE TALKIN' BODY PARTS.
I WILL LEAVE YOU TO YOUR "WORK," DOCTORS.
PLEASE KEEP IN MIND THE SAYING "MONKEY SEE, MONKEY DO."
YETI ARE QUICK LEARNERS AND MIMIC WHAT THEY SEE, DR. ROBIDOUX.

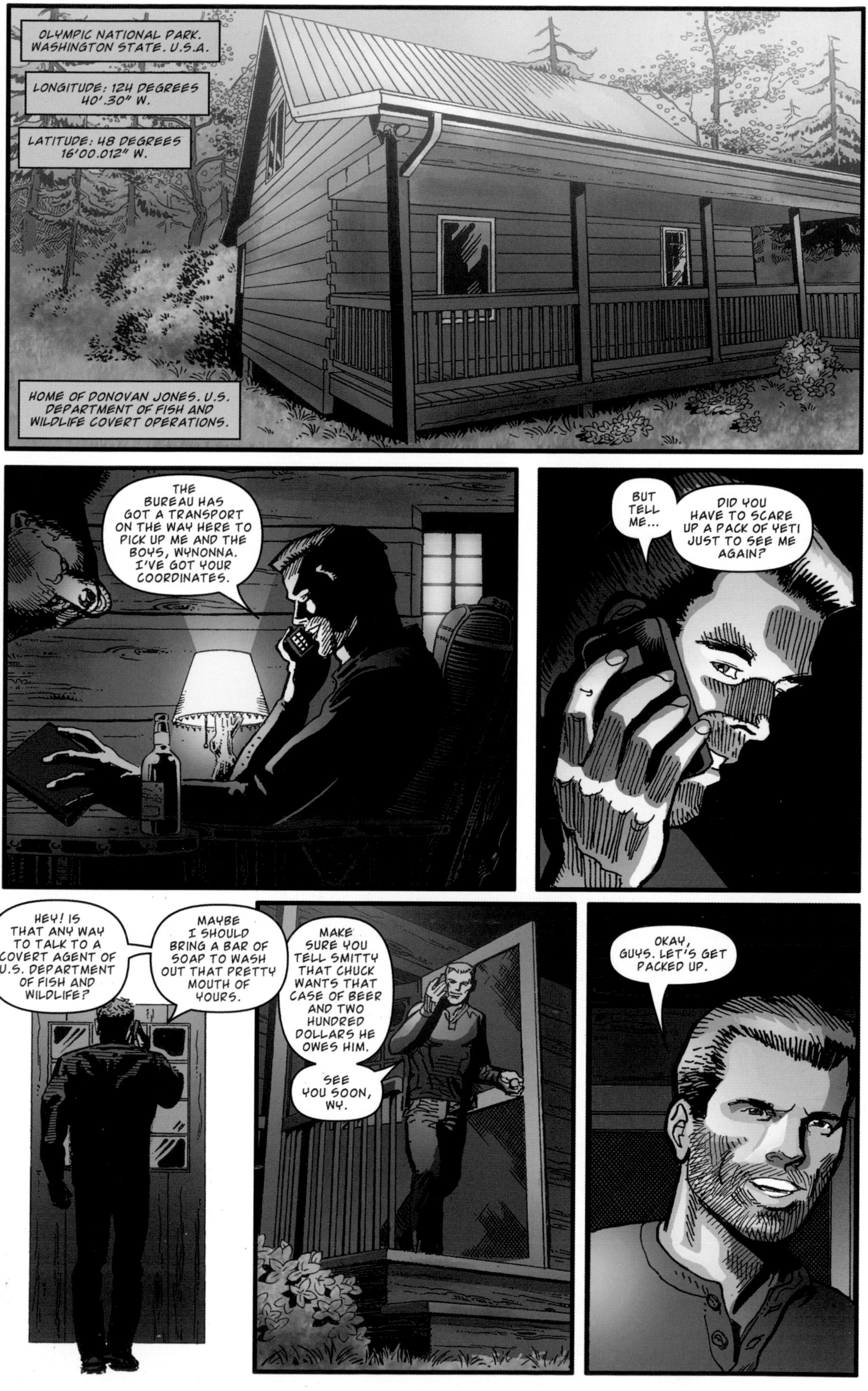

OLYMPIC NATIONAL PARK. WASHINGTON STATE. U.S.A.
LONGITUDE: 124 DEGREES 40'.30" W.
LATITUDE: 48 DEGREES 16'00.012" W.
HOME OF DONOVAN JONES. U.S. DEPARTMENT OF FISH AND WILDLIFE COVERT OPERATIONS.
THE BUREAU HAS GOT A TRANSPORT ON THE WAY HERE TO PICK UP ME AND THE BOYS, WYNONNA. I'VE GOT YOUR COORDINATES.
BUT TELL ME...
DID YOU HAVE TO SCARE UP A PACK OF YETI JUST TO SEE ME AGAIN?
HEY! IS THAT ANY WAY TO TALK TO A COVERT AGENT OF U.S. DEPARTMENT OF FISH AND WILDLIFE?
MAYBE I SHOULD BRING A BAR OF SOAP TO WASH OUT THAT PRETTY MOUTH OF YOURS.
MAKE SURE YOU TELL SMITTY THAT CHUCK WANTS THAT CASE OF BEER AND TWO HUNDRED DOLLARS HE OWES HIM.
SEE YOU SOON, WY.
OKAY, GUYS. LET'S GET PACKED UP.

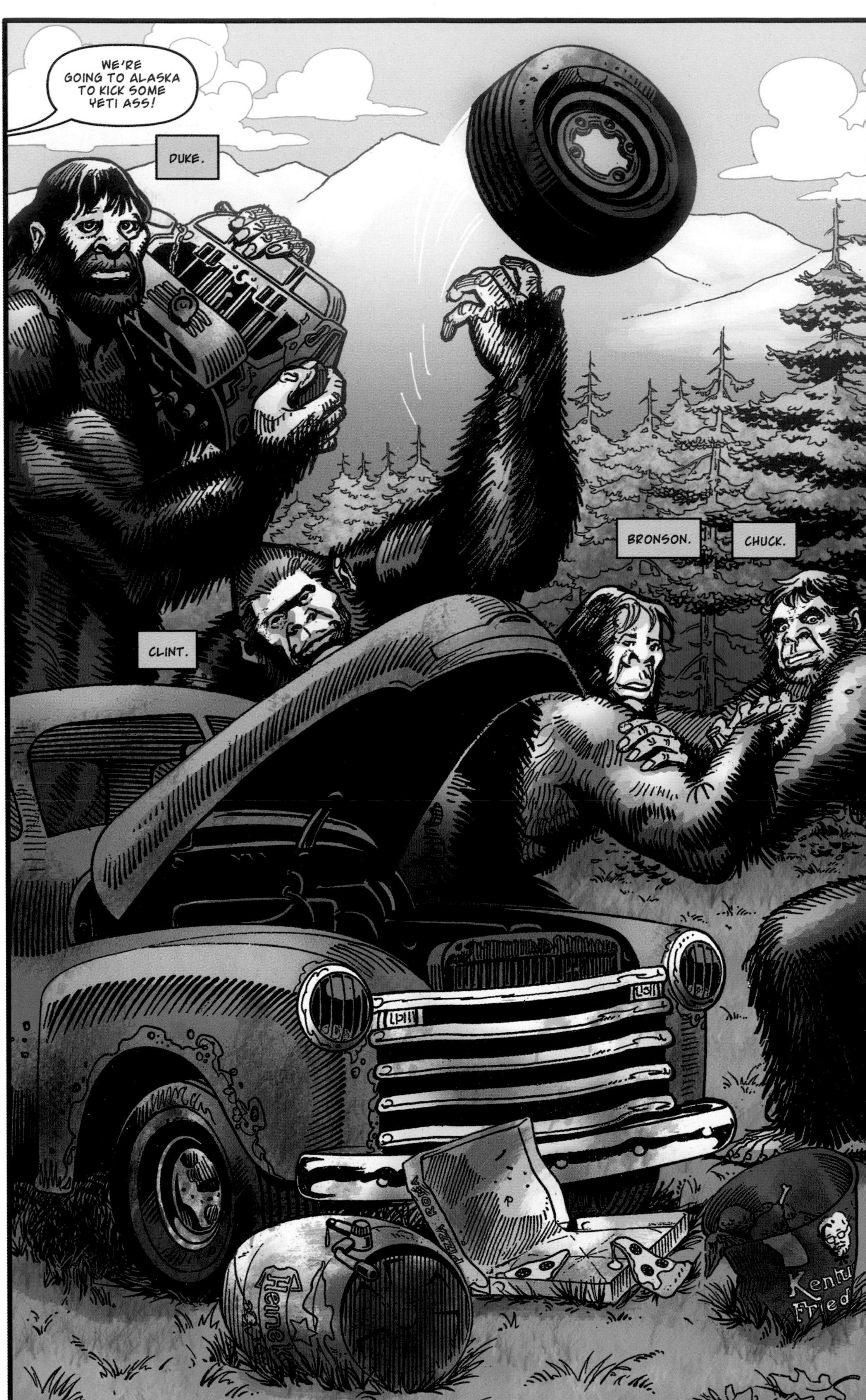
WE'RE GOING TO ALASKA TO KICK SOME YETI ASS!
DUKE.
BRONSON.
CHUCK.
CLINT.
PIZZA ROMA
Heinek
Kentu
Fried

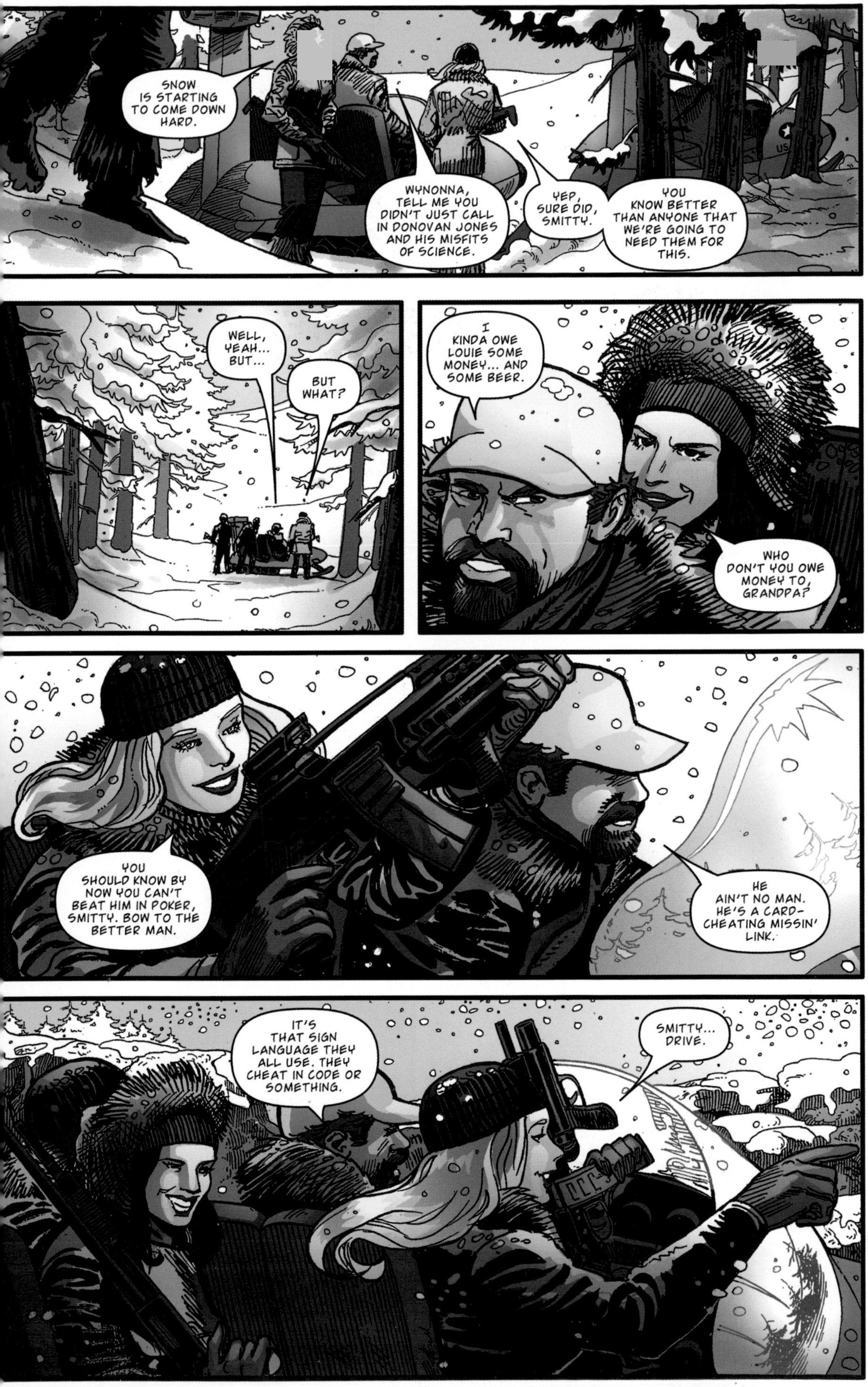
SNOW IS STARTING TO COME DOWN HARD.
WYNONNA, TELL ME YOU DIDN'T JUST CALL IN DONOVAN JONES AND HIS MISFITS OF SCIENCE.
YEP, SURE DID, SMITTY.
YOU KNOW BETTER THAN ANYONE THAT WE'RE GOING TO NEED THEM FOR THIS.
WELL, YEAH... BUT...
BUT WHAT?
I KINDA OWE LOUIE SOME MONEY... AND SOME BEER.
WHO DON'T YOU OWE MONEY TO, GRANDPA?
YOU SHOULD KNOW BY NOW YOU CAN'T BEAT HIM IN POKER, SMITTY. BOW TO THE BETTER MAN.
HE AIN'T NO MAN. HE'S A CARD-CHEATING MISSIN' LINK.
IT'S THAT SIGN LANGUAGE THEY ALL USE. THEY CHEAT IN CODE OR SOMETHING.
SMITTY... DRIVE.

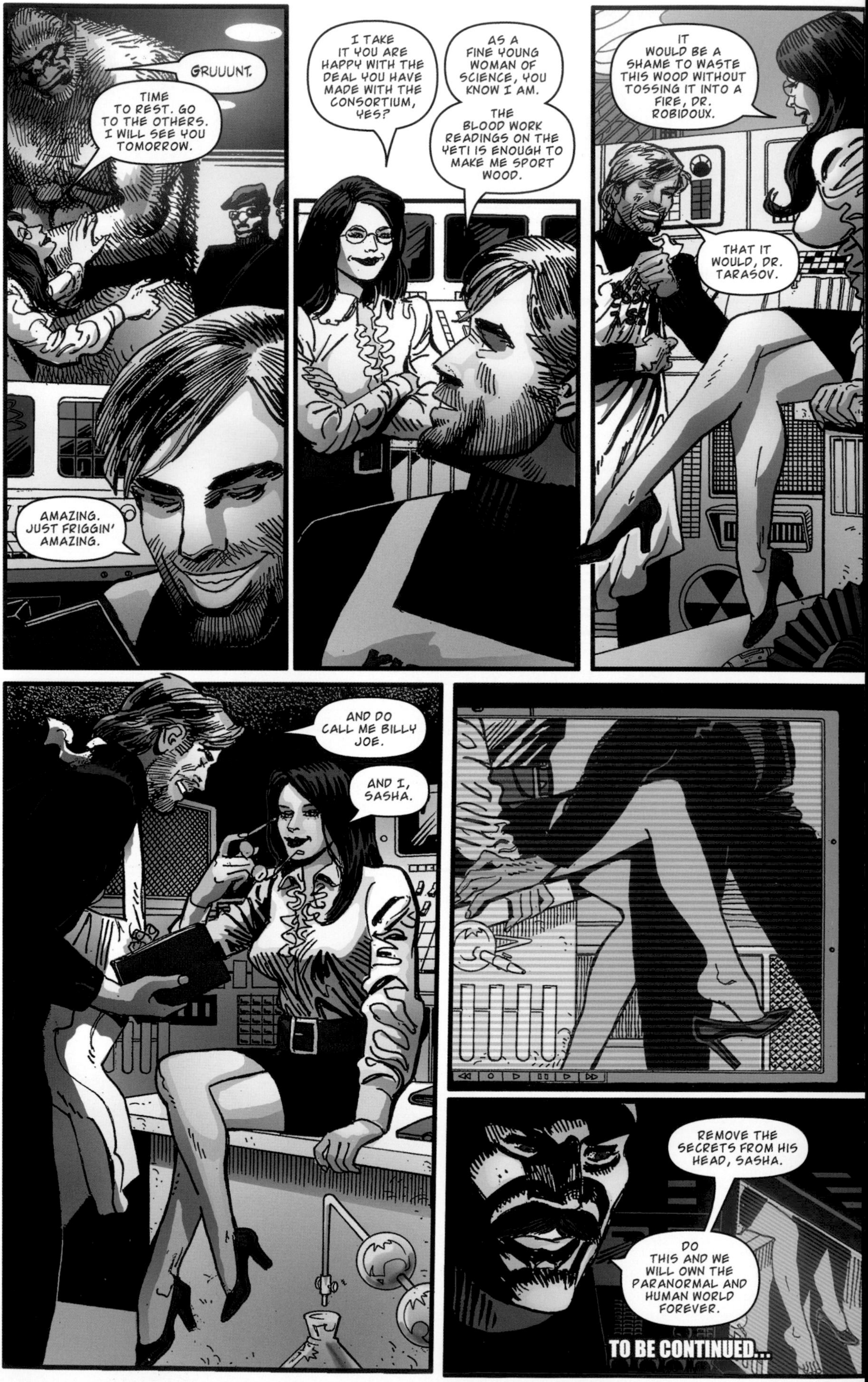
GRUUUNT.
TIME TO REST. GO TO THE OTHERS. I WILL SEE YOU TOMORROW.
AMAZING. JUST FRIGGIN' AMAZING.
I TAKE IT YOU ARE HAPPY WITH THE DEAL YOU HAVE MADE WITH THE CONSORTIUM, YES?
AS A FINE YOUNG WOMAN OF SCIENCE, YOU KNOW I AM.
THE BLOOD WORK READINGS ON THE YETI IS ENOUGH TO MAKE ME SPORT WOOD.
IT WOULD BE A SHAME TO WASTE THIS WOOD WITHOUT TOSSING IT INTO A FIRE, DR. ROBIDOUX.
THAT IT WOULD, DR. TARASOV.
AND DO CALL ME BILLY JOE.
AND I, SASHA.
REMOVE THE SECRETS FROM HIS HEAD, SASHA.
DO THIS AND WE WILL OWN THE PARANORMAL AND HUMAN WORLD FOREVER.
TO BE CONTINUED...

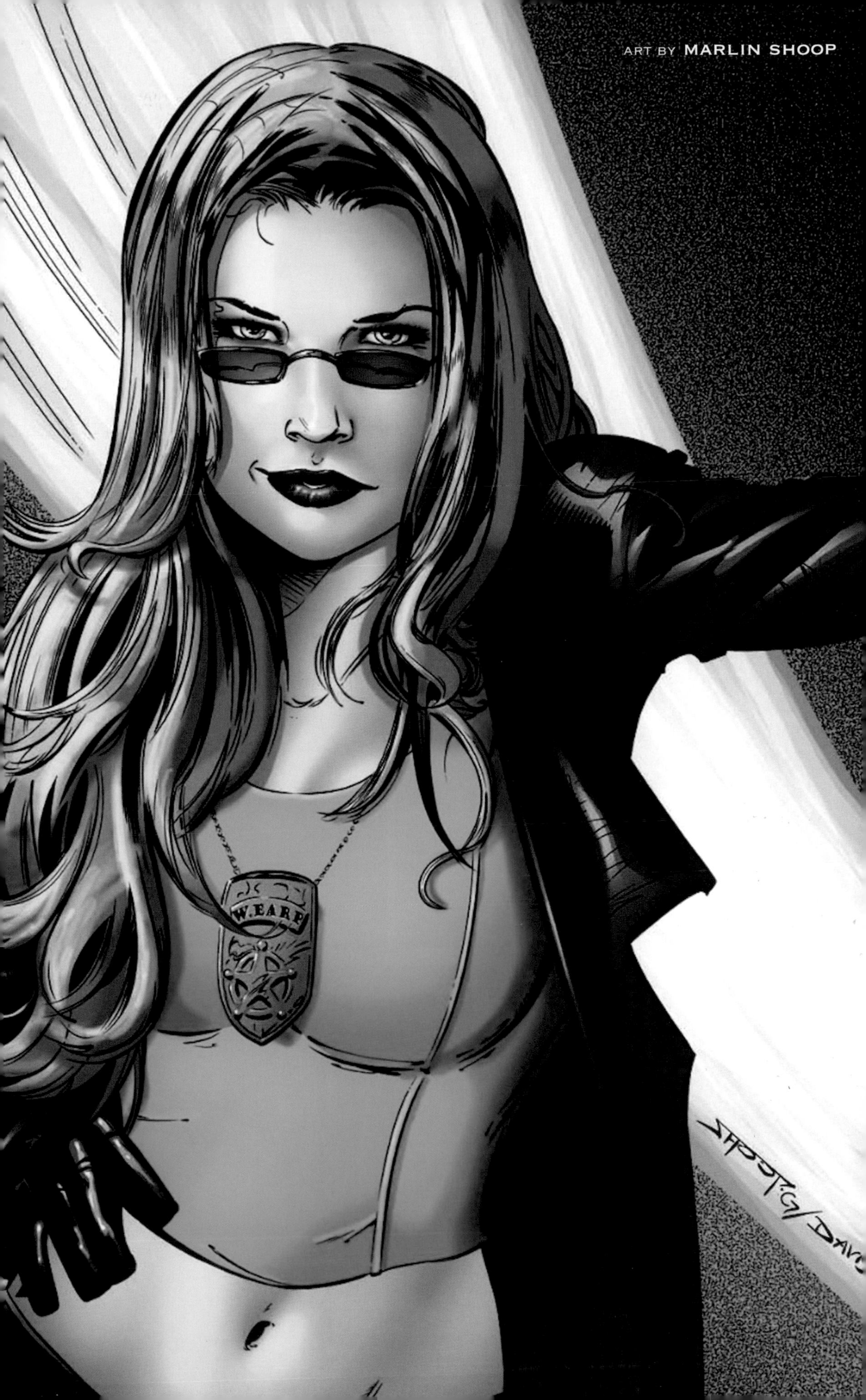
W.EARP
ART BY **MARLIN SHOOP**

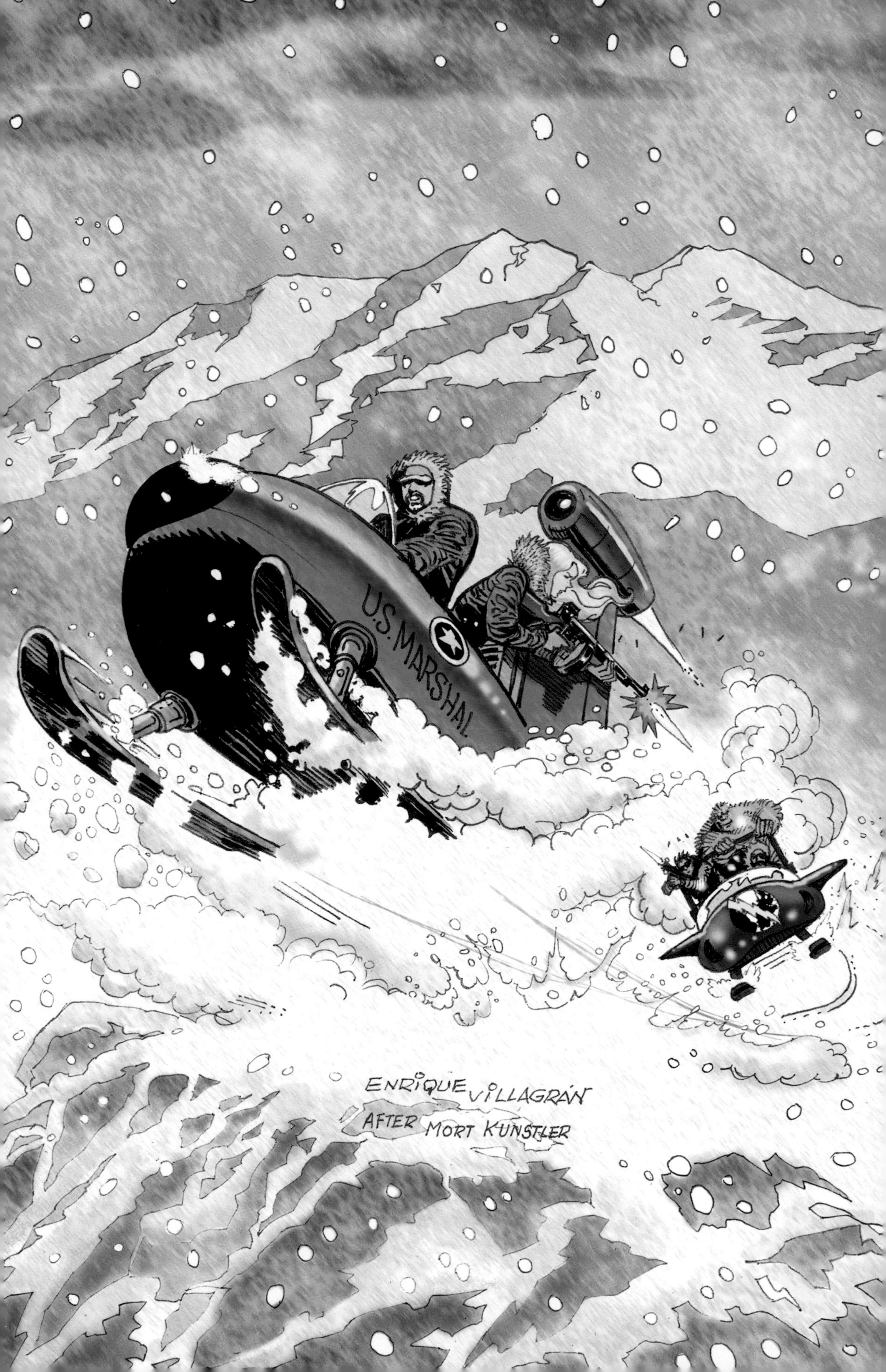
U.S. MARSHAL
ENRIQUE VILLAGRAN
AFTER MORT KUNSTLER

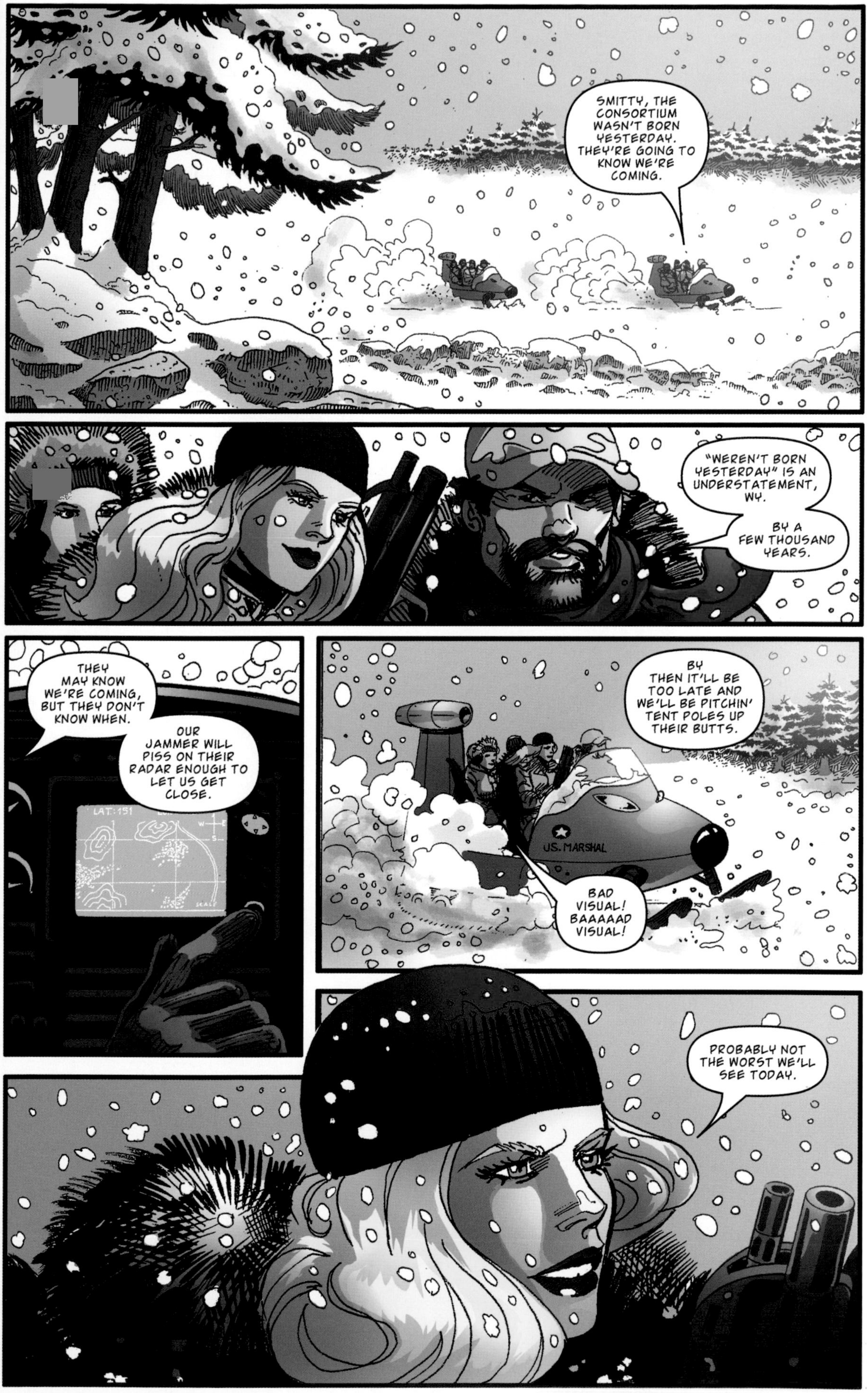
SMITTY, THE CONSORTIUM WASN'T BORN YESTERDAY. THEY'RE GOING TO KNOW WE'RE COMING.
"WEREN'T BORN YESTERDAY" IS AN UNDERSTATEMENT, WY.
BY A FEW THOUSAND YEARS.
THEY MAY KNOW WE'RE COMING, BUT THEY DON'T KNOW WHEN.
OUR JAMMER WILL PISS ON THEIR RADAR ENOUGH TO LET US GET CLOSE.
LAT: 151
BY THEN IT'LL BE TOO LATE AND WE'LL BE PITCHIN' TENT POLES UP THEIR BUTTS.
U.S. MARSHAL
BAD VISUAL! BAAAAAD VISUAL!
PROBABLY NOT THE WORST WE'LL SEE TODAY.

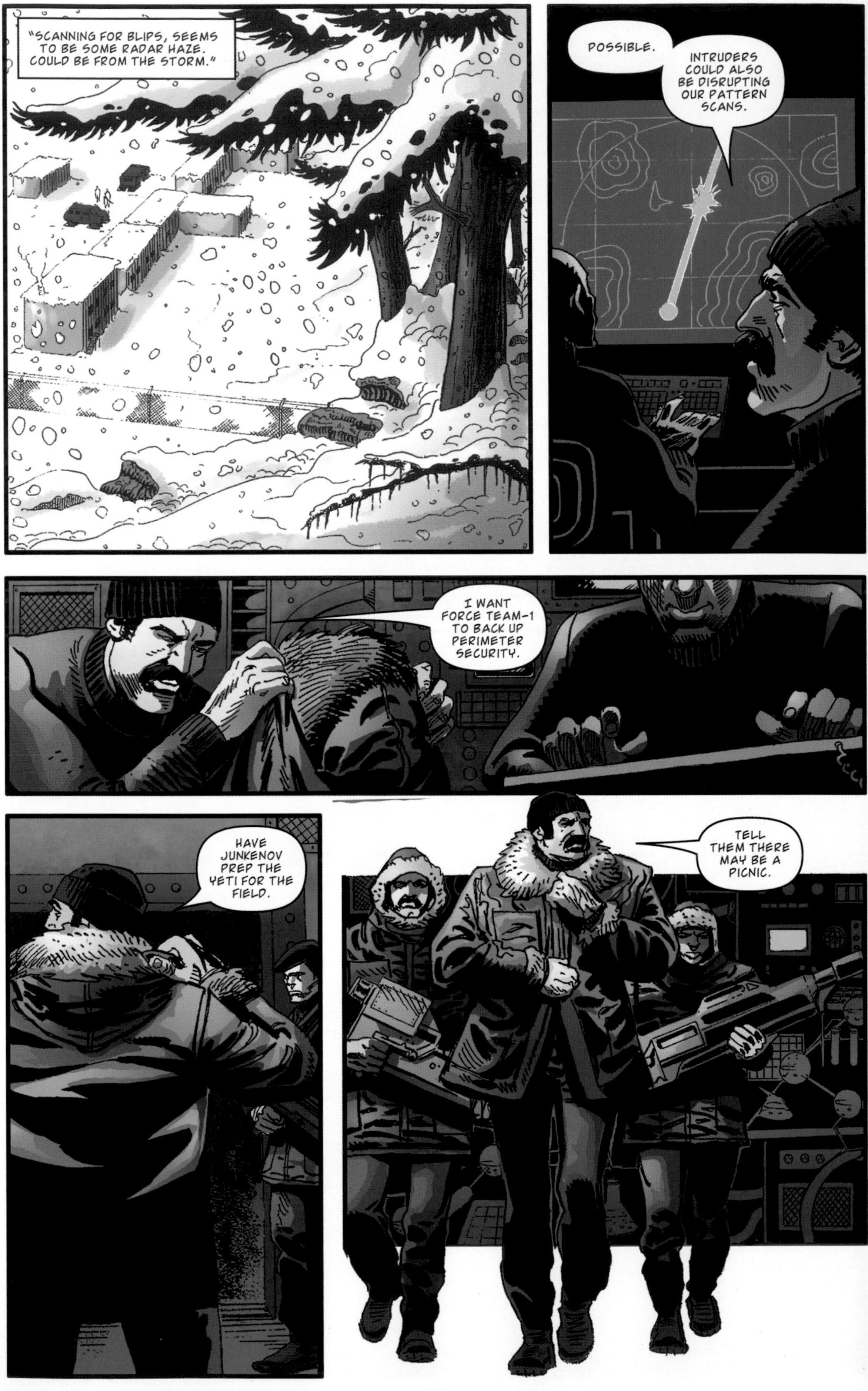
"SCANNING FOR BLIPS, SEEMS TO BE SOME RADAR HAZE. COULD BE FROM THE STORM."
POSSIBLE.
INTRUDERS COULD ALSO BE DISRUPTING OUR PATTERN SCANS.
I WANT FORCE TEAM-1 TO BACK UP PERIMETER SECURITY.
HAVE JUNKENOV PREP THE YETI FOR THE FIELD.
TELL THEM THERE MAY BE A PICNIC.

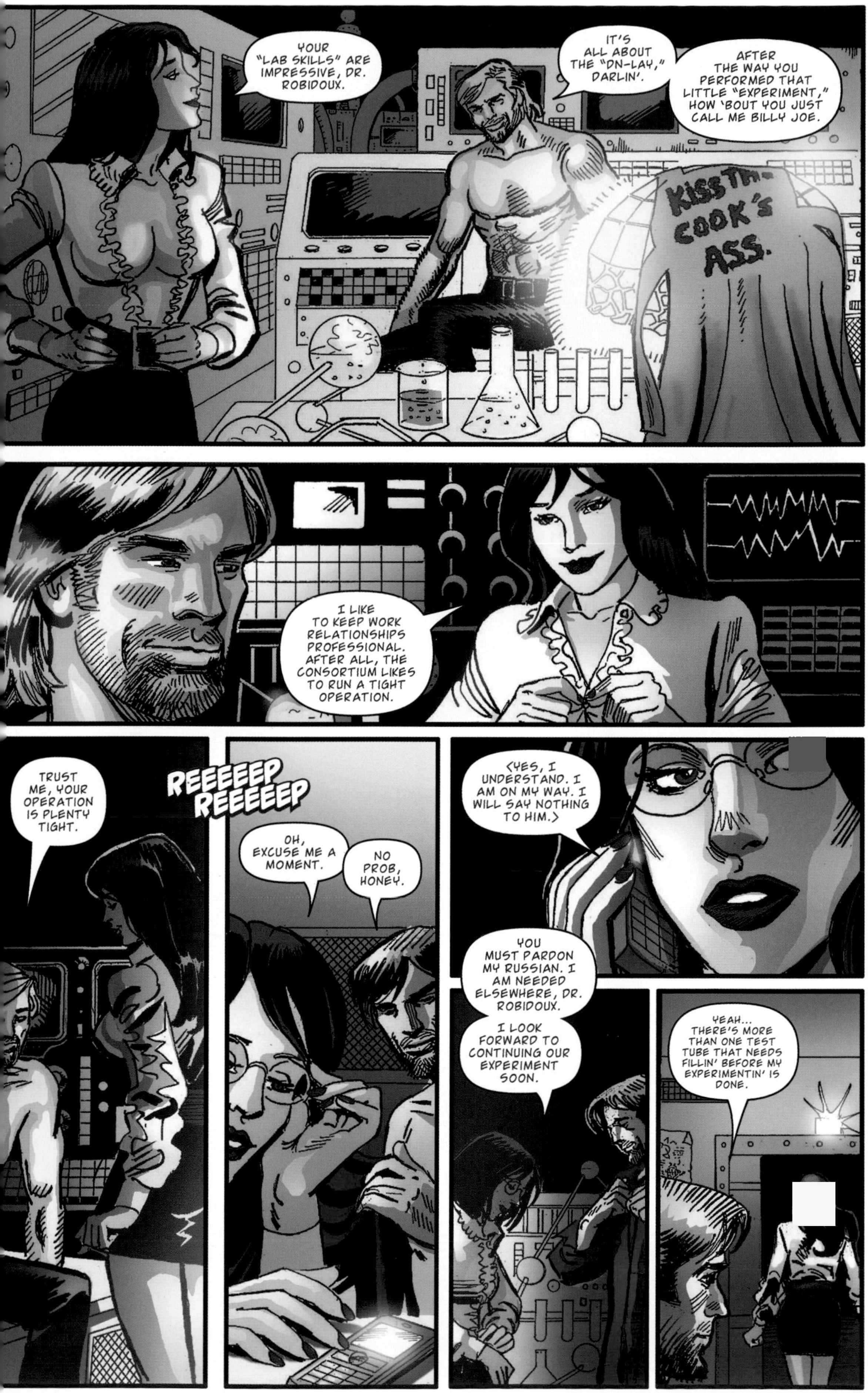
YOUR "LAB SKILLS" ARE IMPRESSIVE, DR. ROBIDOUX.
IT'S ALL ABOUT THE "DN-LAY," DARLIN'.
AFTER THE WAY YOU PERFORMED THAT LITTLE "EXPERIMENT," HOW 'BOUT YOU JUST CALL ME BILLY JOE.
KISS TH- COOK'S ASS.
I LIKE TO KEEP WORK RELATIONSHIPS PROFESSIONAL. AFTER ALL, THE CONSORTIUM LIKES TO RUN A TIGHT OPERATION.
TRUST ME, YOUR OPERATION IS PLENTY TIGHT.
REEEEEP REEEEEP
OH, EXCUSE ME A MOMENT.
NO PROB, HONEY.
<YES, I UNDERSTAND. I AM ON MY WAY. I WILL SAY NOTHING TO HIM.>
YOU MUST PARDON MY RUSSIAN. I AM NEEDED ELSEWHERE, DR. ROBIDOUX.
I LOOK FORWARD TO CONTINUING OUR EXPERIMENT SOON.
YEAH... THERE'S MORE THAN ONE TEST TUBE THAT NEEDS FILLIN' BEFORE MY EXPERIMENTIN' IS DONE.

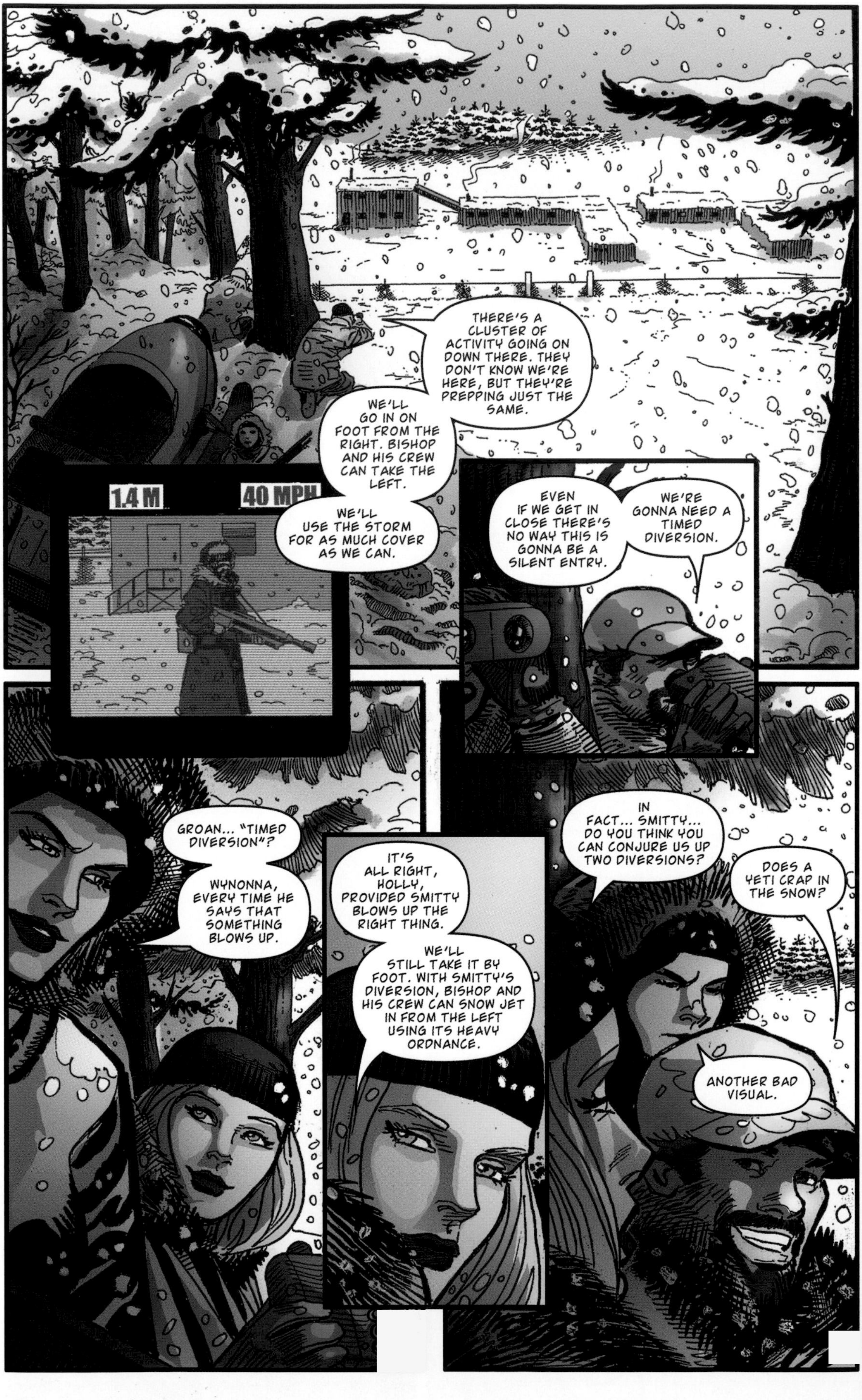
THERE'S A CLUSTER OF ACTIVITY GOING ON DOWN THERE. THEY DON'T KNOW WE'RE HERE, BUT THEY'RE PREPPING JUST THE SAME.
WE'LL GO IN ON FOOT FROM THE RIGHT. BISHOP AND HIS CREW CAN TAKE THE LEFT.
WE'LL USE THE STORM FOR AS MUCH COVER AS WE CAN.
1.4 M
40 MPH
EVEN IF WE GET IN CLOSE THERE'S NO WAY THIS IS GONNA BE A SILENT ENTRY.
WE'RE GONNA NEED A TIMED DIVERSION.
GROAN... "TIMED DIVERSION"?
WYNONNA, EVERY TIME HE SAYS THAT SOMETHING BLOWS UP.
IT'S ALL RIGHT, HOLLY, PROVIDED SMITTY BLOWS UP THE RIGHT THING.
WE'LL STILL TAKE IT BY FOOT. WITH SMITTY'S DIVERSION, BISHOP AND HIS CREW CAN SNOW JET IN FROM THE LEFT USING ITS HEAVY ORDNANCE.
IN FACT... SMITTY... DO YOU THINK YOU CAN CONJURE US UP TWO DIVERSIONS?
DOES A YETI CRAP IN THE SNOW?
ANOTHER BAD VISUAL.

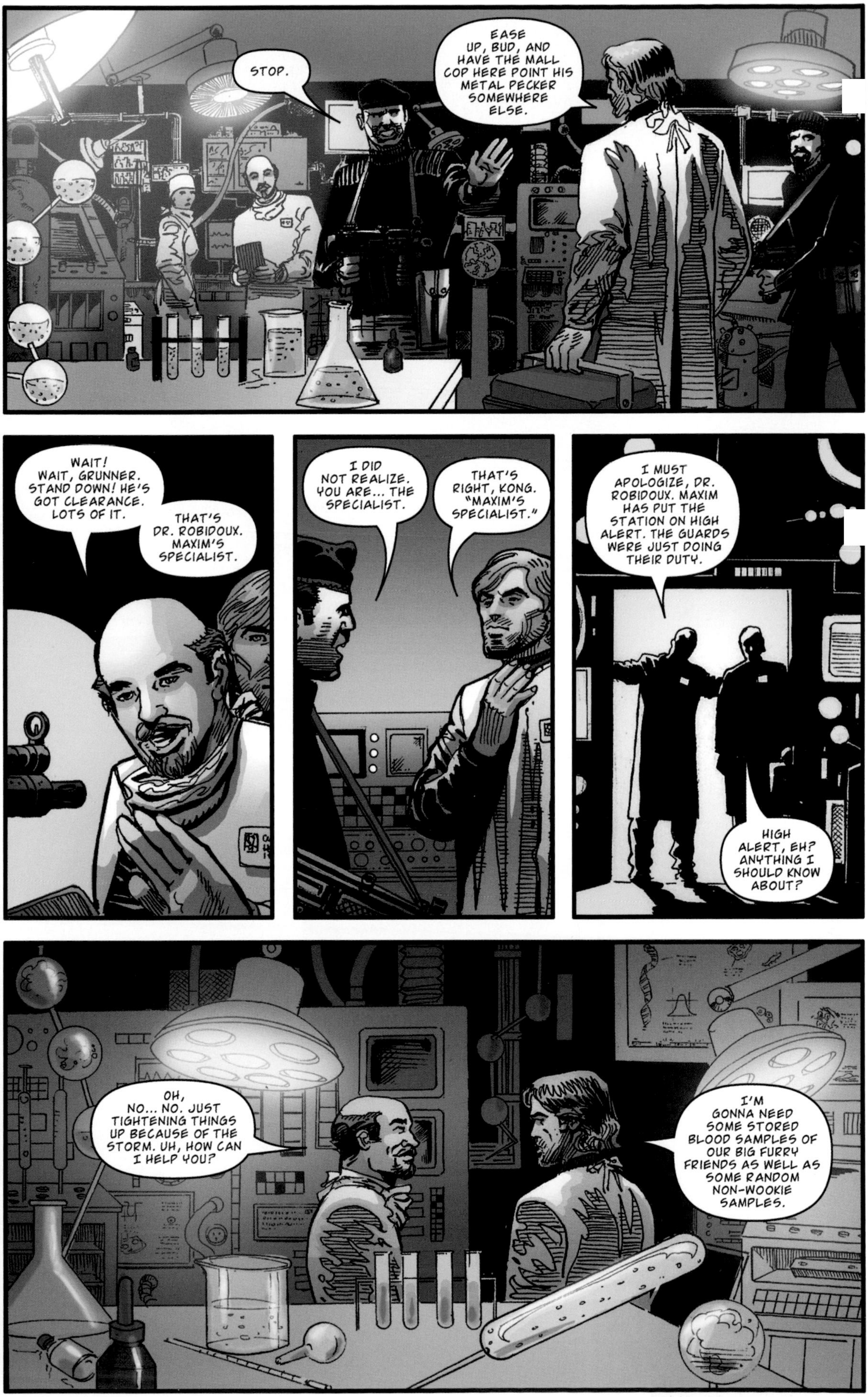
STOP.
EASE UP, BUD, AND HAVE THE MALL COP HERE POINT HIS METAL PECKER SOMEWHERE ELSE.
WAIT! WAIT, GRUNNER. STAND DOWN! HE'S GOT CLEARANCE. LOTS OF IT.
THAT'S DR. ROBIDOUX. MAXIM'S SPECIALIST.
I DID NOT REALIZE. YOU ARE... THE SPECIALIST.
THAT'S RIGHT, KONG. "MAXIM'S SPECIALIST."
I MUST APOLOGIZE, DR. ROBIDOUX. MAXIM HAS PUT THE STATION ON HIGH ALERT. THE GUARDS WERE JUST DOING THEIR DUTY.
HIGH ALERT, EH? ANYTHING I SHOULD KNOW ABOUT?
OH, NO... NO. JUST TIGHTENING THINGS UP BECAUSE OF THE STORM. UH, HOW CAN I HELP YOU?
I'M GONNA NEED SOME STORED BLOOD SAMPLES OF OUR BIG FURRY FRIENDS AS WELL AS SOME RANDOM NON-WOOKIE SAMPLES.

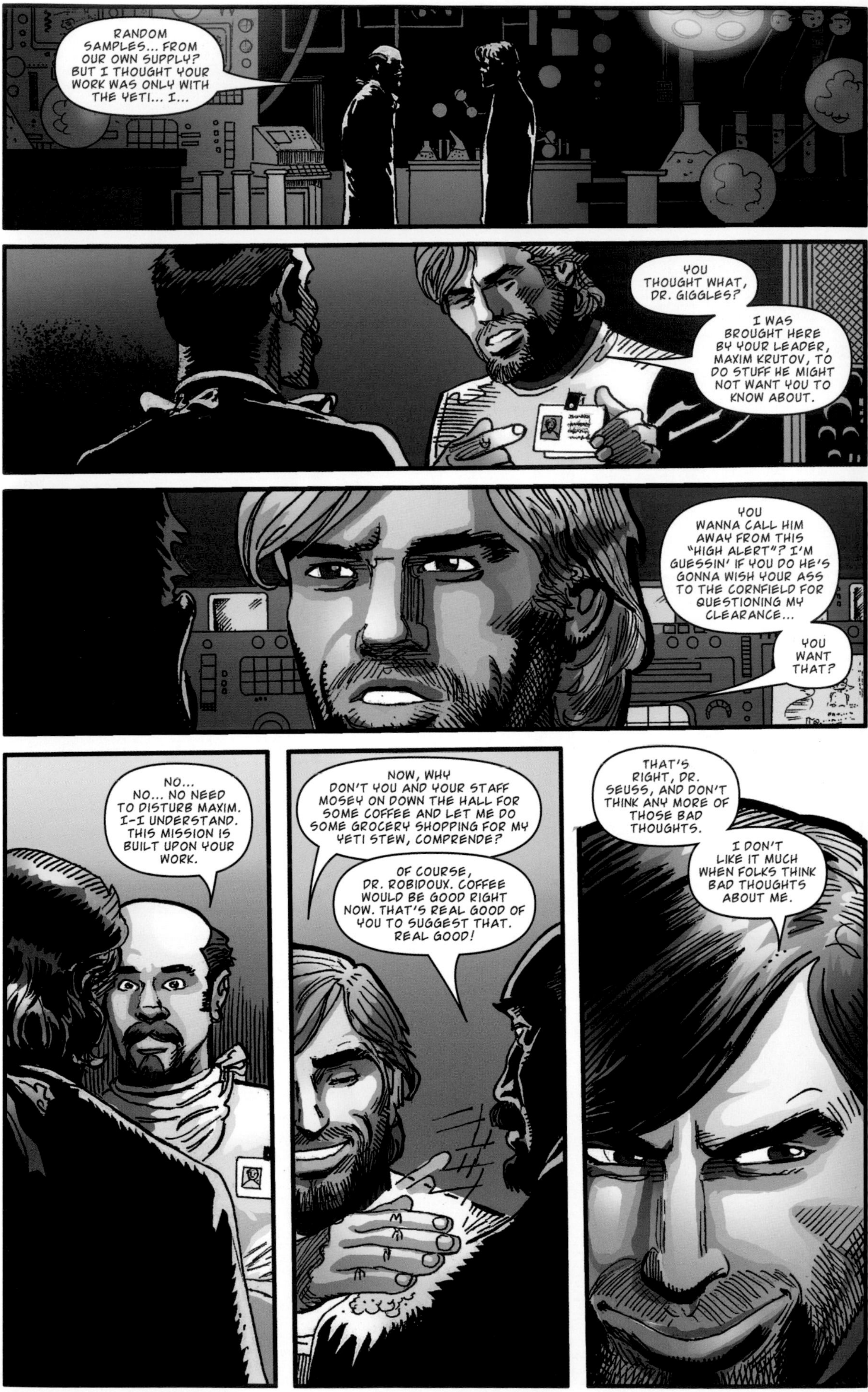
RANDOM SAMPLES... FROM OUR OWN SUPPLY? BUT I THOUGHT YOUR WORK WAS ONLY WITH THE YETI... I...
YOU THOUGHT WHAT, DR. GIGGLES?
I WAS BROUGHT HERE BY YOUR LEADER, MAXIM KRUTOV, TO DO STUFF HE MIGHT NOT WANT YOU TO KNOW ABOUT.
YOU WANNA CALL HIM AWAY FROM THIS "HIGH ALERT"? I'M GUESSIN' IF YOU DO HE'S GONNA WISH YOUR ASS TO THE CORNFIELD FOR QUESTIONING MY CLEARANCE...
YOU WANT THAT?
NO... NO... NO NEED TO DISTURB MAXIM. I-I UNDERSTAND. THIS MISSION IS BUILT UPON YOUR WORK.
NOW, WHY DON'T YOU AND YOUR STAFF MOSEY ON DOWN THE HALL FOR SOME COFFEE AND LET ME DO SOME GROCERY SHOPPING FOR MY YETI STEW, COMPRENDE?
OF COURSE, DR. ROBIDOUX. COFFEE WOULD BE GOOD RIGHT NOW. THAT'S REAL GOOD OF YOU TO SUGGEST THAT. REAL GOOD!
THAT'S RIGHT, DR. SEUSS, AND DON'T THINK ANY MORE OF THOSE BAD THOUGHTS.
I DON'T LIKE IT MUCH WHEN FOLKS THINK BAD THOUGHTS ABOUT ME.

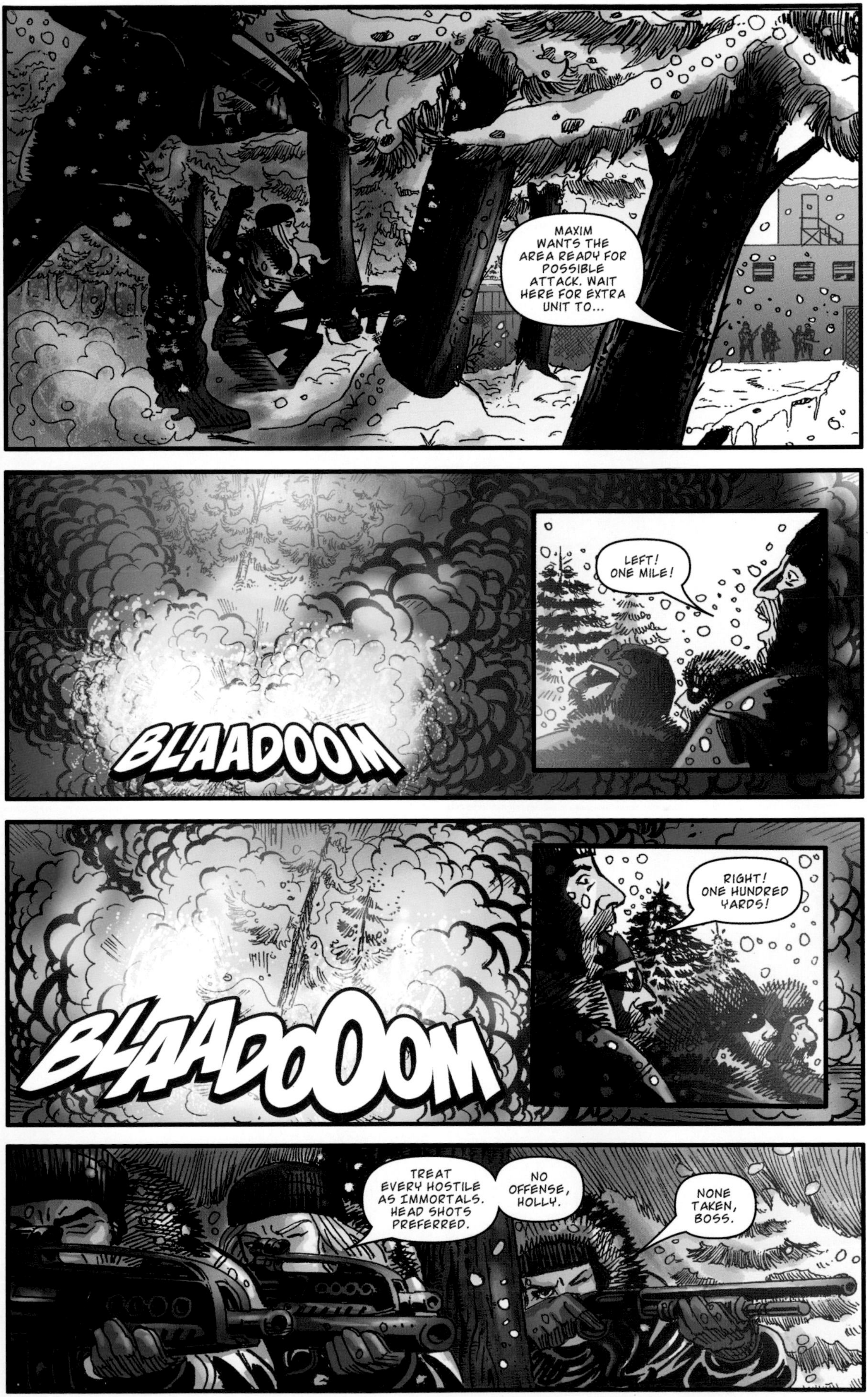
MAXIM WANTS THE AREA READY FOR POSSIBLE ATTACK. WAIT HERE FOR EXTRA UNIT TO...
LEFT! ONE MILE!
BLAADOOM
RIGHT! ONE HUNDRED YARDS!
BLAADOOOM
TREAT EVERY HOSTILE AS IMMORTALS. HEAD SHOTS PREFERRED.
NO OFFENSE, HOLLY.
NONE TAKEN, BOSS.

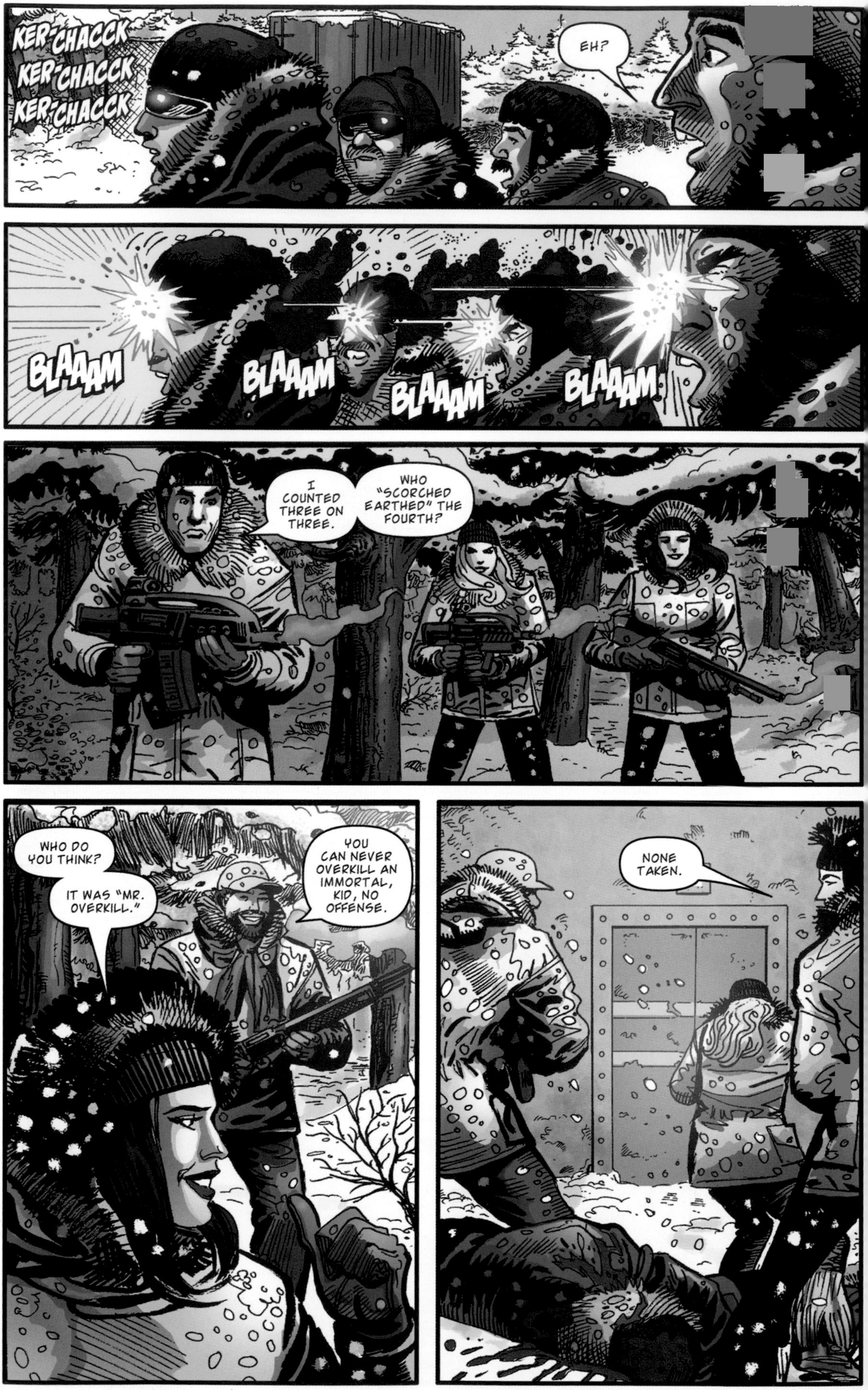
KER-CHACCK
KER-CHACCK
KER-CHACCK
EH?
BLAAAM
BLAAAM
BLAAAM
BLAAAM
I COUNTED THREE ON THREE.
WHO "SCORCHED EARTHED" THE FOURTH?
WHO DO YOU THINK?
IT WAS "MR. OVERKILL."
YOU CAN NEVER OVERKILL AN IMMORTAL, KID, NO OFFENSE.
NONE TAKEN.

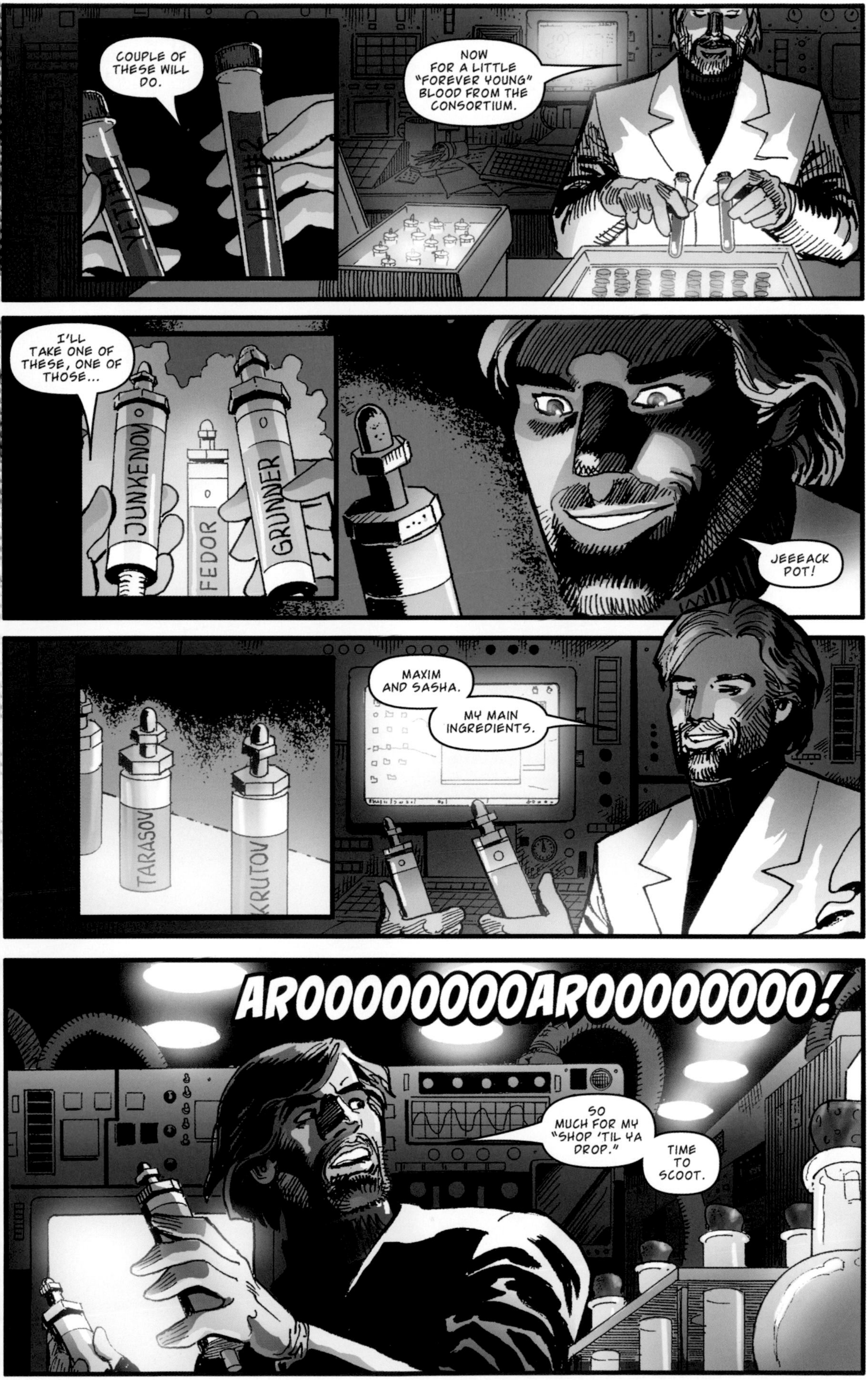
COUPLE OF THESE WILL DO.
YETI #1
YETI #2
NOW FOR A LITTLE "FOREVER YOUNG" BLOOD FROM THE CONSORTIUM.
I'LL TAKE ONE OF THESE, ONE OF THOSE...
JUNKENOV
FEDOR
GRUNNER
JEEEACK POT!
TARASOV
KRUTOV
MAXIM AND SASHA.
MY MAIN INGREDIENTS.
AROOOOOOOOAROOOOOOOO!
SO MUCH FOR MY "SHOP 'TIL YA DROP."
TIME TO SCOOT.

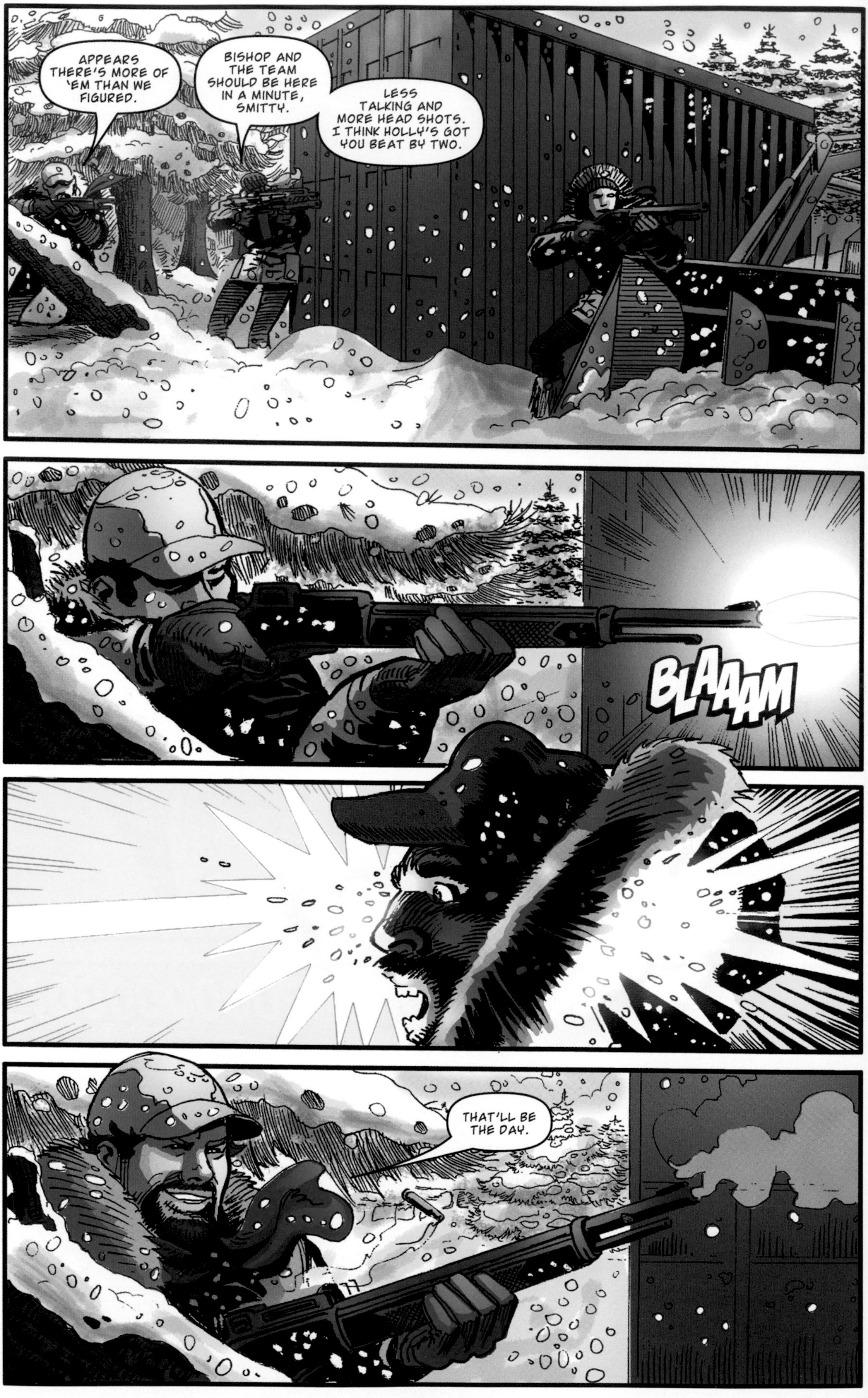
APPEARS THERE'S MORE OF 'EM THAN WE FIGURED.
BISHOP AND THE TEAM SHOULD BE HERE IN A MINUTE, SMITTY.
LESS TALKING AND MORE HEAD SHOTS. I THINK HOLLY'S GOT YOU BEAT BY TWO.
BLAAAM
THAT'LL BE THE DAY.

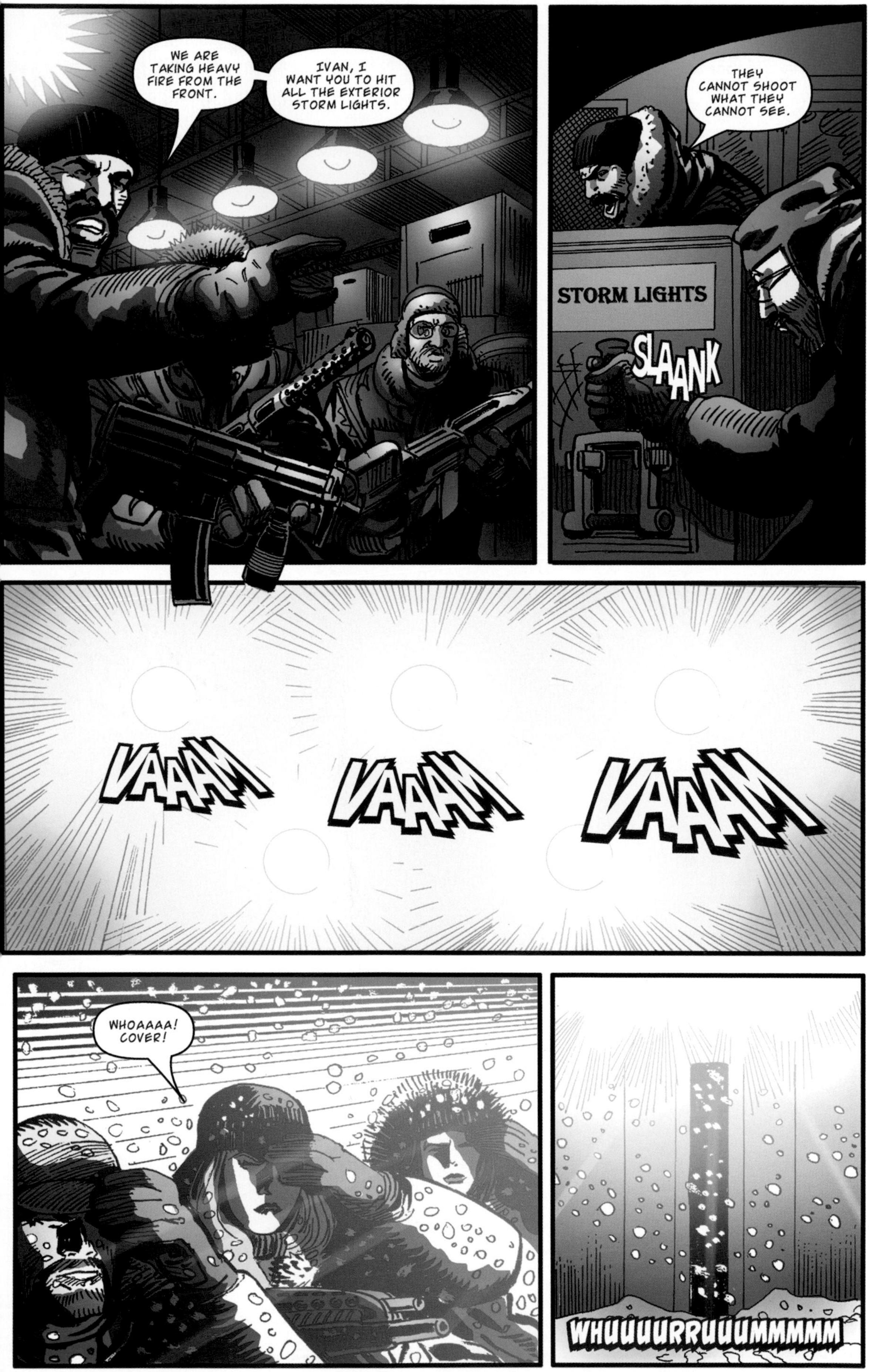
WE ARE TAKING HEAVY FIRE FROM THE FRONT.
IVAN, I WANT YOU TO HIT ALL THE EXTERIOR STORM LIGHTS.
THEY CANNOT SHOOT WHAT THEY CANNOT SEE.
STORM LIGHTS
SLAANK
VAAAM
VAAAM
VAAAM
WHOAAAA! COVER!
WHUUUURRUUUMMMMM

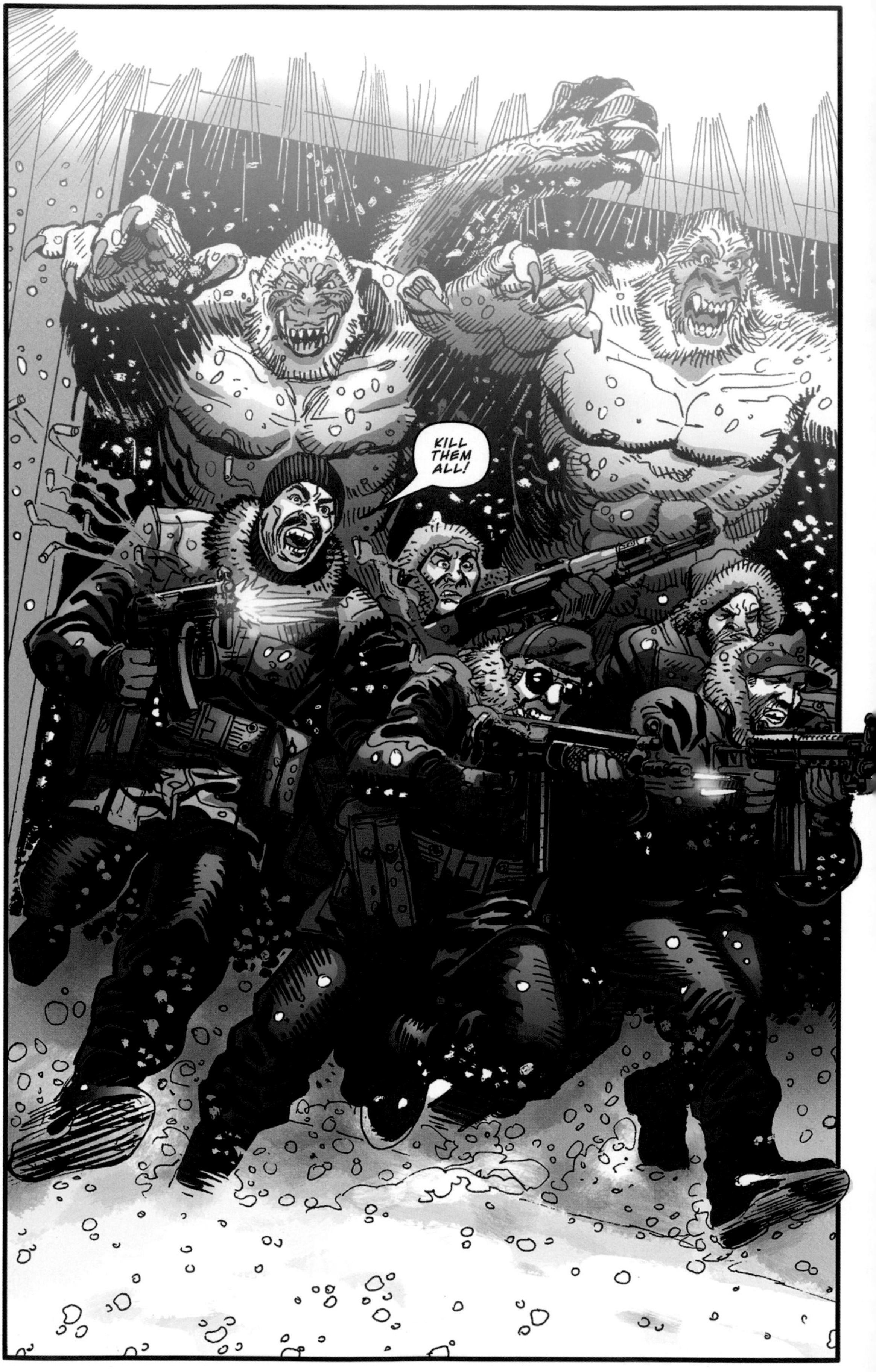
KILL THEM ALL!

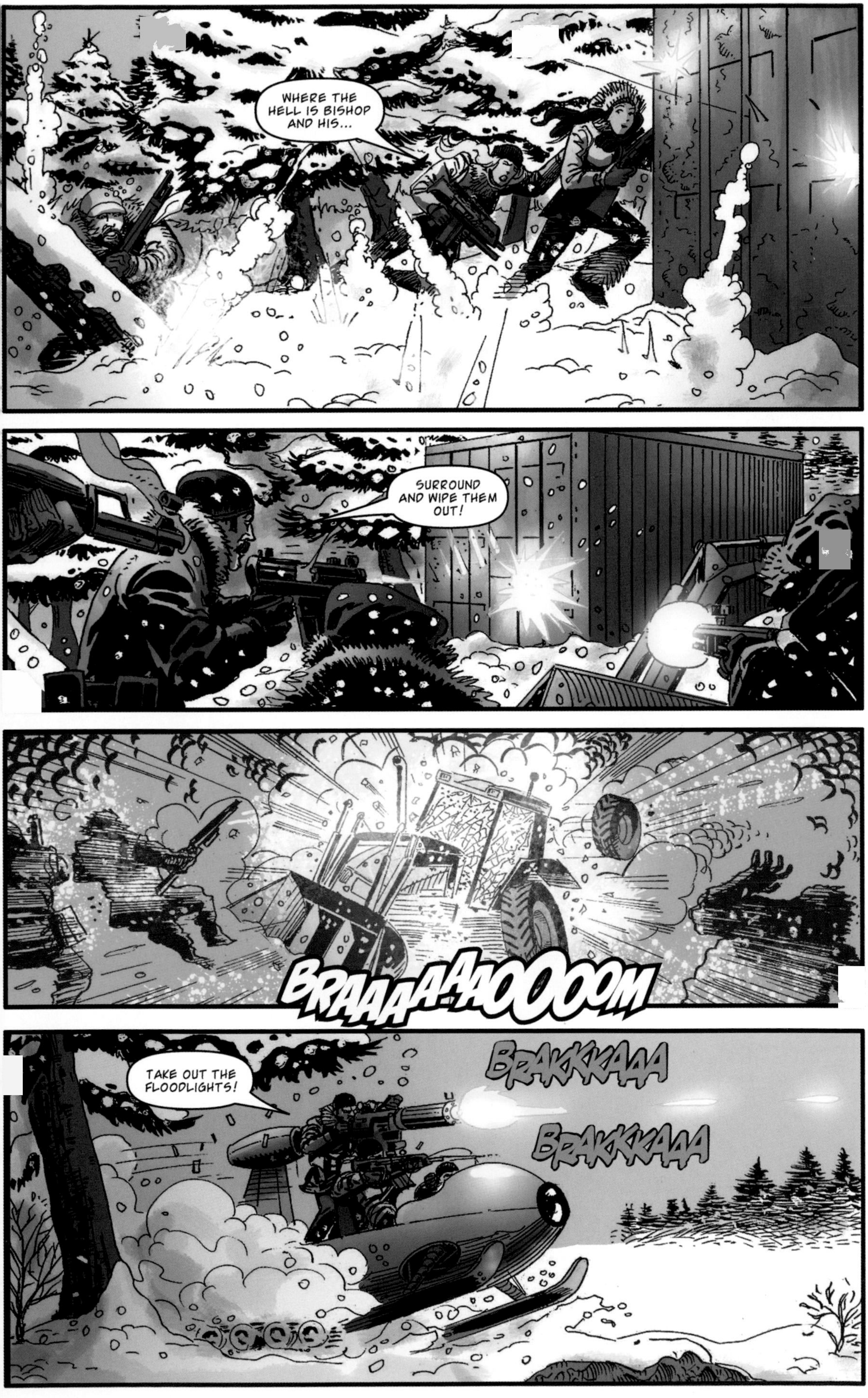
WHERE THE HELL IS BISHOP AND HIS...
SURROUND AND WIPE THEM OUT!
BRAAAAAAOOOOOM
TAKE OUT THE FLOODLIGHTS!
BRAKKKAAA
BRAKKKAAA

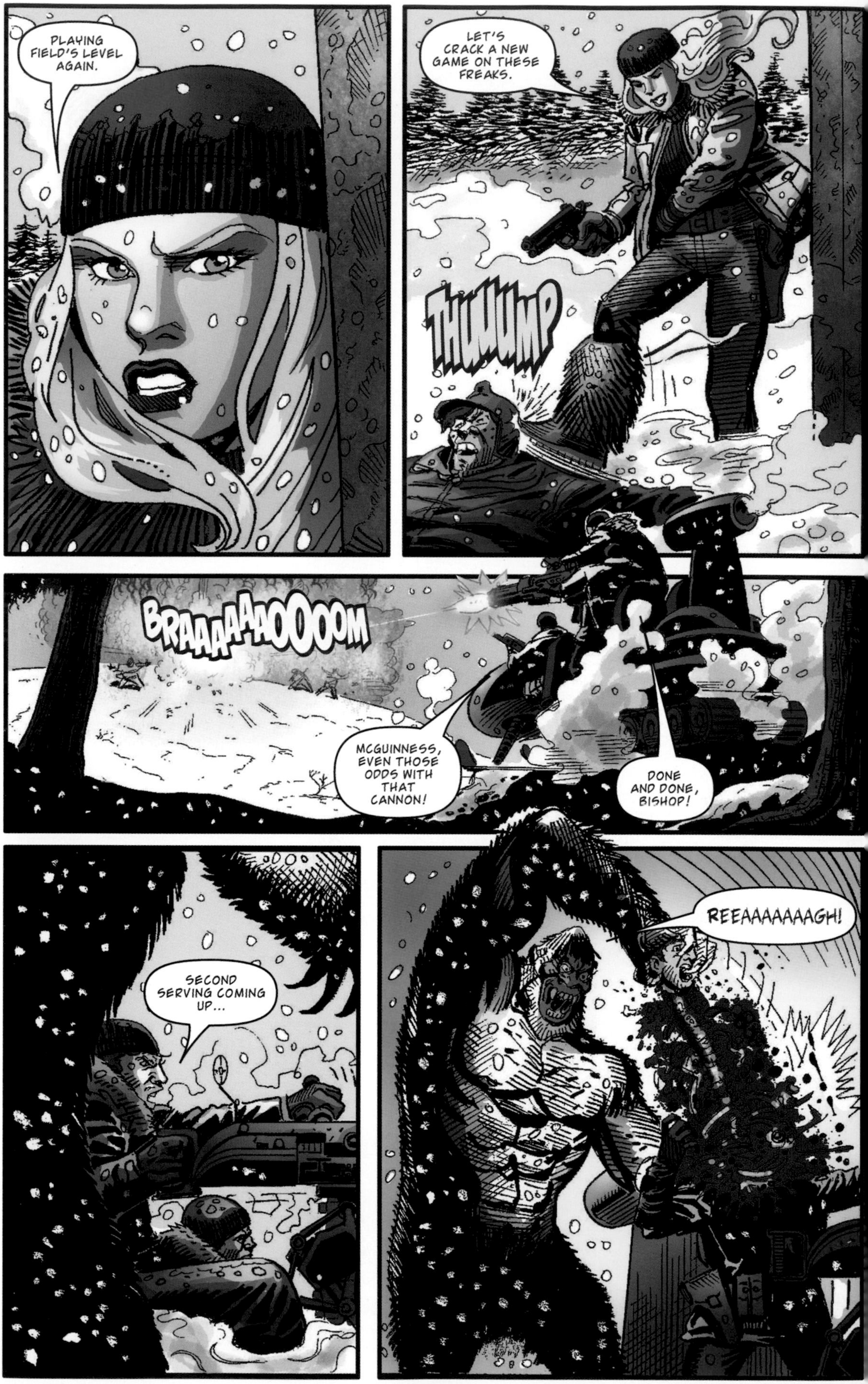
PLAYING FIELD'S LEVEL AGAIN.
LET'S CRACK A NEW GAME ON THESE FREAKS.
THUUUMP
BRAAAAAAOOOOM
MCGUINNESS, EVEN THOSE ODDS WITH THAT CANNON!
DONE AND DONE, BISHOP!
SECOND SERVING COMING UP...
REEAAAAAAAGH!

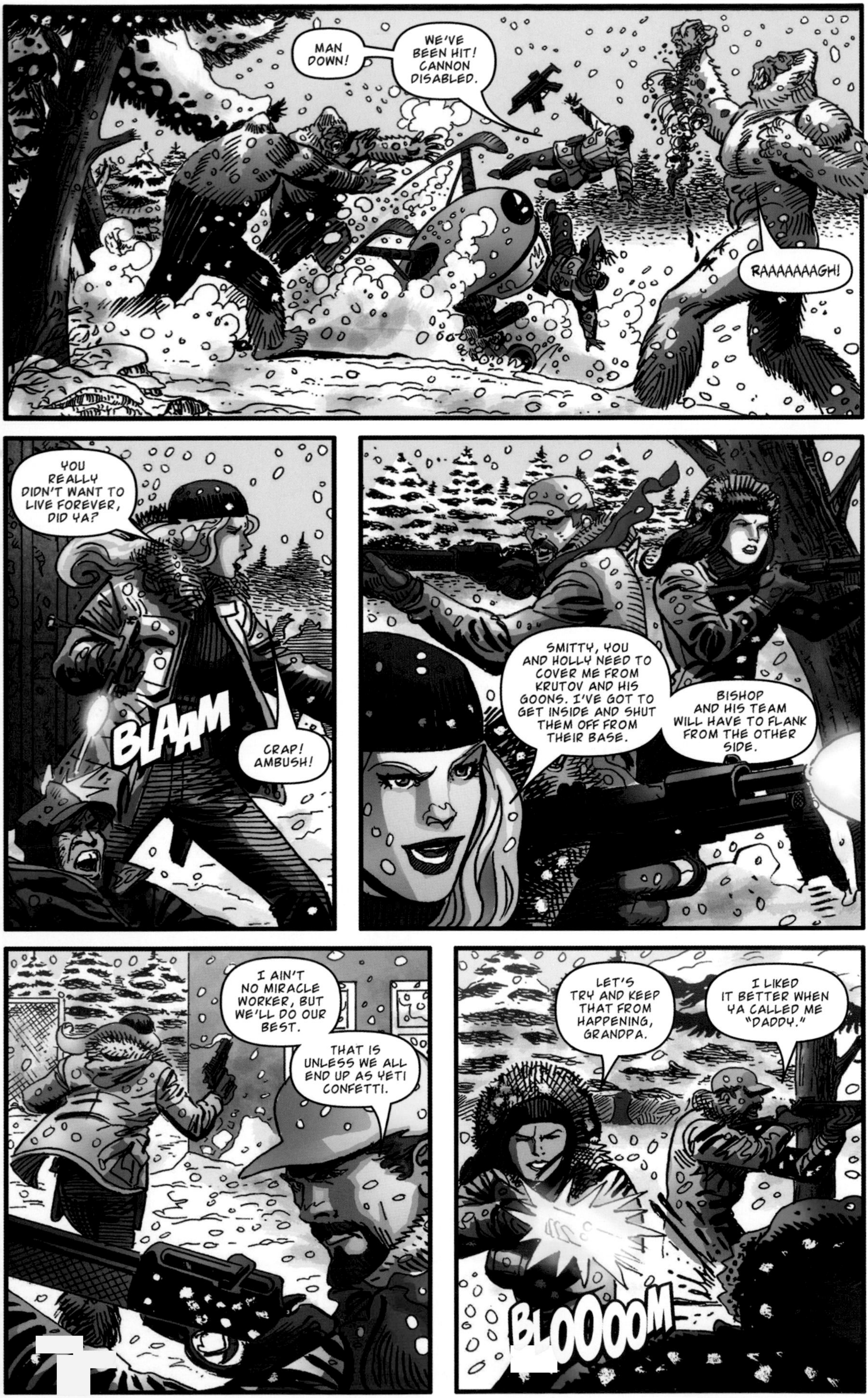

MAN DOWN!
WE'VE BEEN HIT! CANNON DISABLED.
RAAAAAAAGH!
YOU REALLY DIDN'T WANT TO LIVE FOREVER, DID YA?
BLAAM
CRAP! AMBUSH!
SMITTY, YOU AND HOLLY NEED TO COVER ME FROM KRUTOV AND HIS GOONS. I'VE GOT TO GET INSIDE AND SHUT THEM OFF FROM THEIR BASE.
BISHOP AND HIS TEAM WILL HAVE TO FLANK FROM THE OTHER SIDE.
I AIN'T NO MIRACLE WORKER, BUT WE'LL DO OUR BEST.
THAT IS UNLESS WE ALL END UP AS YETI CONFETTI.
LET'S TRY AND KEEP THAT FROM HAPPENING, GRANDPA.
I LIKED IT BETTER WHEN YA CALLED ME "DADDY."
BLOOOOM

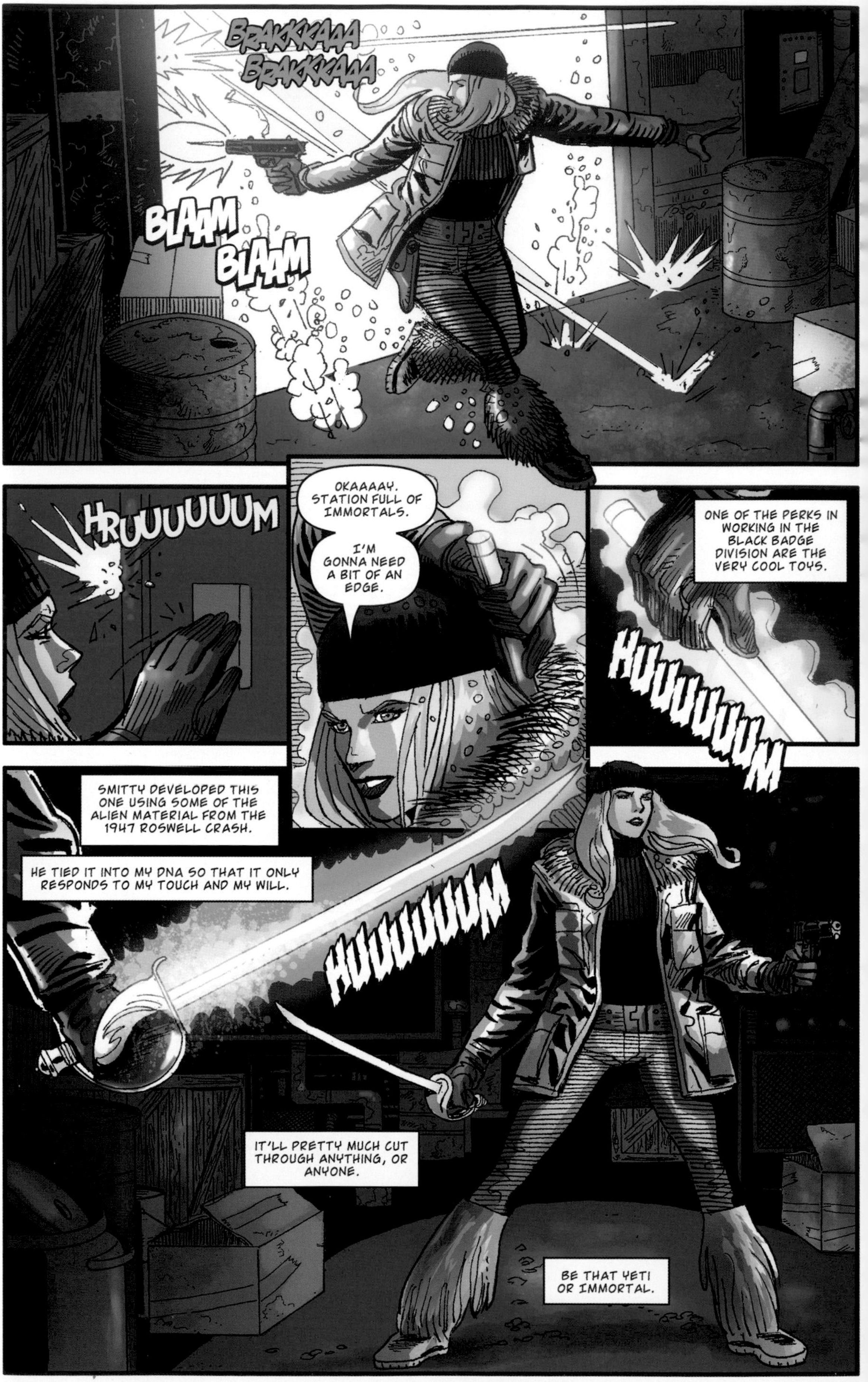
BRAKKKAAA
BRAKKKAAA
BLAAM
BLAAM
HRUUUUUUM
OKAAAAY. STATION FULL OF IMMORTALS.
I'M GONNA NEED A BIT OF AN EDGE.
ONE OF THE PERKS IN WORKING IN THE BLACK BADGE DIVISION ARE THE VERY COOL TOYS.
HUUUUUUUM
SMITTY DEVELOPED THIS ONE USING SOME OF THE ALIEN MATERIAL FROM THE 1947 ROSWELL CRASH.
HE TIED IT INTO MY DNA SO THAT IT ONLY RESPONDS TO MY TOUCH AND MY WILL.
HUUUUUUM
IT'LL PRETTY MUCH CUT THROUGH ANYTHING, OR ANYONE.
BE THAT YETI OR IMMORTAL.

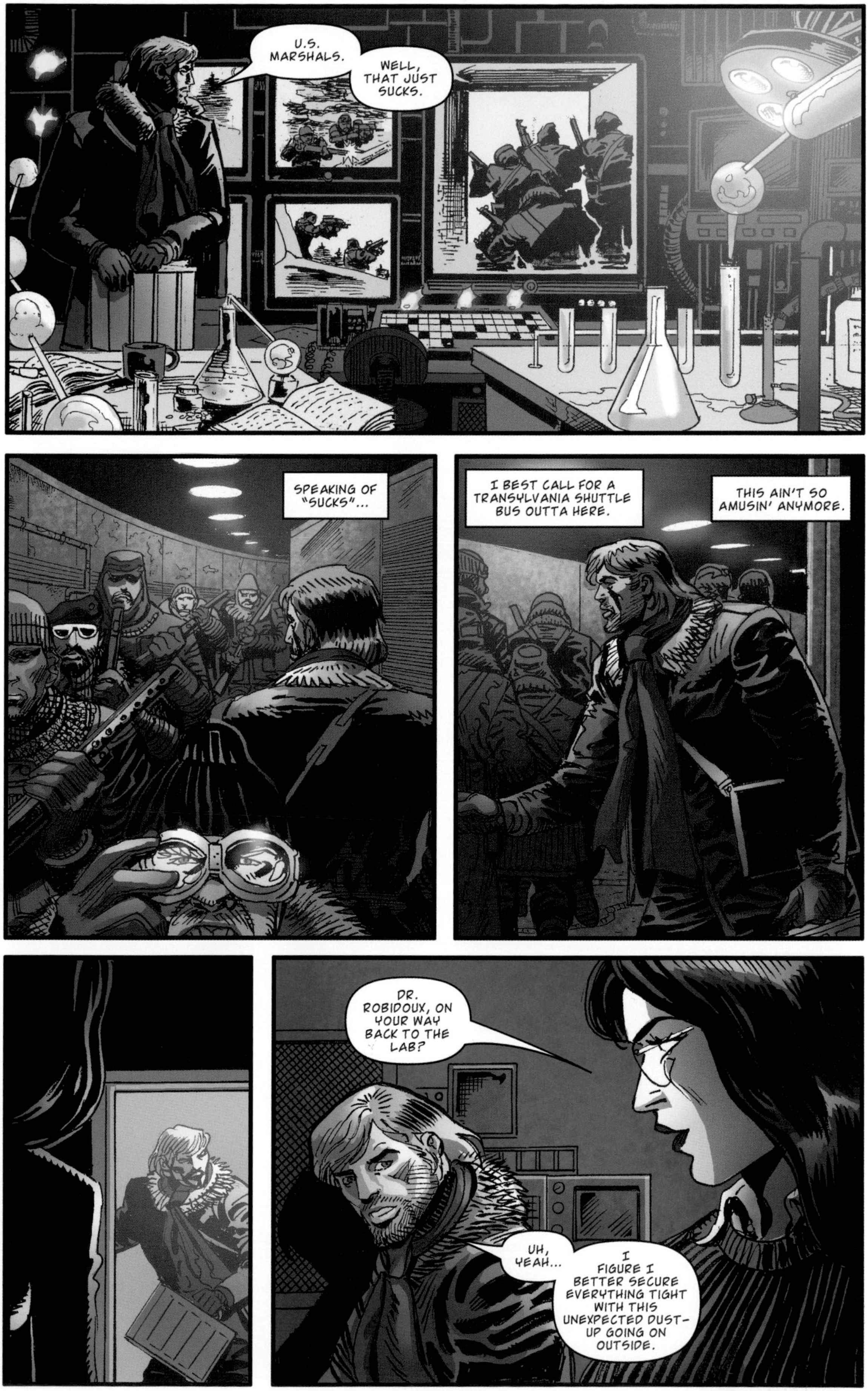
U.S. MARSHALS.
WELL, THAT JUST SUCKS.
SPEAKING OF "SUCKS"...
I BEST CALL FOR A TRANSYLVANIA SHUTTLE BUS OUTTA HERE.
THIS AIN'T SO AMUSIN' ANYMORE.
DR. ROBIDOUX, ON YOUR WAY BACK TO THE LAB?
UH, YEAH...
I FIGURE I BETTER SECURE EVERYTHING TIGHT WITH THIS UNEXPECTED DUST-UP GOING ON OUTSIDE.

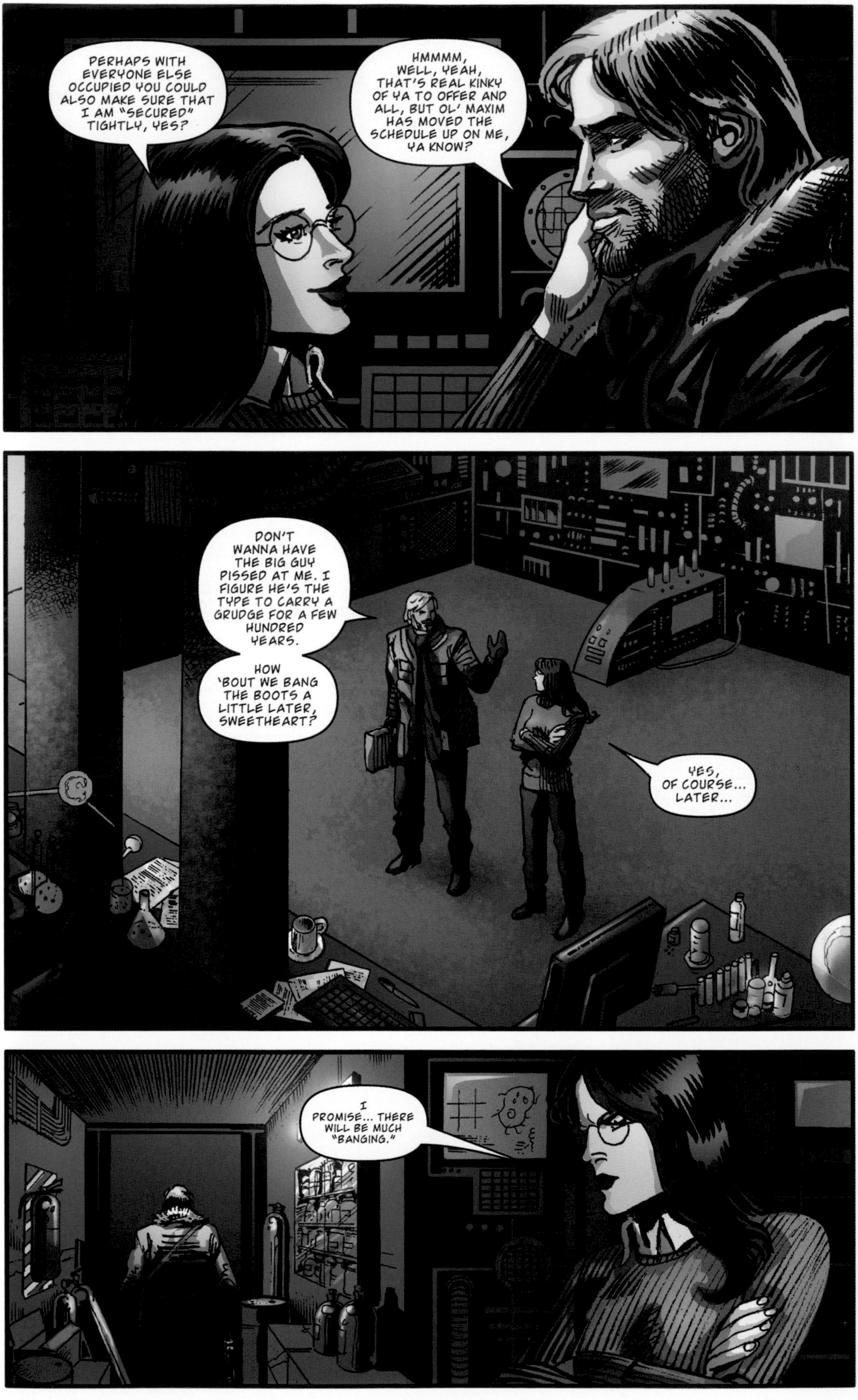
PERHAPS WITH EVERYONE ELSE OCCUPIED YOU COULD ALSO MAKE SURE THAT I AM "SECURED" TIGHTLY, YES?
HMMMM, WELL, YEAH, THAT'S REAL KINKY OF YA TO OFFER AND ALL, BUT OL' MAXIM HAS MOVED THE SCHEDULE UP ON ME, YA KNOW?
DON'T WANNA HAVE THE BIG GUY PISSED AT ME. I FIGURE HE'S THE TYPE TO CARRY A GRUDGE FOR A FEW HUNDRED YEARS.
HOW 'BOUT WE BANG THE BOOTS A LITTLE LATER, SWEETHEART?
YES, OF COURSE... LATER...
I PROMISE... THERE WILL BE MUCH "BANGING."

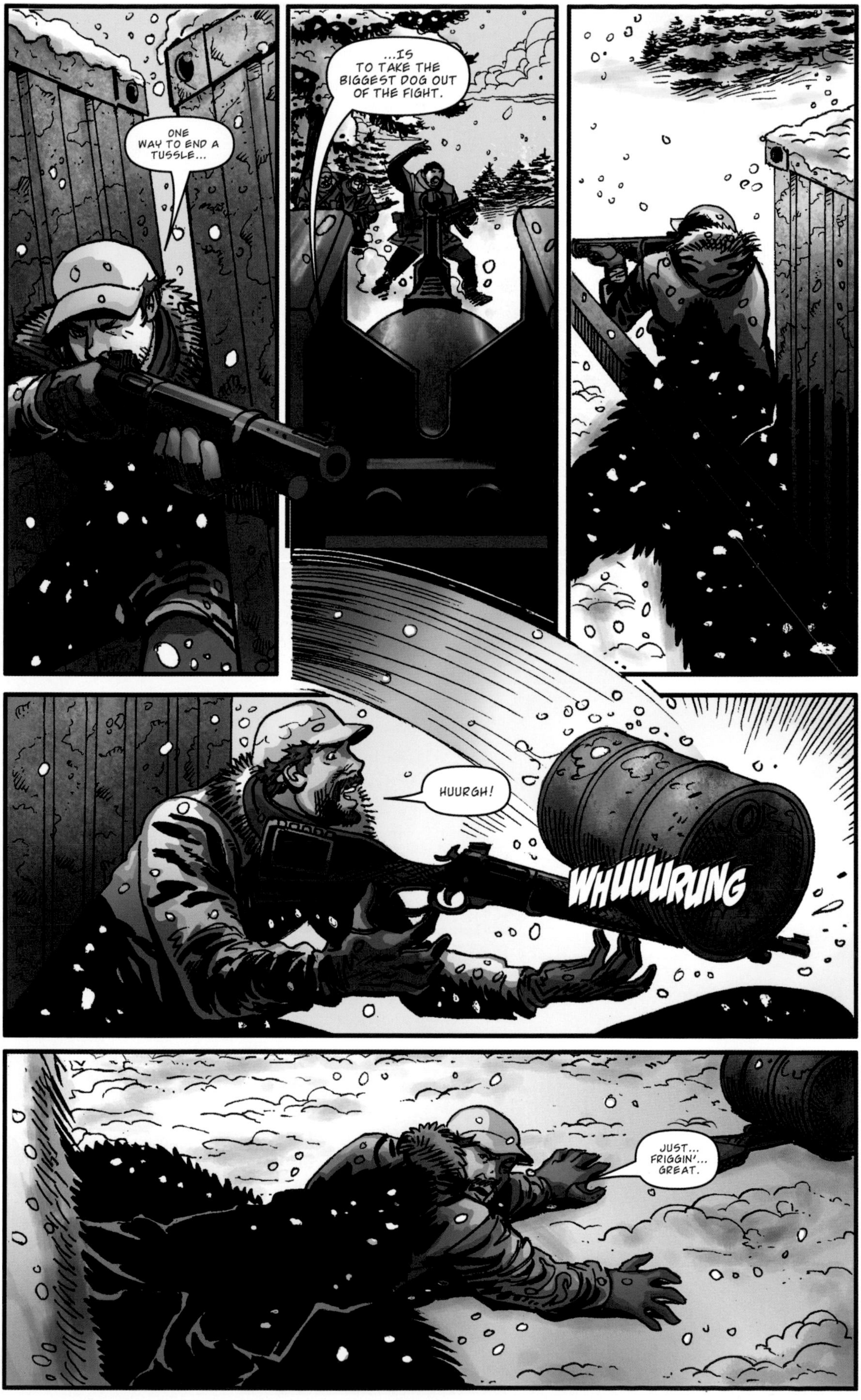
ONE WAY TO END A TUSSLE...
...IS TO TAKE THE BIGGEST DOG OUT OF THE FIGHT.
HUURGH!
WHUUURUNG
JUST... FRIGGIN'... GREAT.

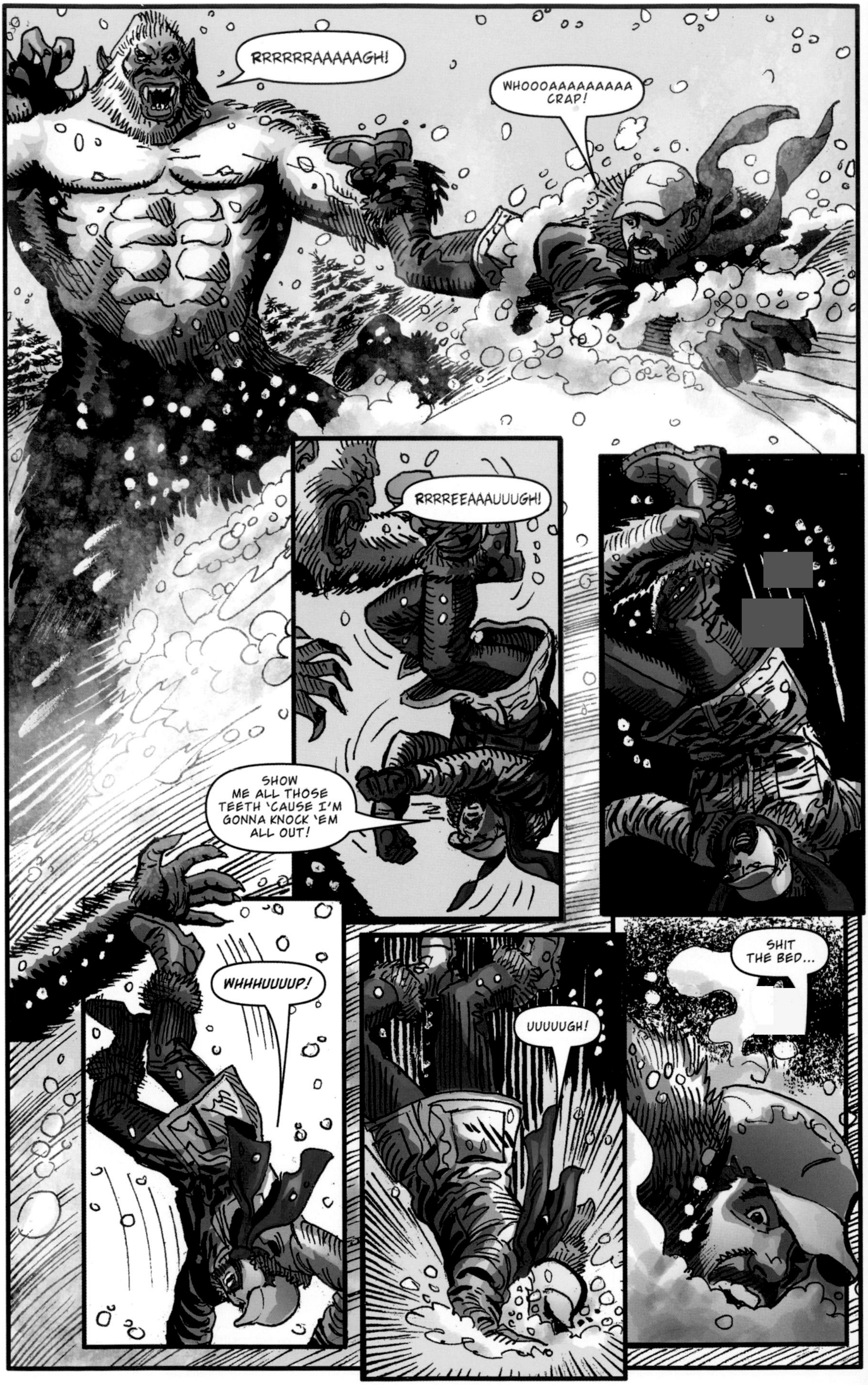
RRRRRRAAAAAGH!
WHOOOAAAAAAAAA CRAP!
RRRREEAAAUUUGH!
SHOW ME ALL THOSE TEETH 'CAUSE I'M GONNA KNOCK 'EM ALL OUT!
WHHHUUUUP!
UUUUUGH!
SHIT THE BED...

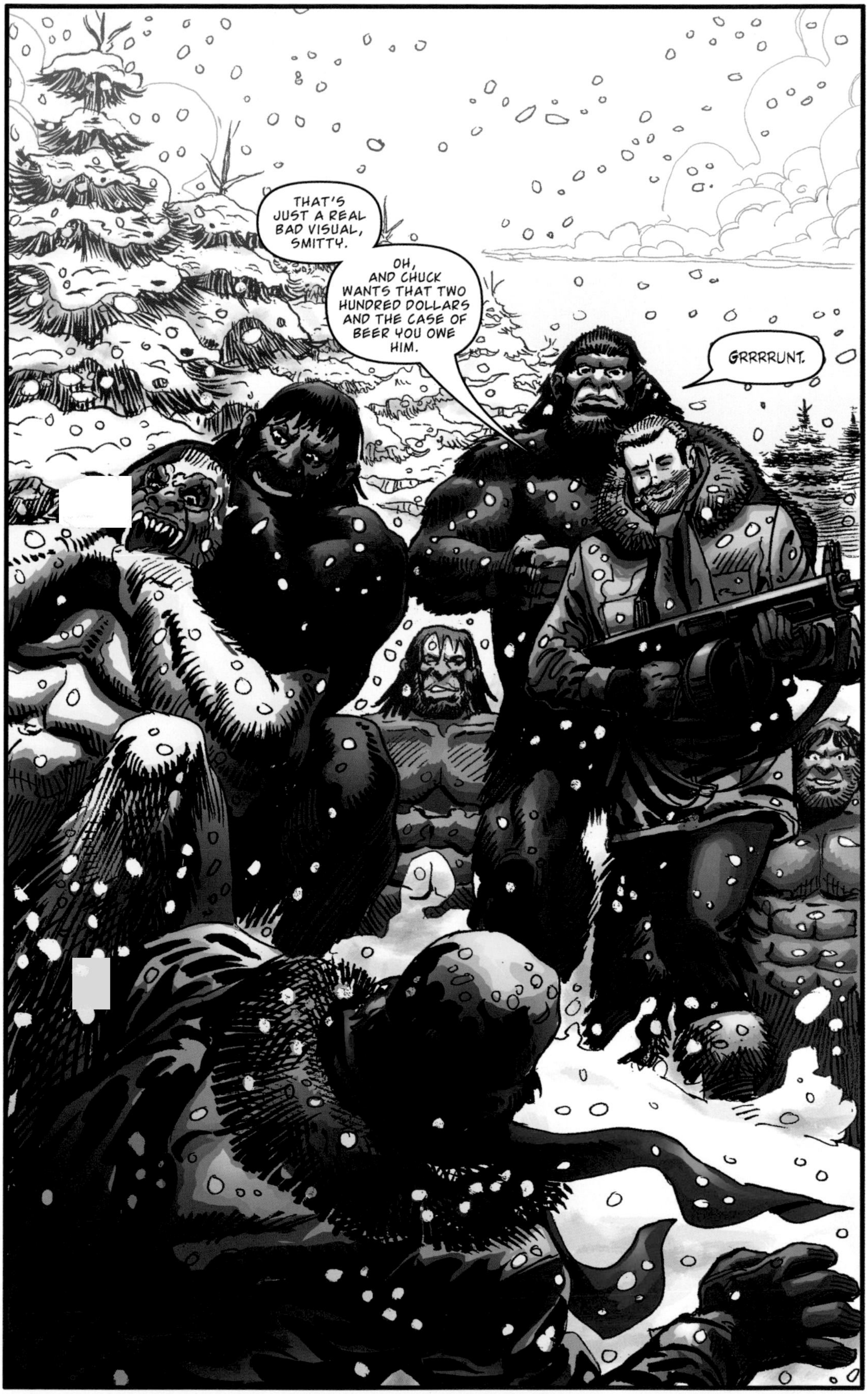
THAT'S JUST A REAL BAD VISUAL, SMITTY.
OH, AND CHUCK WANTS THAT TWO HUNDRED DOLLARS AND THE CASE OF BEER YOU OWE HIM.
GRRRRUNT.

GUURGLE...
ACK!

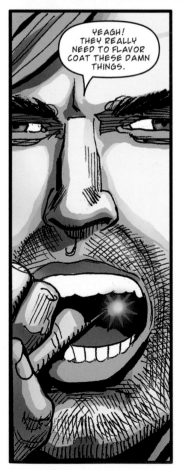

YEAGH!
THEY REALLY
NEED TO FLAVOR
COAT THESE DAMN
THINGS.

DYNACORE TECHNOLOGY
HEADQUARTERS.

MR.
FARNSWORTH,
ROBIDOUX'S
EXTRACTION
ALARM HAS BEEN
IGNITED.

ALERT
THE TEAM-1 FOR
AN IMMEDIATE
EXTRACTION OF DR.
ROBIDOUX.

GET HIM
BACK HERE AT
ANY COST.

TO BE
CONTINUED...

ART BY **SCOTT JAMES**

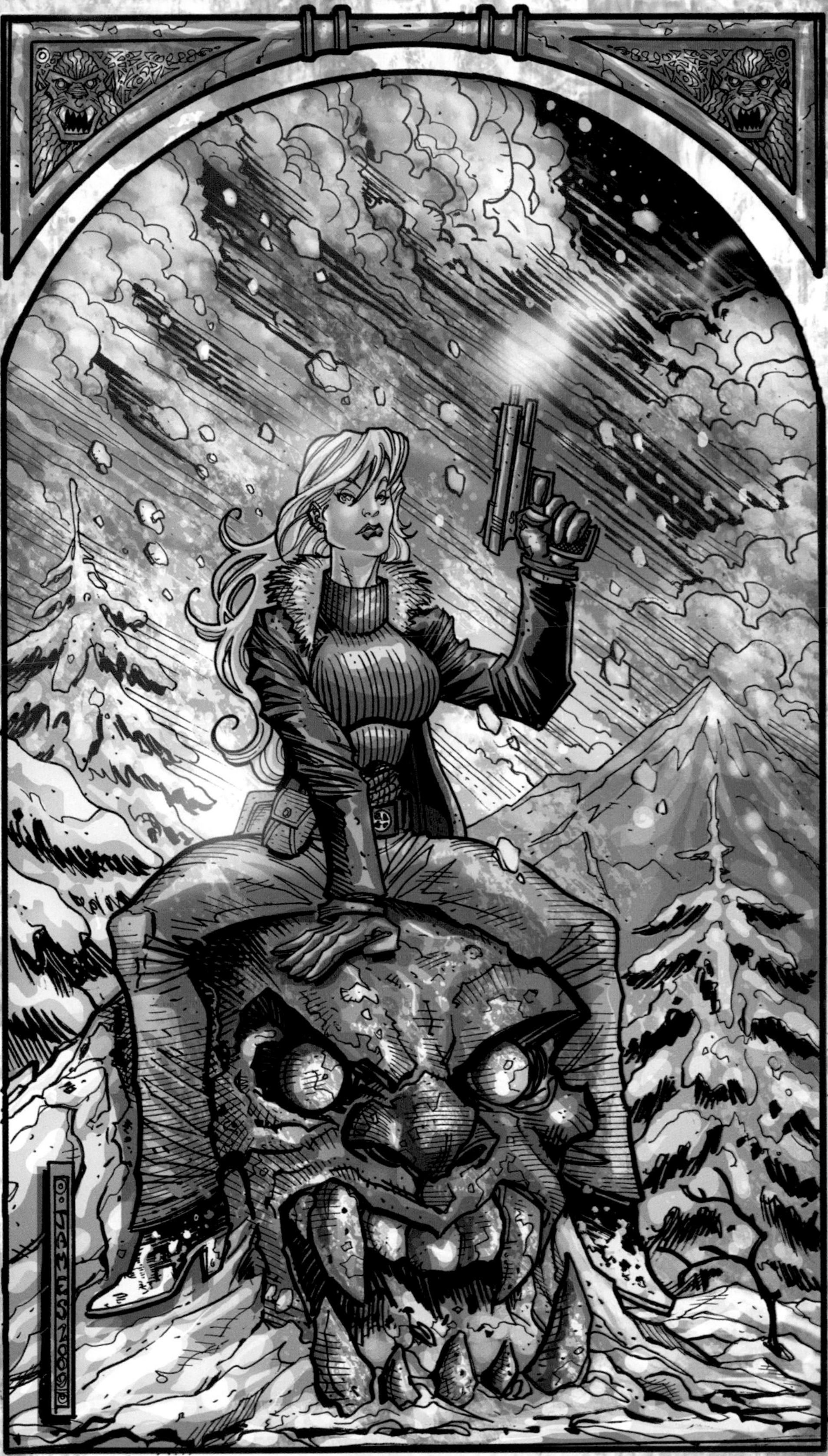

ART BY ENRIQUE VILLAGRAN

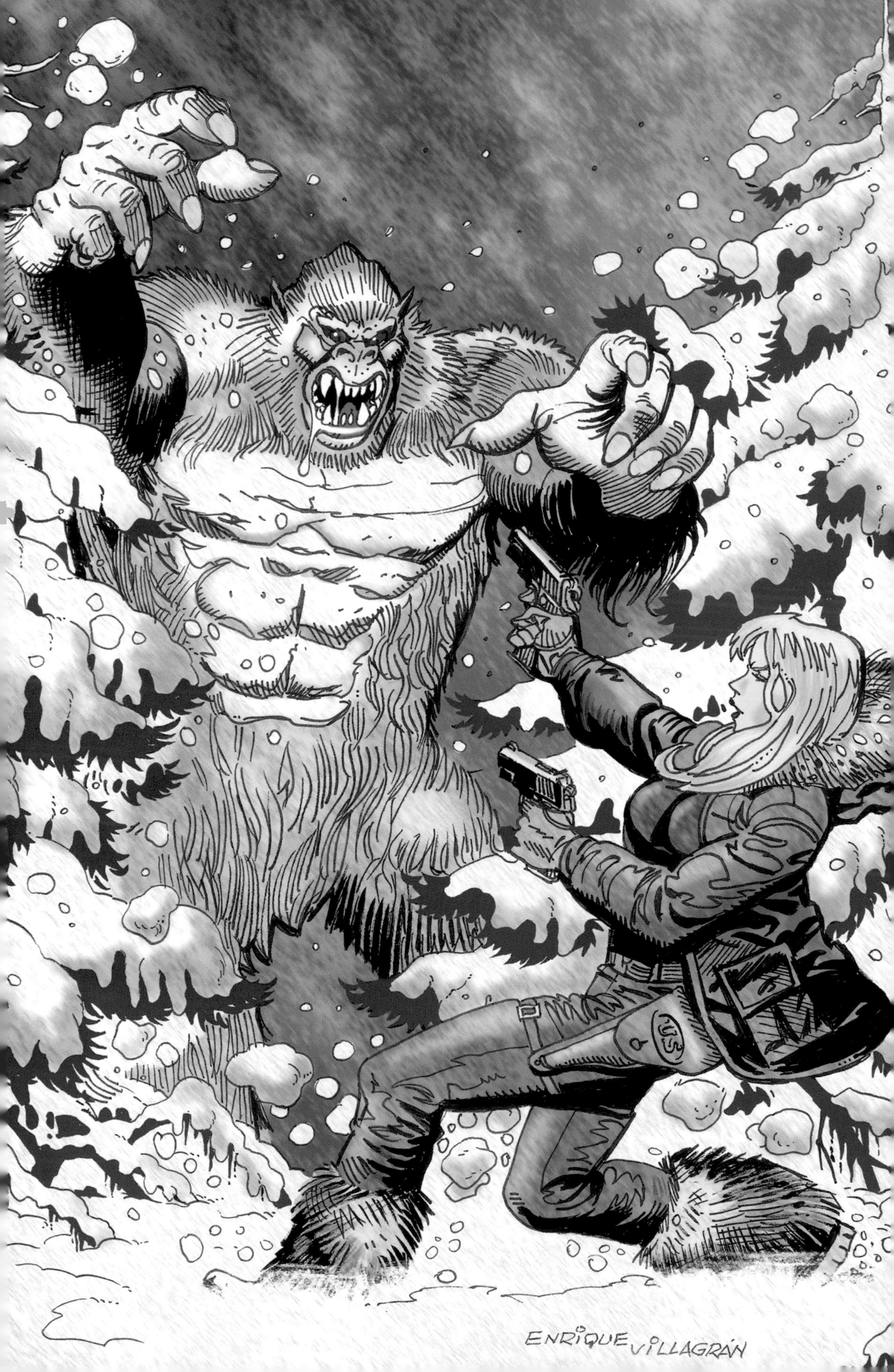

"US"
ENRIQUE VILLAGRAN

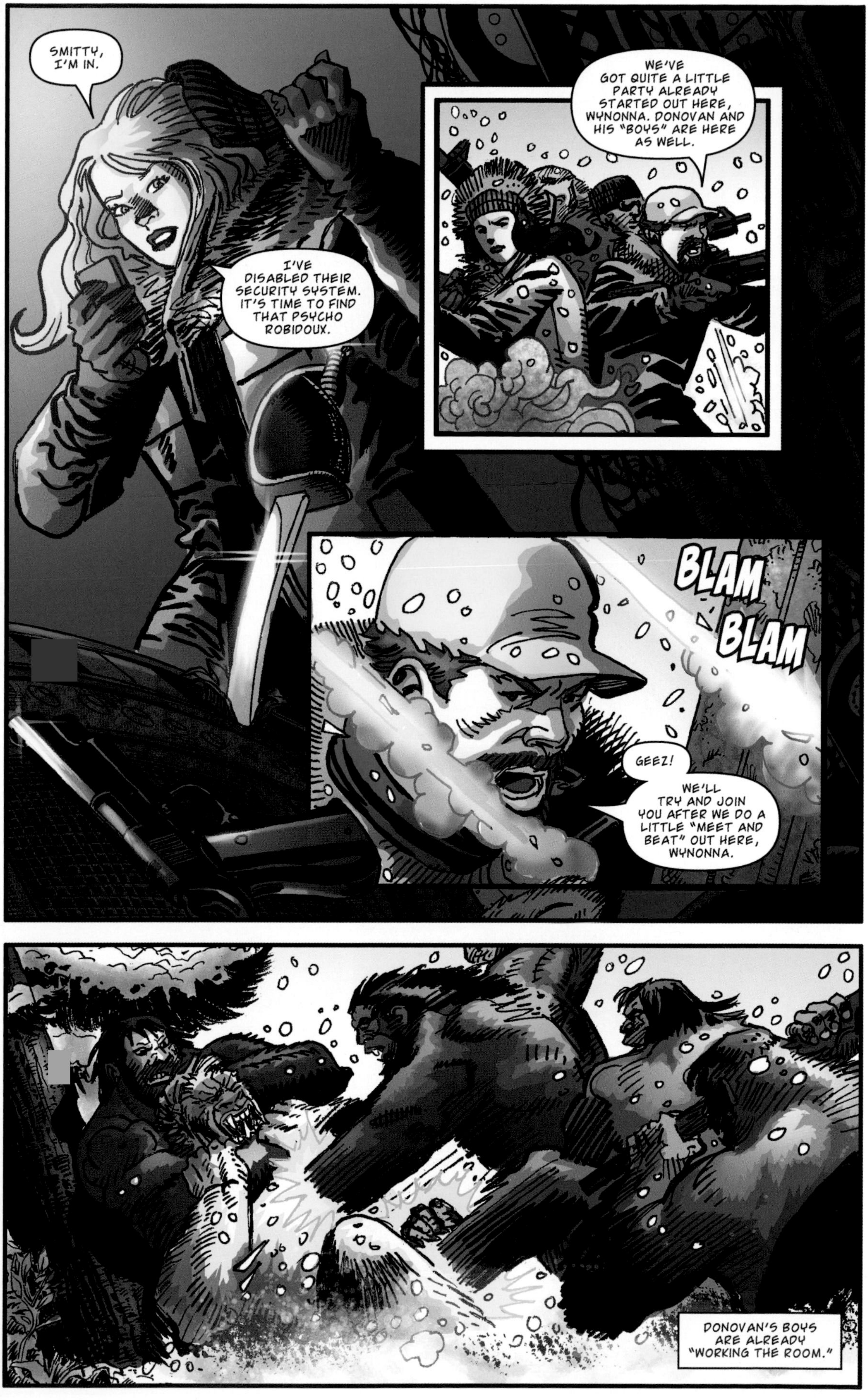
SMITTY, I'M IN.
I'VE DISABLED THEIR SECURITY SYSTEM. IT'S TIME TO FIND THAT PSYCHO ROBIDOUX.
WE'VE GOT QUITE A LITTLE PARTY ALREADY STARTED OUT HERE, WYNONNA. DONOVAN AND HIS "BOYS" ARE HERE AS WELL.
BLAM
BLAM
GEEZ!
WE'LL TRY AND JOIN YOU AFTER WE DO A LITTLE "MEET AND BEAT" OUT HERE, WYNONNA.
DONOVAN'S BOYS ARE ALREADY "WORKING THE ROOM."

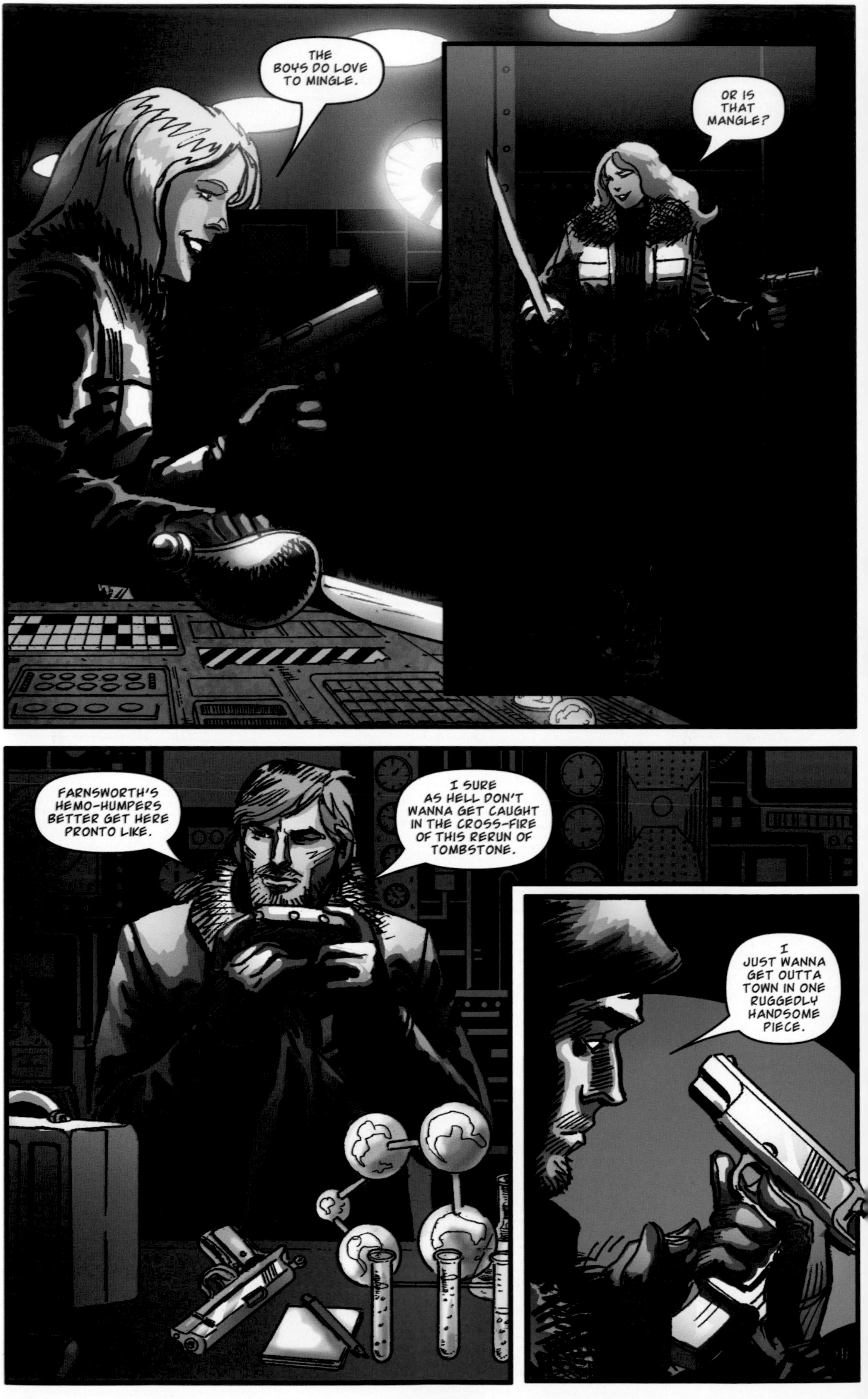
THE BOYS DO LOVE TO MINGLE.
OR IS THAT MANGLE?
FARNSWORTH'S HEMO-HUMPERS BETTER GET HERE PRONTO LIKE.
I SURE AS HELL DON'T WANNA GET CAUGHT IN THE CROSS-FIRE OF THIS RERUN OF TOMBSTONE.
I JUST WANNA GET OUTTA TOWN IN ONE RUGGEDLY HANDSOME PIECE.

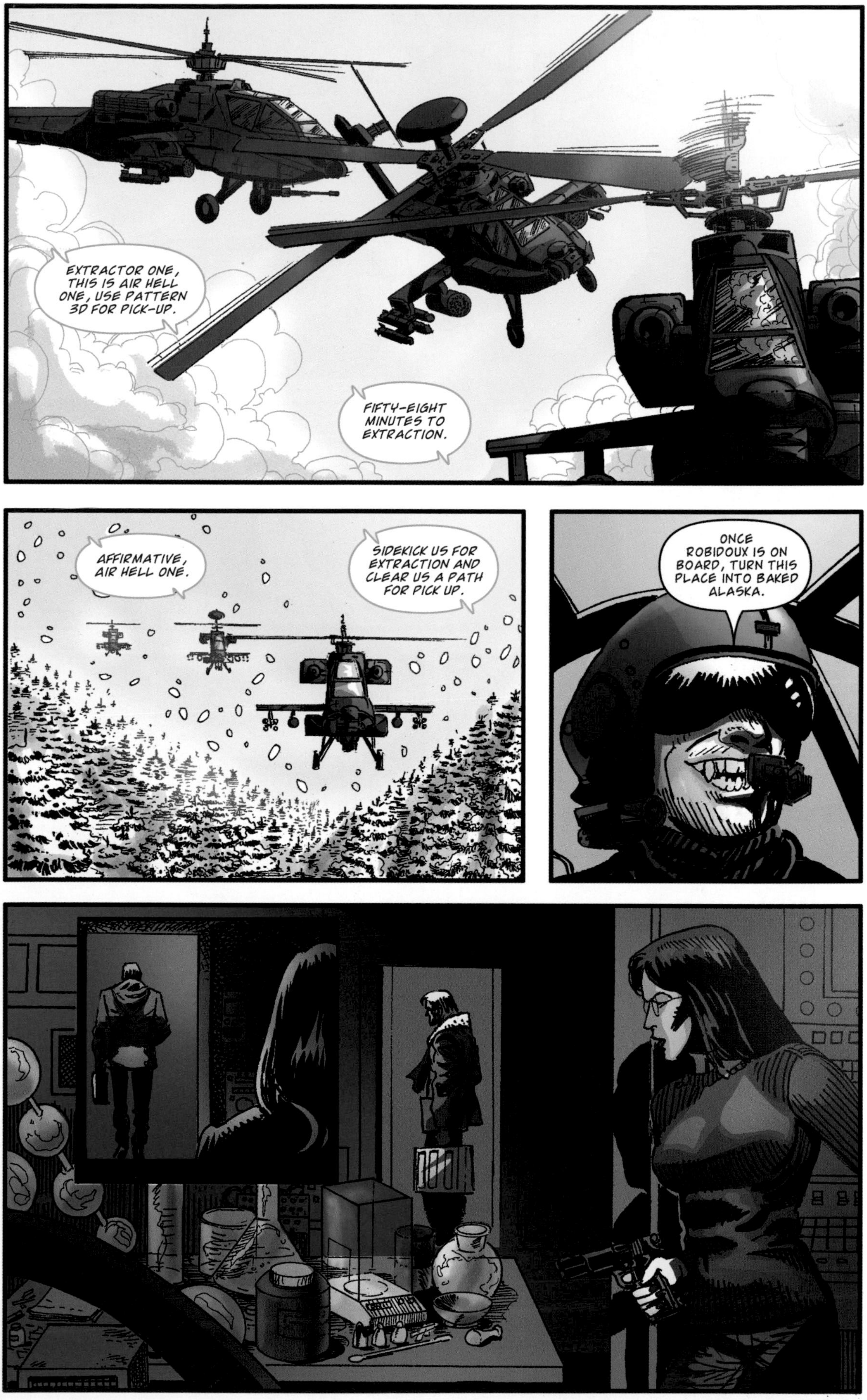
EXTRACTOR ONE, THIS IS AIR HELL ONE, USE PATTERN 3D FOR PICK-UP.
FIFTY-EIGHT MINUTES TO EXTRACTION.
AFFIRMATIVE, AIR HELL ONE.
SIDEKICK US FOR EXTRACTION AND CLEAR US A PATH FOR PICK UP.
ONCE ROBIDOUX IS ON BOARD, TURN THIS PLACE INTO BAKED ALASKA.

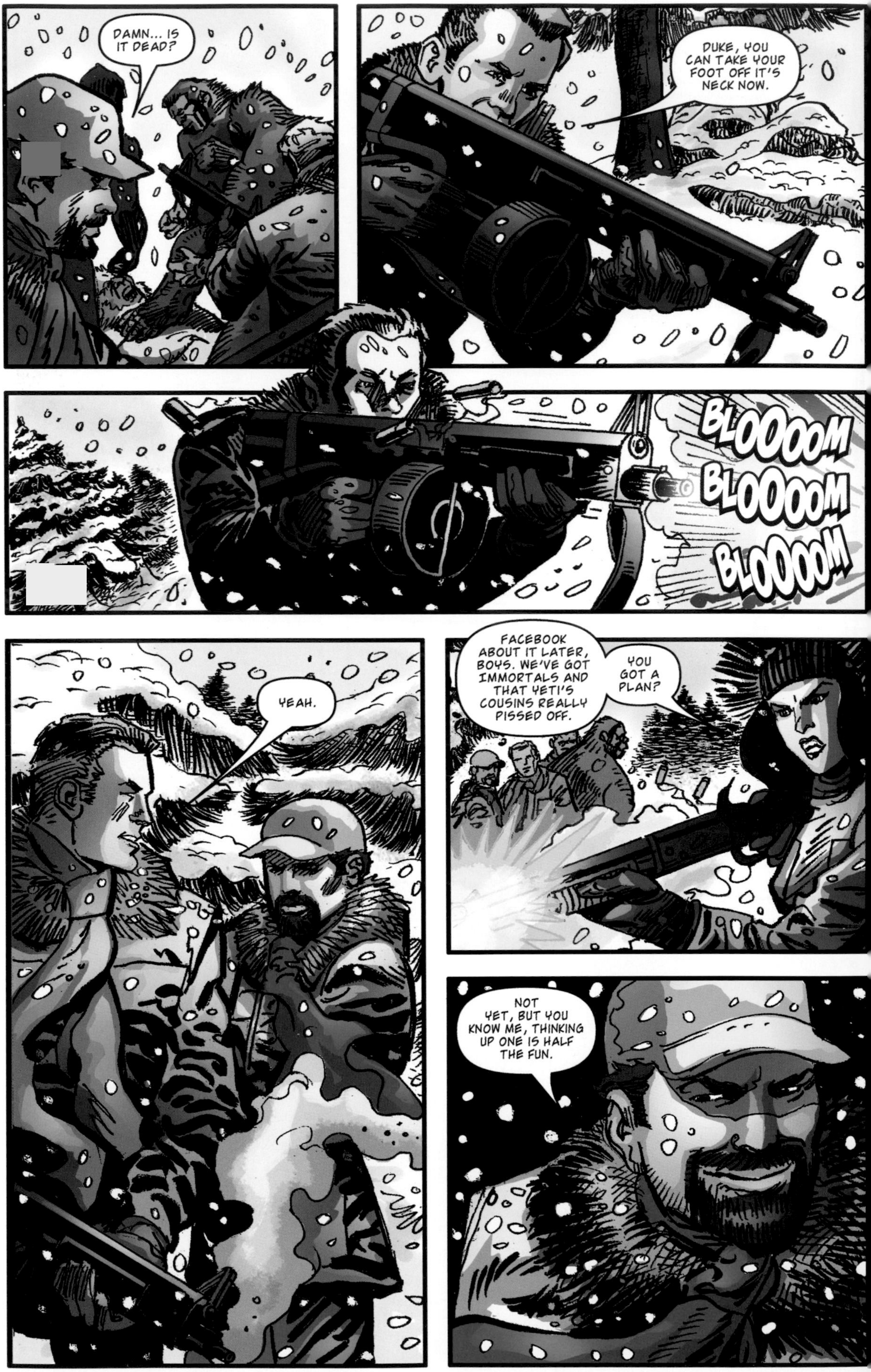
DAMN... IS IT DEAD?
DUKE, YOU CAN TAKE YOUR FOOT OFF IT'S NECK NOW.
BLOOOOOM BLOOOOM BLOOOOM
YEAH.
FACEBOOK ABOUT IT LATER, BOYS. WE'VE GOT IMMORTALS AND THAT YETI'S COUSINS REALLY PISSED OFF.
YOU GOT A PLAN?
NOT YET, BUT YOU KNOW ME, THINKING UP ONE IS HALF THE FUN.

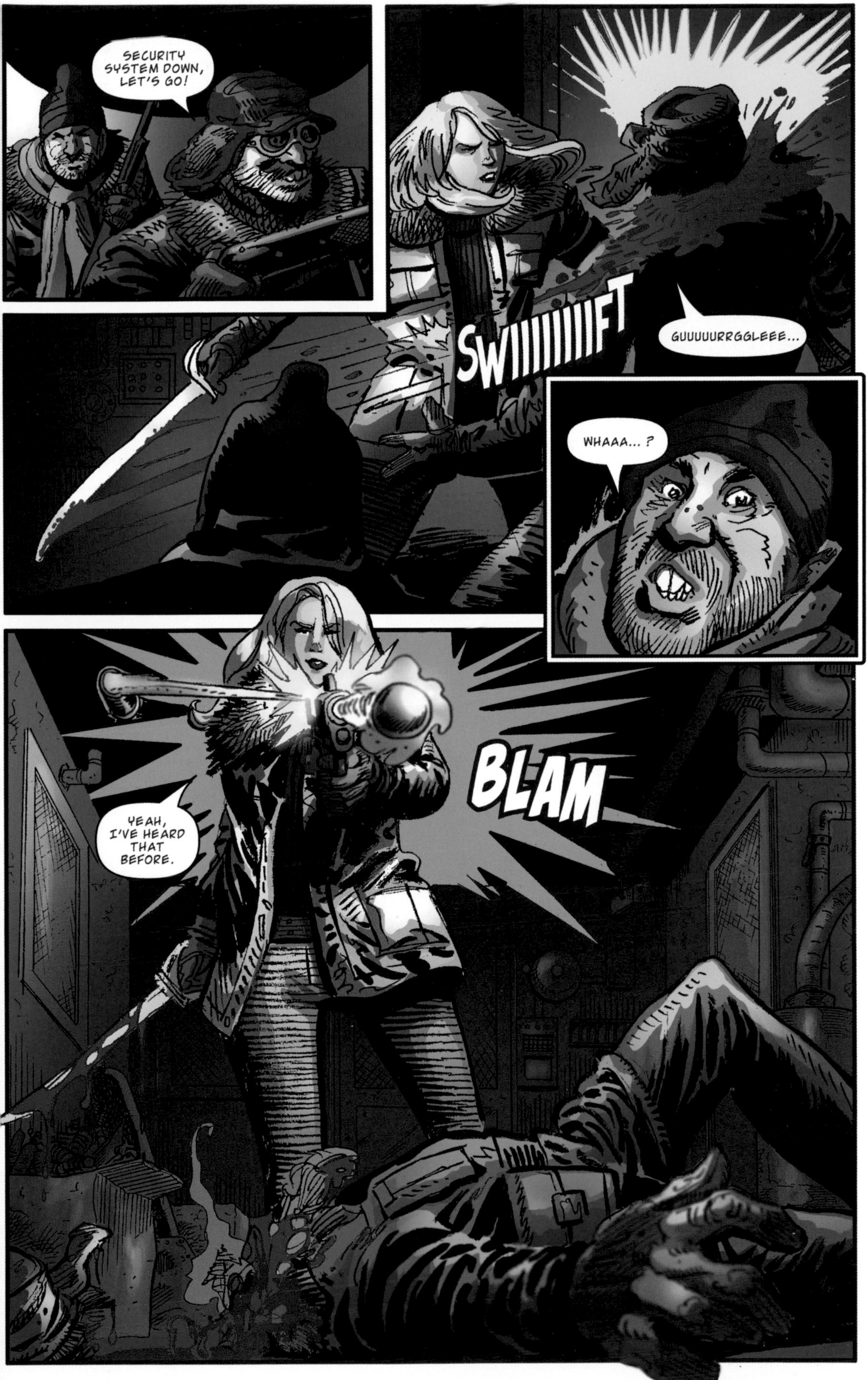
SECURITY SYSTEM DOWN, LET'S GO!
SWIIIIIIIFT
GUUUUURRGGLEEE...
WHAAA... ?
BLAM
YEAH, I'VE HEARD THAT BEFORE.

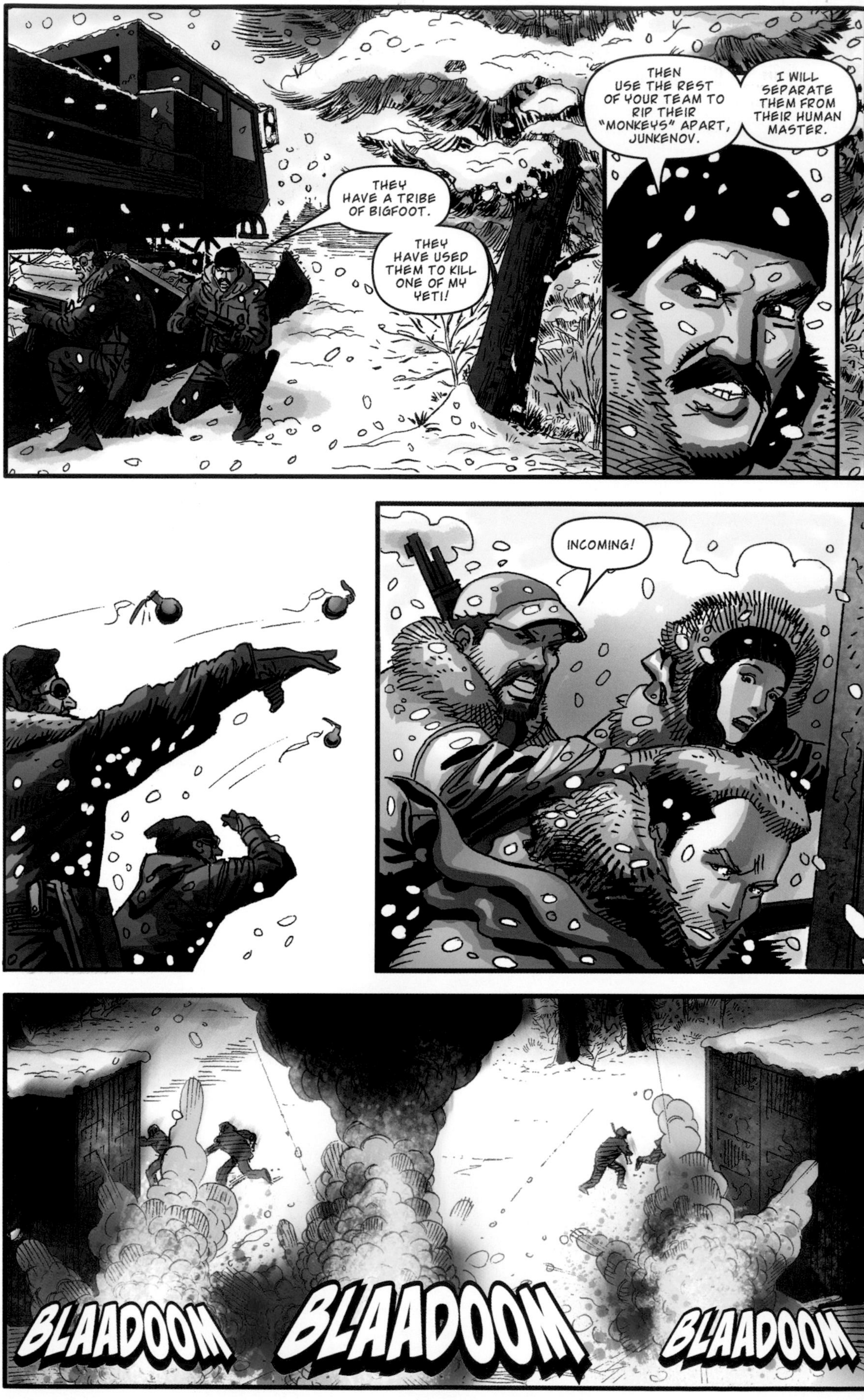
THEY HAVE A TRIBE OF BIGFOOT.
THEY HAVE USED THEM TO KILL ONE OF MY YETI!
THEN USE THE REST OF YOUR TEAM TO RIP THEIR "MONKEYS" APART, JUNKENOV.
I WILL SEPARATE THEM FROM THEIR HUMAN MASTER.
INCOMING!
BLAADOOM
BLAADOOM
BLAADOOM

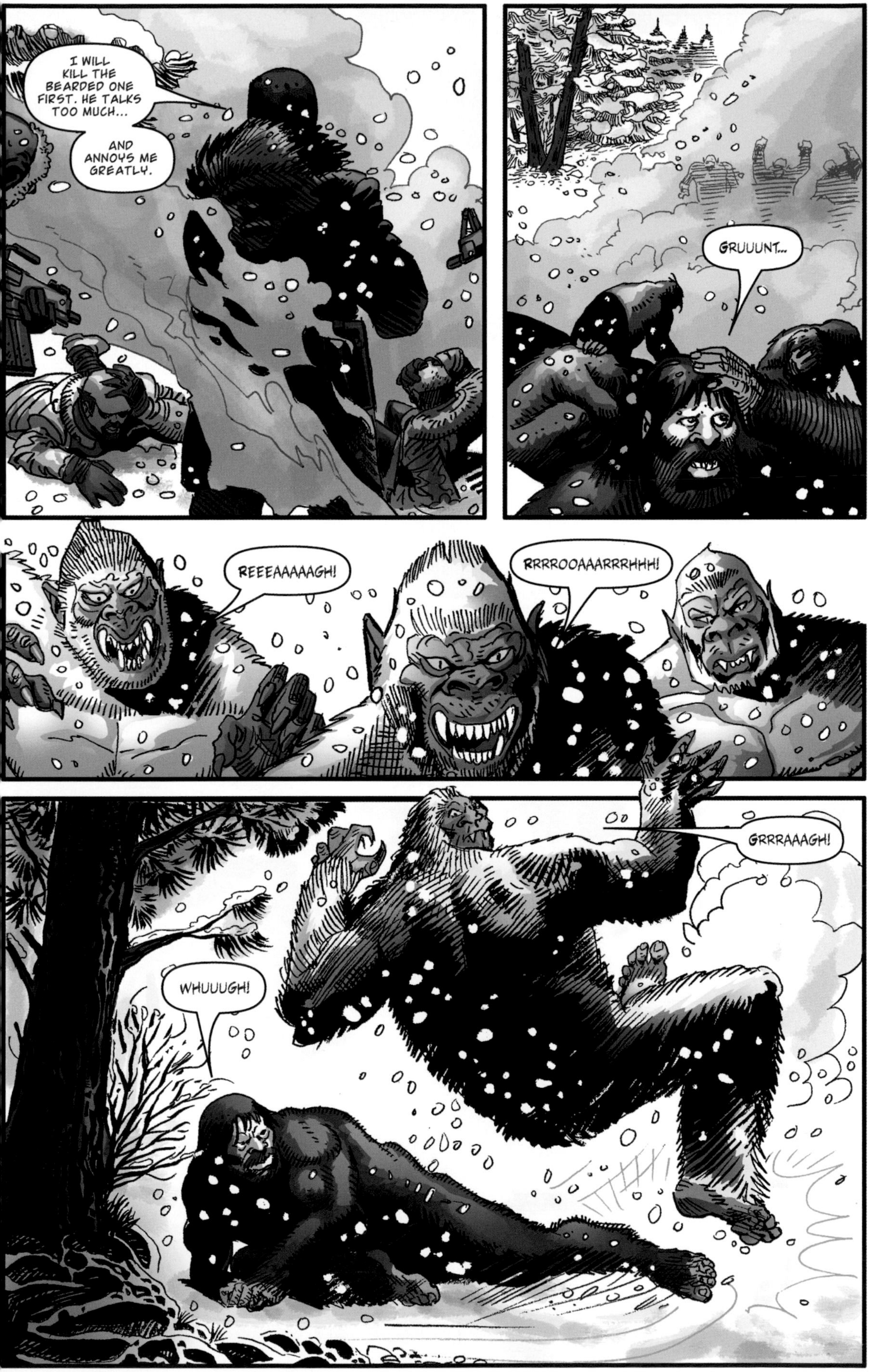
I WILL KILL THE BEARDED ONE FIRST. HE TALKS TOO MUCH...
AND ANNOYS ME GREATLY.
GRUUUNT...
REEEAAAAAAGH!
RRRROOAAARRRHHH!
GRRRAAAGH!
WHUUUGH!

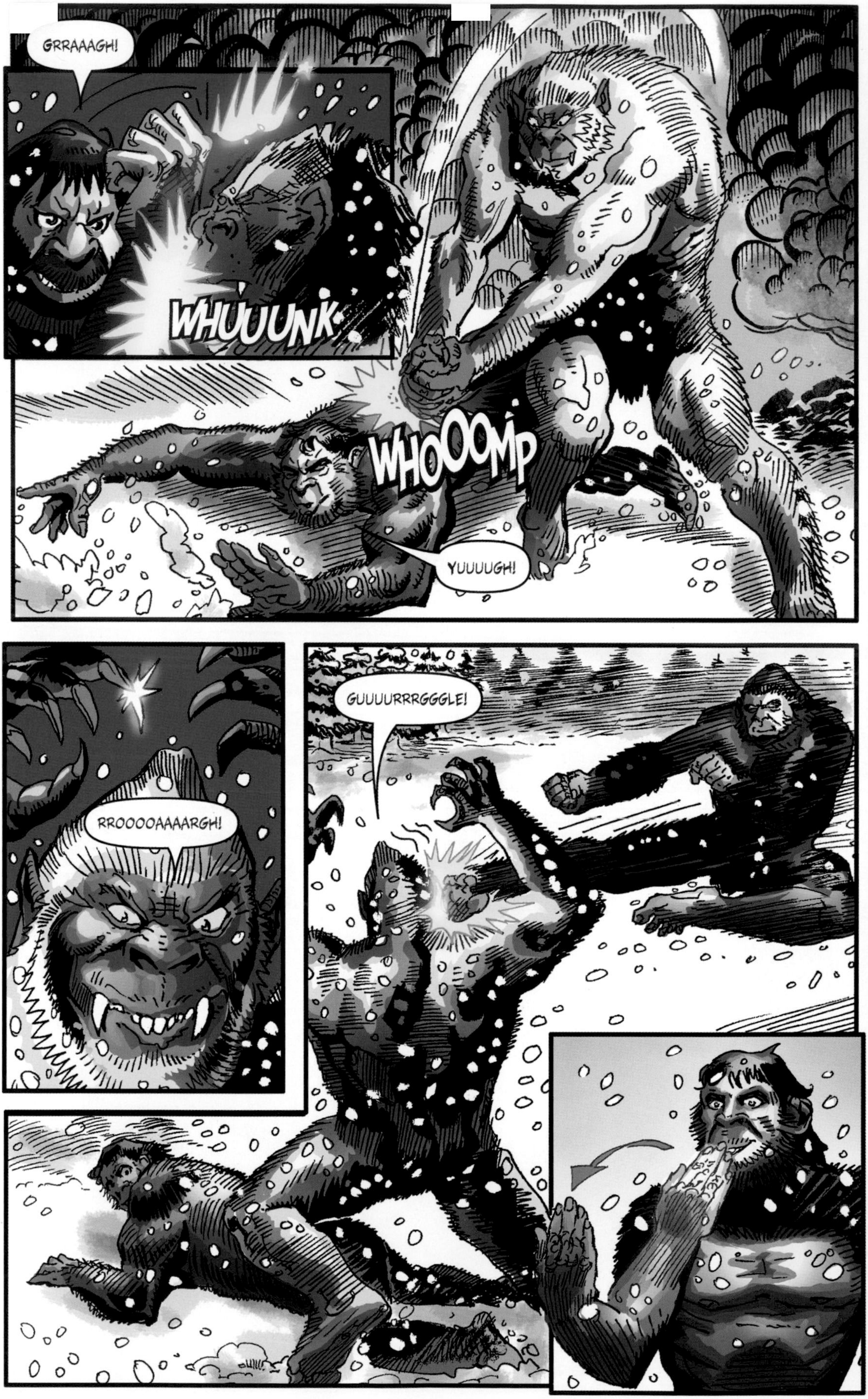
GRRAAAGH!
WHUUUNK
WHOOOMP
YUUUUGH!
RROOOOAAAARGH!
GUUUURRRGGGLE!

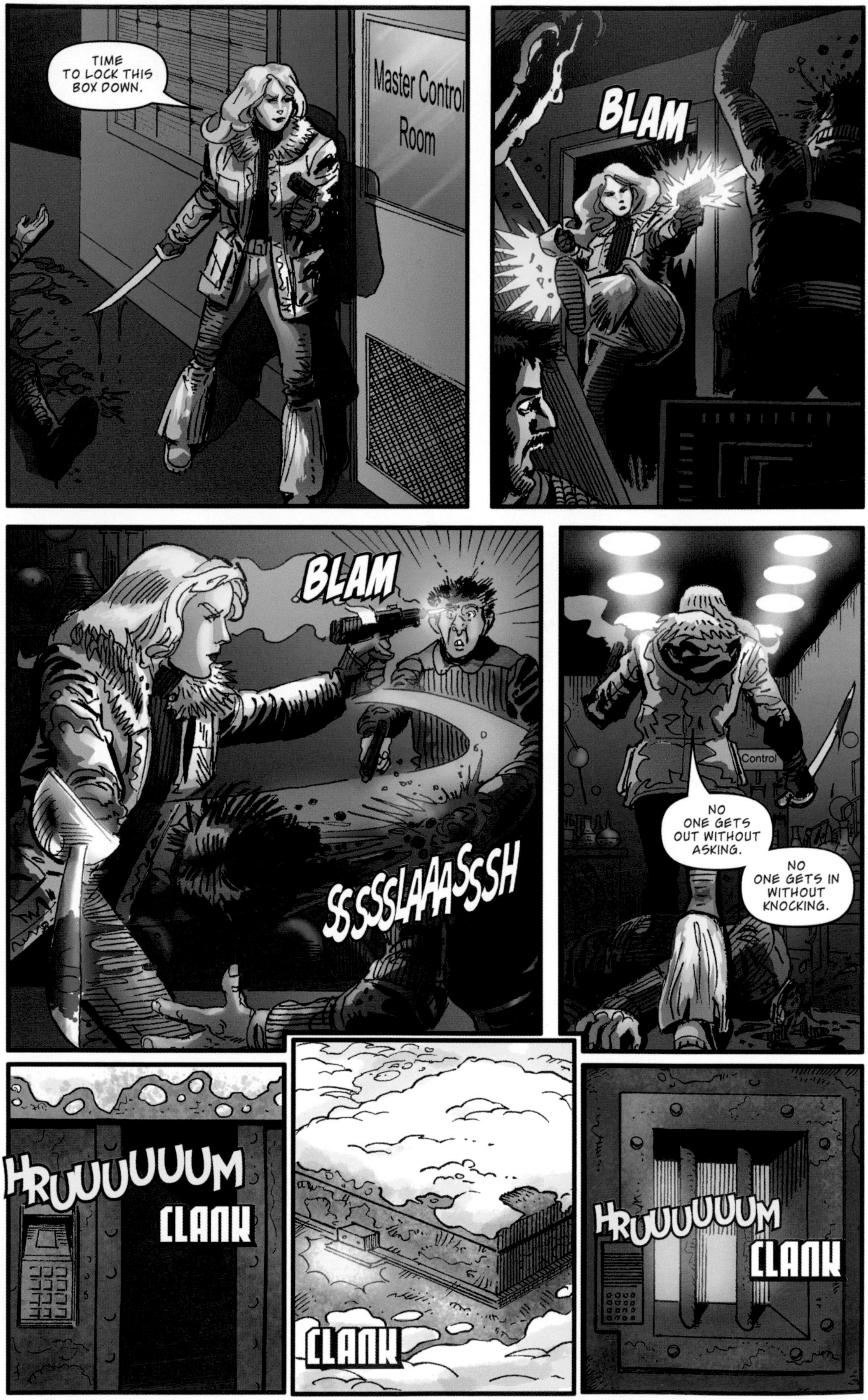
TIME TO LOCK THIS BOX DOWN.
Master Control Room
BLAM
BLAM
SSSSSLAAASSSH
Control
NO ONE GETS OUT WITHOUT ASKING.
NO ONE GETS IN WITHOUT KNOCKING.
HRUUUUUUM
CLANK
CLANK
HRUUUUUUM
CLANK

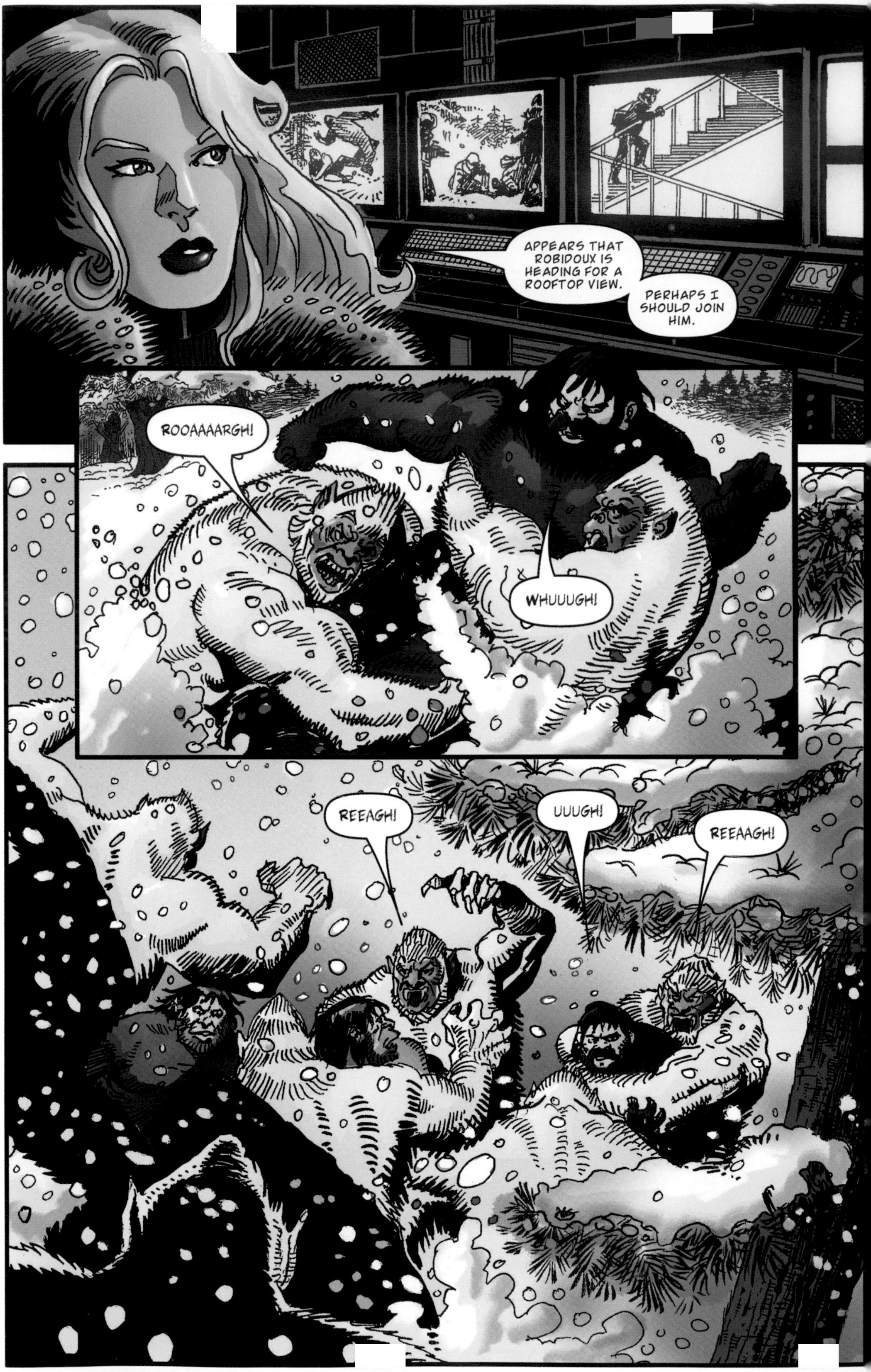
APPEARS THAT ROBIDOUX IS HEADING FOR A ROOFTOP VIEW.
PERHAPS I SHOULD JOIN HIM.
ROOAAAARGH!
WHUUUGH!
REEAGH!
UUUGH!
REEAAGH!

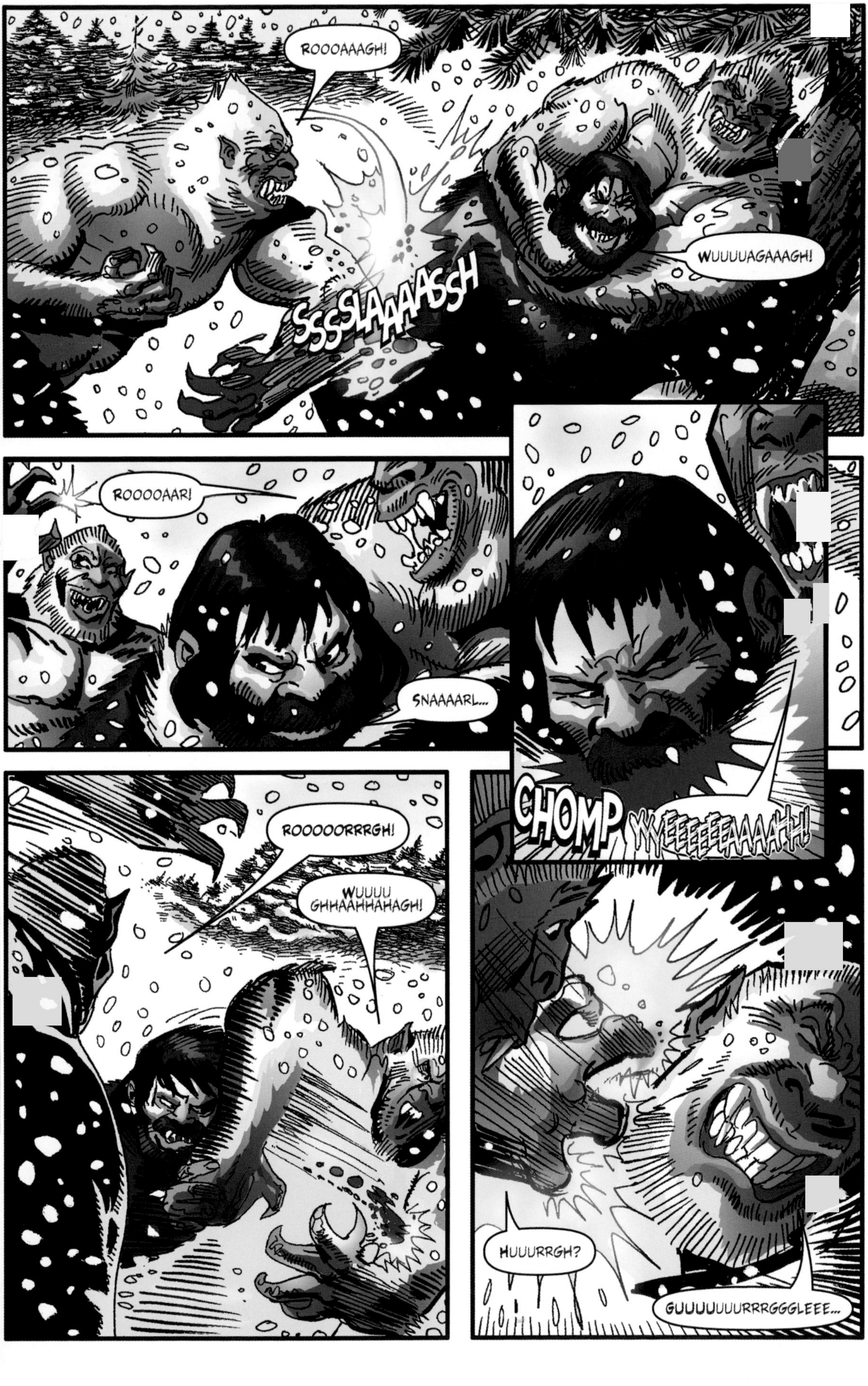
ROOOAAAGH!
WUUUUAGAAAGH!
SSSSLAAAASSH
ROOOOAAR!
SNAAAARL...
CHOMP
YYYEEEEEEAAAAHH!
ROOOOORRRGH!
WUUUU GHHAAHHAHAGH!
HUUURRGH?
GUUUUUUURRRGGGLEEE...

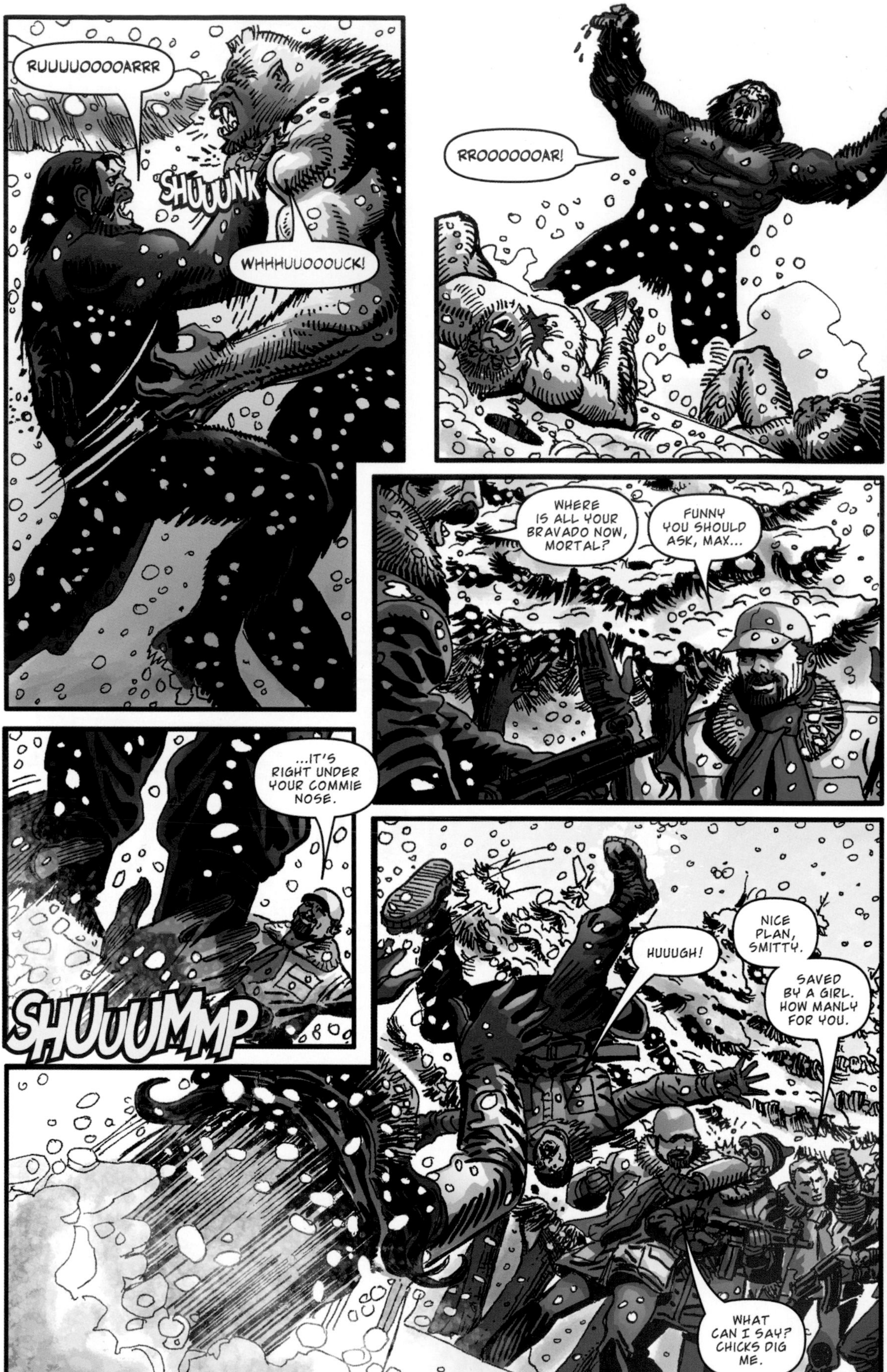
RUUUUOOOOARRR
SHUUUNK
WHHHUUOOOUCK!
RROOOOOOAR!
WHERE IS ALL YOUR BRAVADO NOW, MORTAL?
FUNNY YOU SHOULD ASK, MAX...
...IT'S RIGHT UNDER YOUR COMMIE NOSE.
SHUUUMMP
HUUUGH!
NICE PLAN, SMITTY.
SAVED BY A GIRL. HOW MANLY FOR YOU.
WHAT CAN I SAY? CHICKS DIG ME.

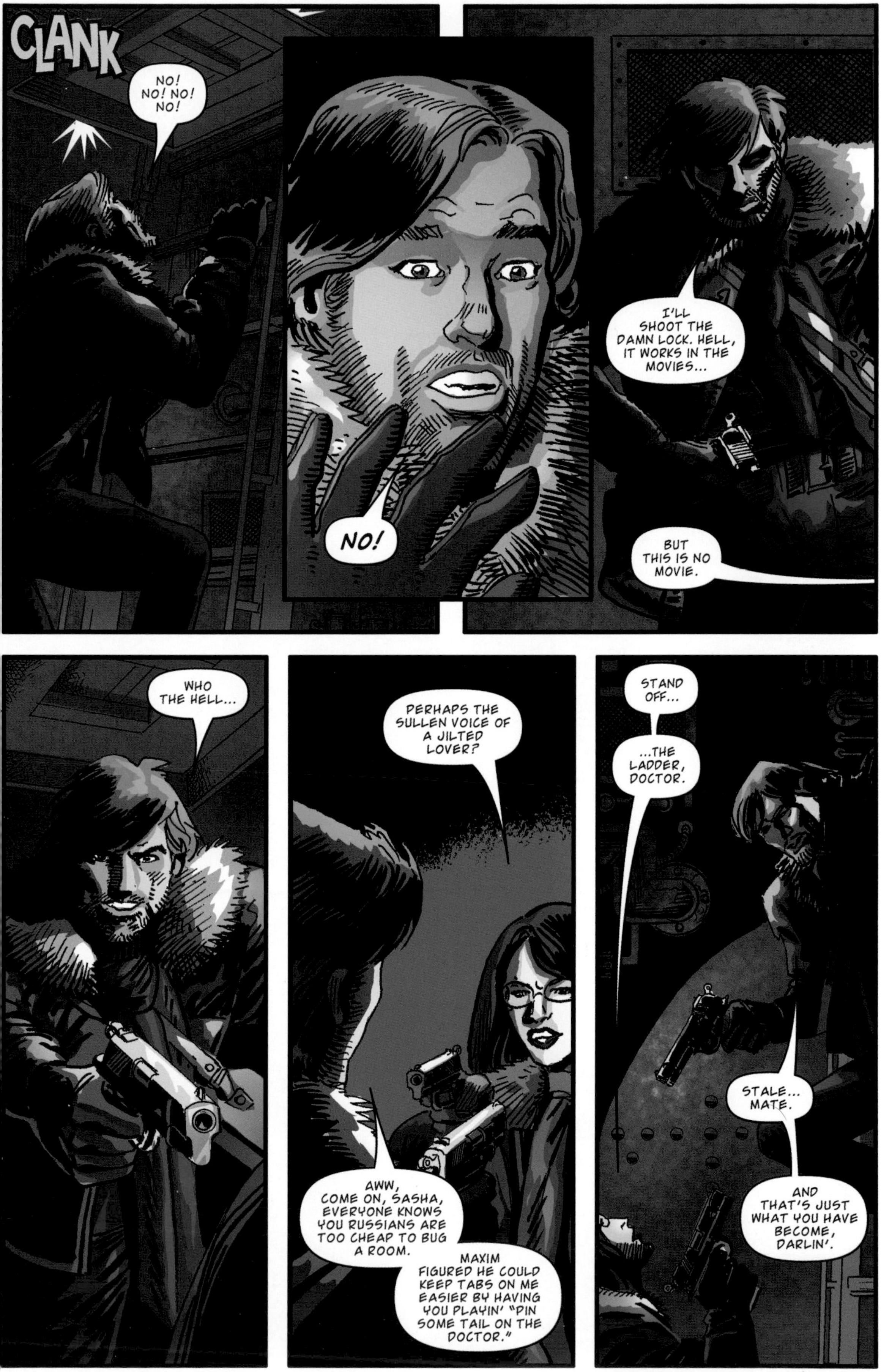
CLANK
NO! NO! NO! NO!
NO!
I'LL SHOOT THE DAMN LOCK. HELL, IT WORKS IN THE MOVIES...
BUT THIS IS NO MOVIE.
WHO THE HELL...
PERHAPS THE SULLEN VOICE OF A JILTED LOVER?
AWW, COME ON, SASHA, EVERYONE KNOWS YOU RUSSIANS ARE TOO CHEAP TO BUG A ROOM.
MAXIM FIGURED HE COULD KEEP TABS ON ME EASIER BY HAVING YOU PLAYIN' "PIN SOME TAIL ON THE DOCTOR."
STAND OFF...
...THE LADDER, DOCTOR.
STALE... MATE.
AND THAT'S JUST WHAT YOU HAVE BECOME, DARLIN'.

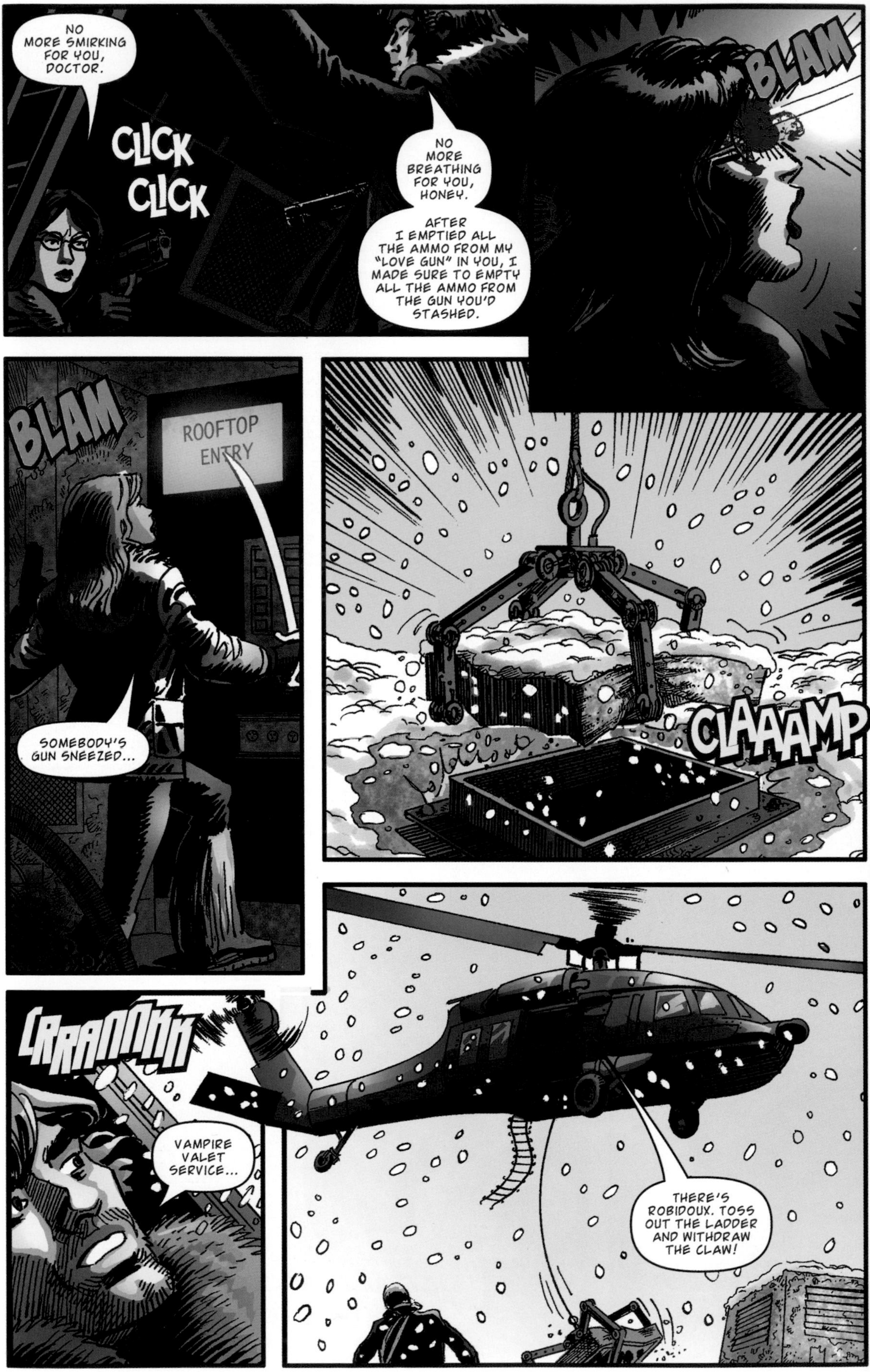
NO MORE SMIRKING FOR YOU, DOCTOR.
CLICK CLICK
NO MORE BREATHING FOR YOU, HONEY.
AFTER I EMPTIED ALL THE AMMO FROM MY "LOVE GUN" IN YOU, I MADE SURE TO EMPTY ALL THE AMMO FROM THE GUN YOU'D STASHED.
BLAM
BLAM
ROOFTOP ENTRY
SOMEBODY'S GUN SNEEZED...
CLAAAMP
CRRANNKK
VAMPIRE VALET SERVICE...
THERE'S ROBIDOUX. TOSS OUT THE LADDER AND WITHDRAW THE CLAW!

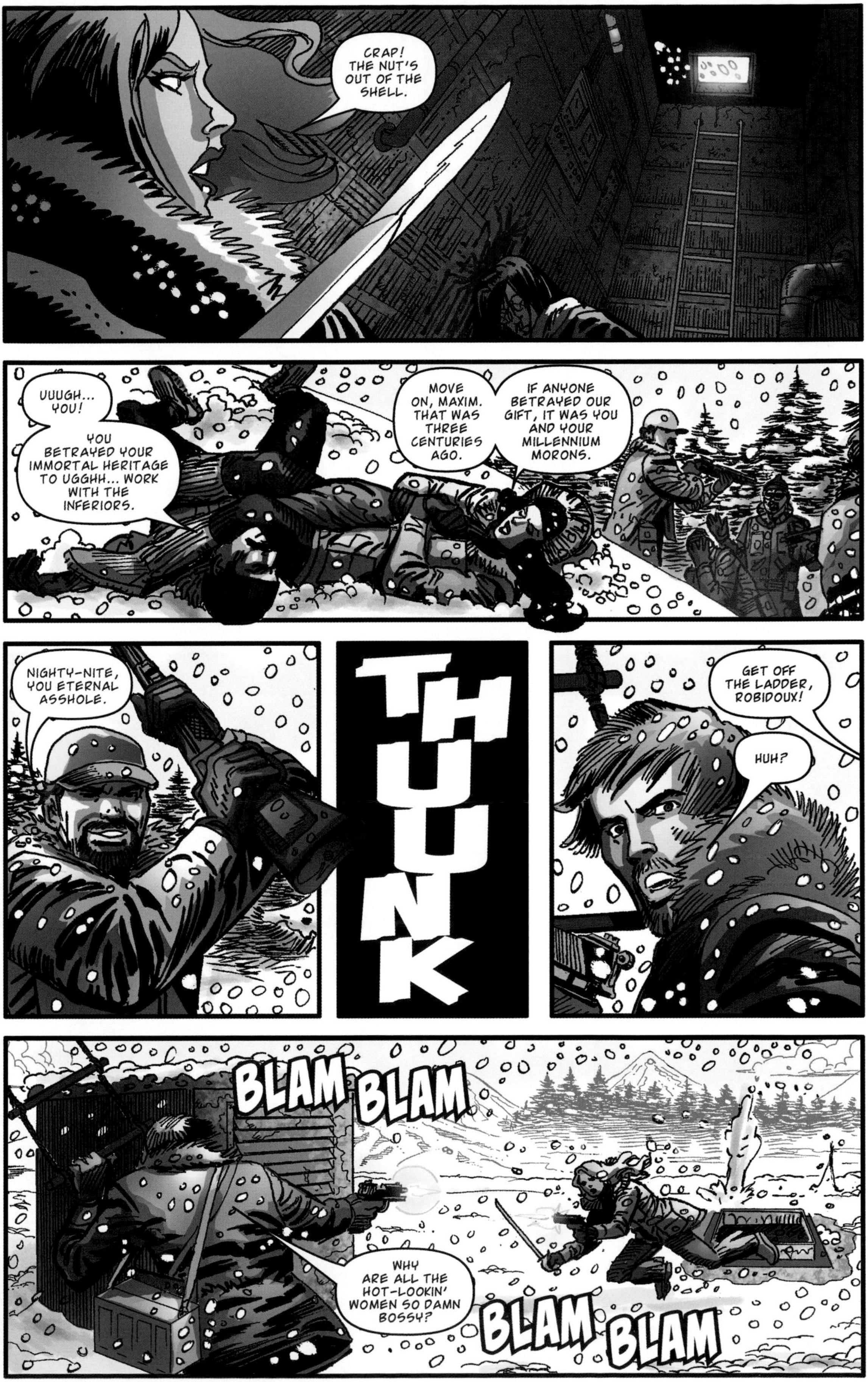
CRAP! THE NUT'S OUT OF THE SHELL.
UUUGH... YOU!
YOU BETRAYED YOUR IMMORTAL HERITAGE TO UGGHH... WORK WITH THE INFERIORS.
MOVE ON, MAXIM. THAT WAS THREE CENTURIES AGO.
IF ANYONE BETRAYED OUR GIFT, IT WAS YOU AND YOUR MILLENNIUM MORONS.
NIGHTY-NITE, YOU ETERNAL ASSHOLE.
THUUNK
GET OFF THE LADDER, ROBIDOUX!
HUH?
BLAM BLAM
WHY ARE ALL THE HOT-LOOKIN' WOMEN SO DAMN BOSSY?
BLAM BLAM

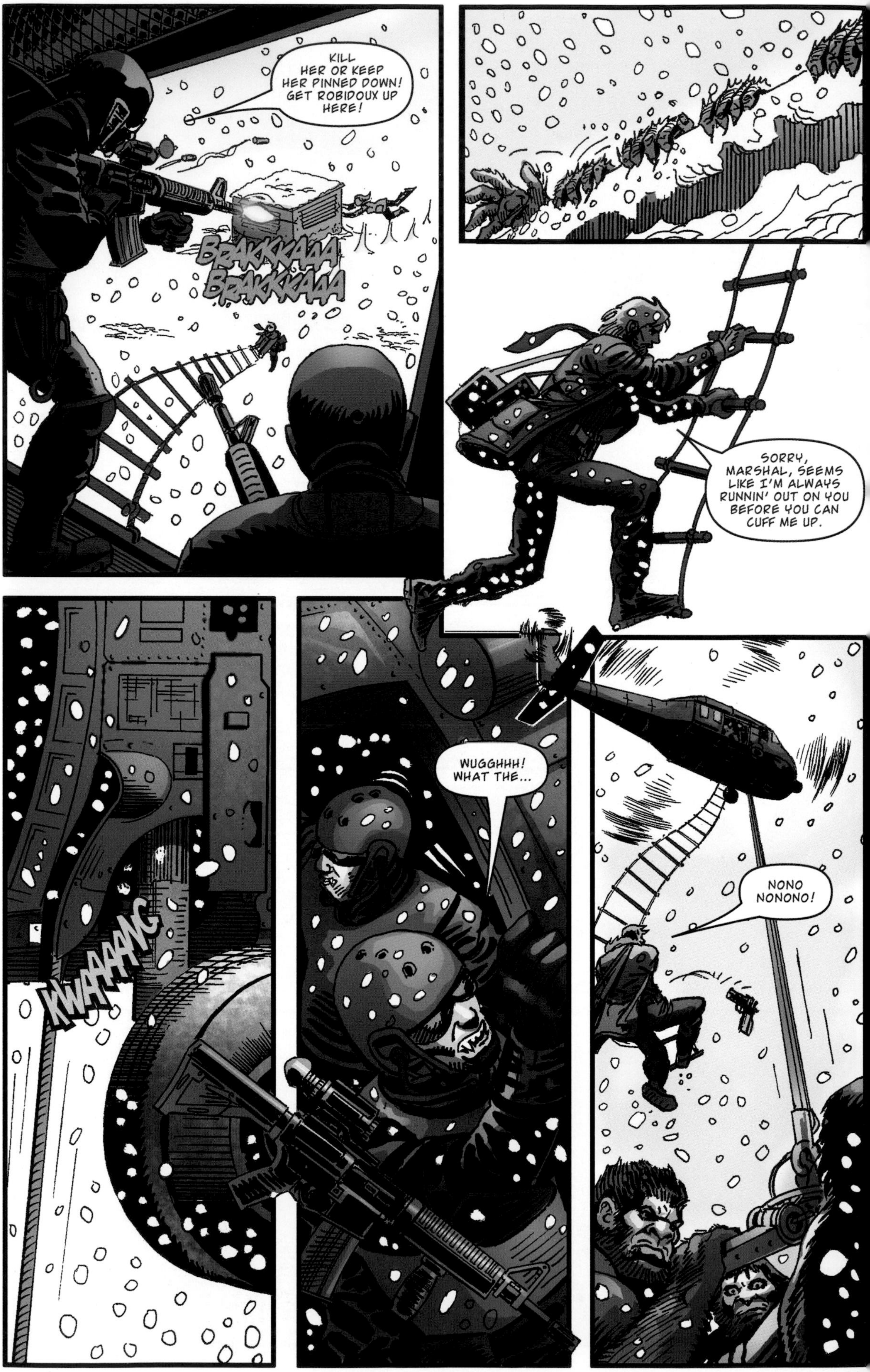
KILL HER OR KEEP HER PINNED DOWN! GET ROBIDOUX UP HERE!
BRAKKKAAA
BRAKKKAAA
SORRY, MARSHAL, SEEMS LIKE I'M ALWAYS RUNNIN' OUT ON YOU BEFORE YOU CAN CUFF ME UP.
KWAAAANG
WUGGHHH! WHAT THE...
NONO NONONO!

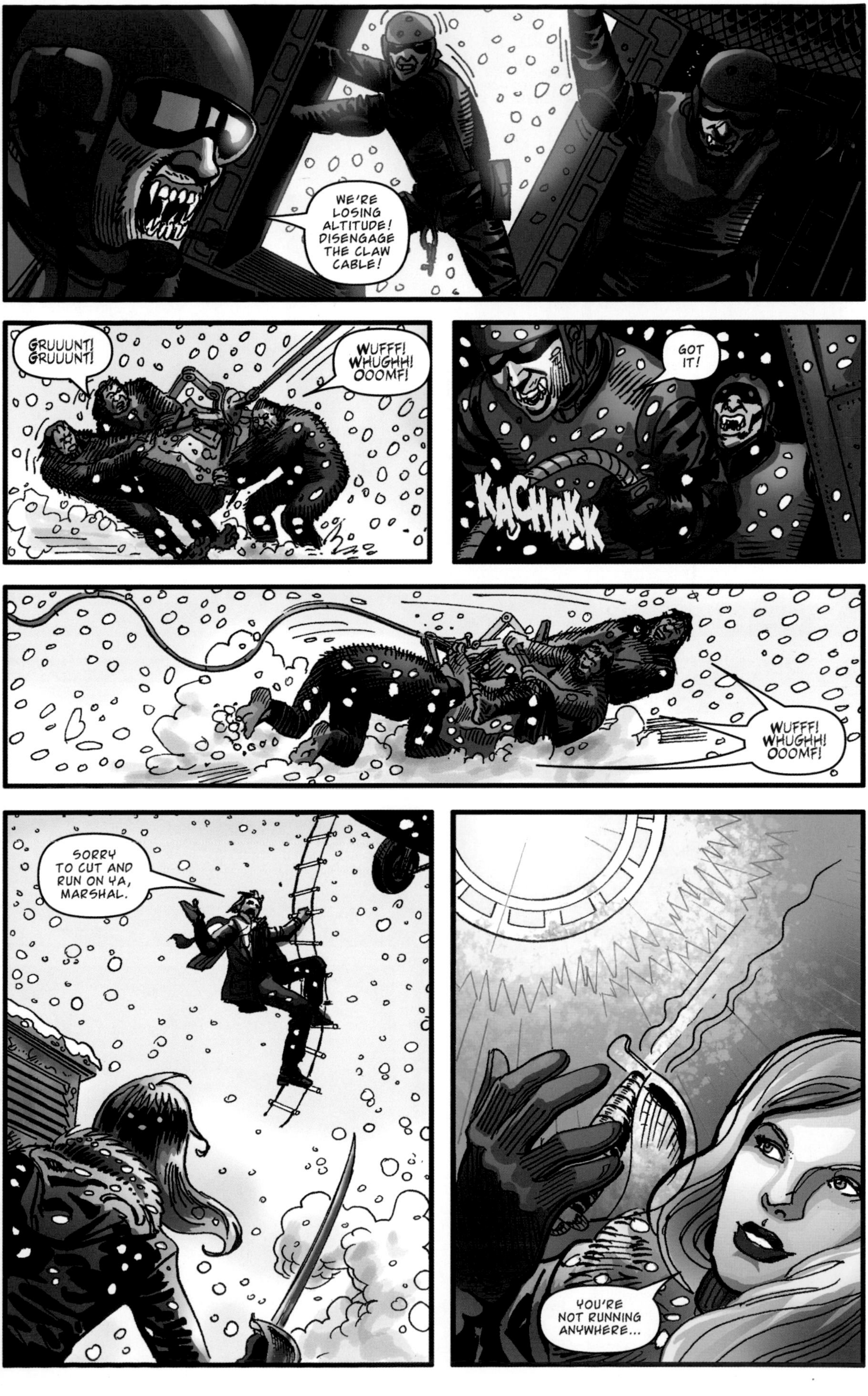
WE'RE LOSING ALTITUDE! DISENGAGE THE CLAW CABLE!
GRUUUNT! GRUUUNT!
WUFFF! WHUGHH! OOOMF!
GOT IT!
KACHAKK
WUFFF! WHUGHH! OOOMF!
SORRY TO CUT AND RUN ON YA, MARSHAL.
YOU'RE NOT RUNNING ANYWHERE...

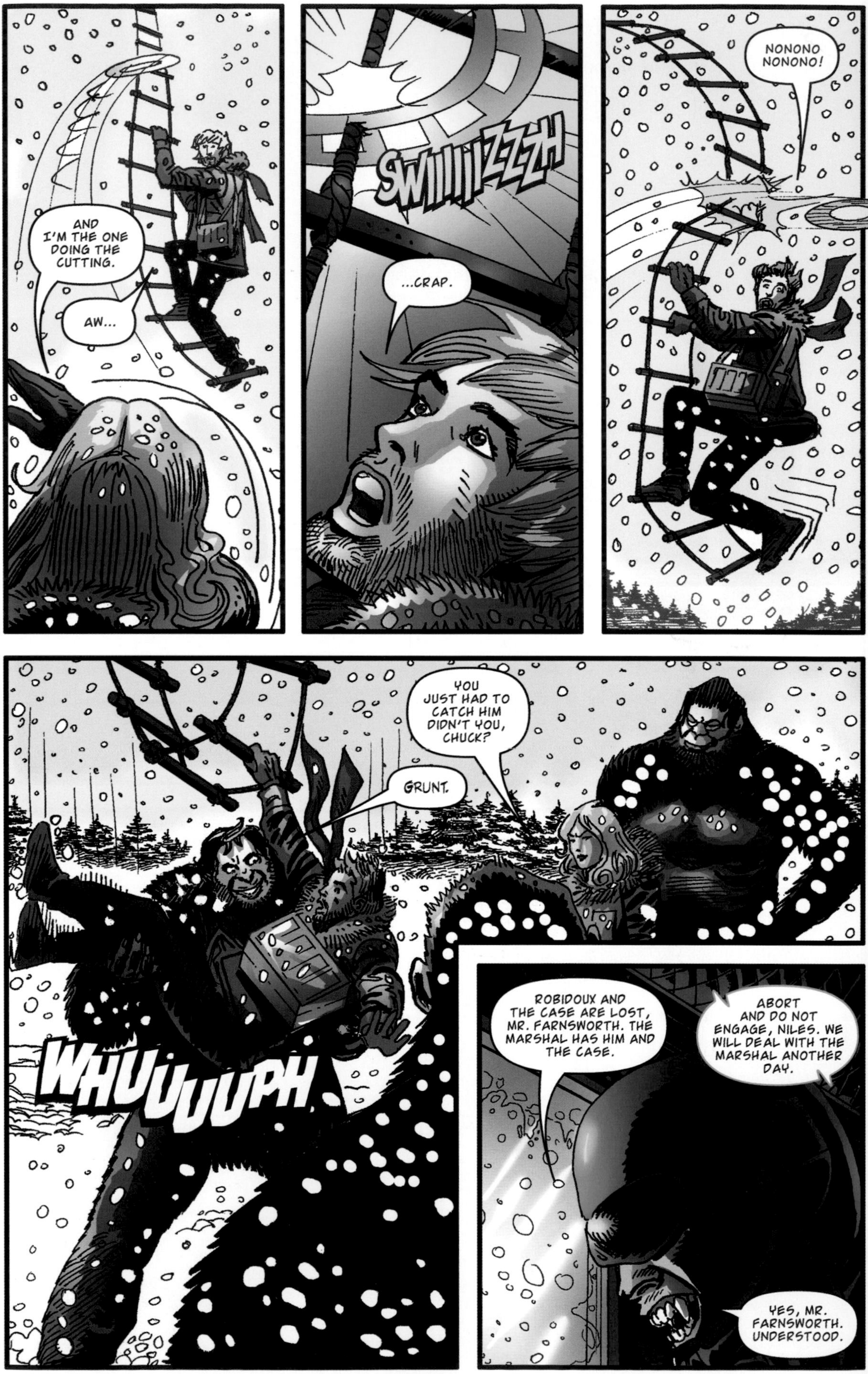
AND I'M THE ONE DOING THE CUTTING.
AW...
SWIIIIIZZZH
...CRAP.
NONONO NONONO!
YOU JUST HAD TO CATCH HIM DIDN'T YOU, CHUCK?
GRUNT.
WHUUUUUPH
ROBIDOUX AND THE CASE ARE LOST, MR. FARNSWORTH. THE MARSHAL HAS HIM AND THE CASE.
ABORT AND DO NOT ENGAGE, NILES. WE WILL DEAL WITH THE MARSHAL ANOTHER DAY.
YES, MR. FARNSWORTH. UNDERSTOOD.

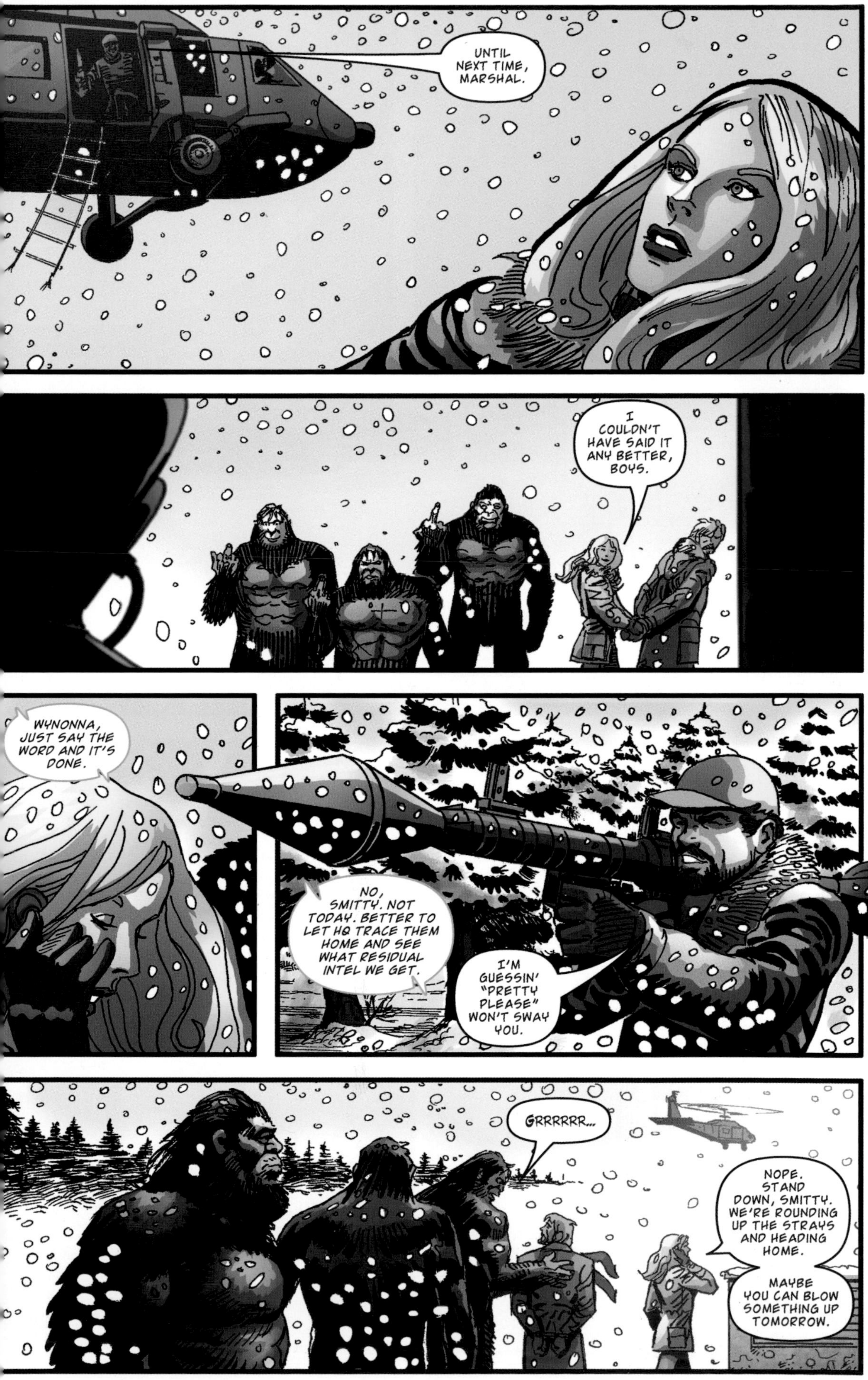
UNTIL NEXT TIME, MARSHAL.
I COULDN'T HAVE SAID IT ANY BETTER, BOYS.
WYNONNA, JUST SAY THE WORD AND IT'S DONE.
NO, SMITTY. NOT TODAY. BETTER TO LET HQ TRACE THEM HOME AND SEE WHAT RESIDUAL INTEL WE GET.
I'M GUESSIN' "PRETTY PLEASE" WON'T SWAY YOU.
GRRRRRR...
NOPE. STAND DOWN, SMITTY. WE'RE ROUNDING UP THE STRAYS AND HEADING HOME.
MAYBE YOU CAN BLOW SOMETHING UP TOMORROW.

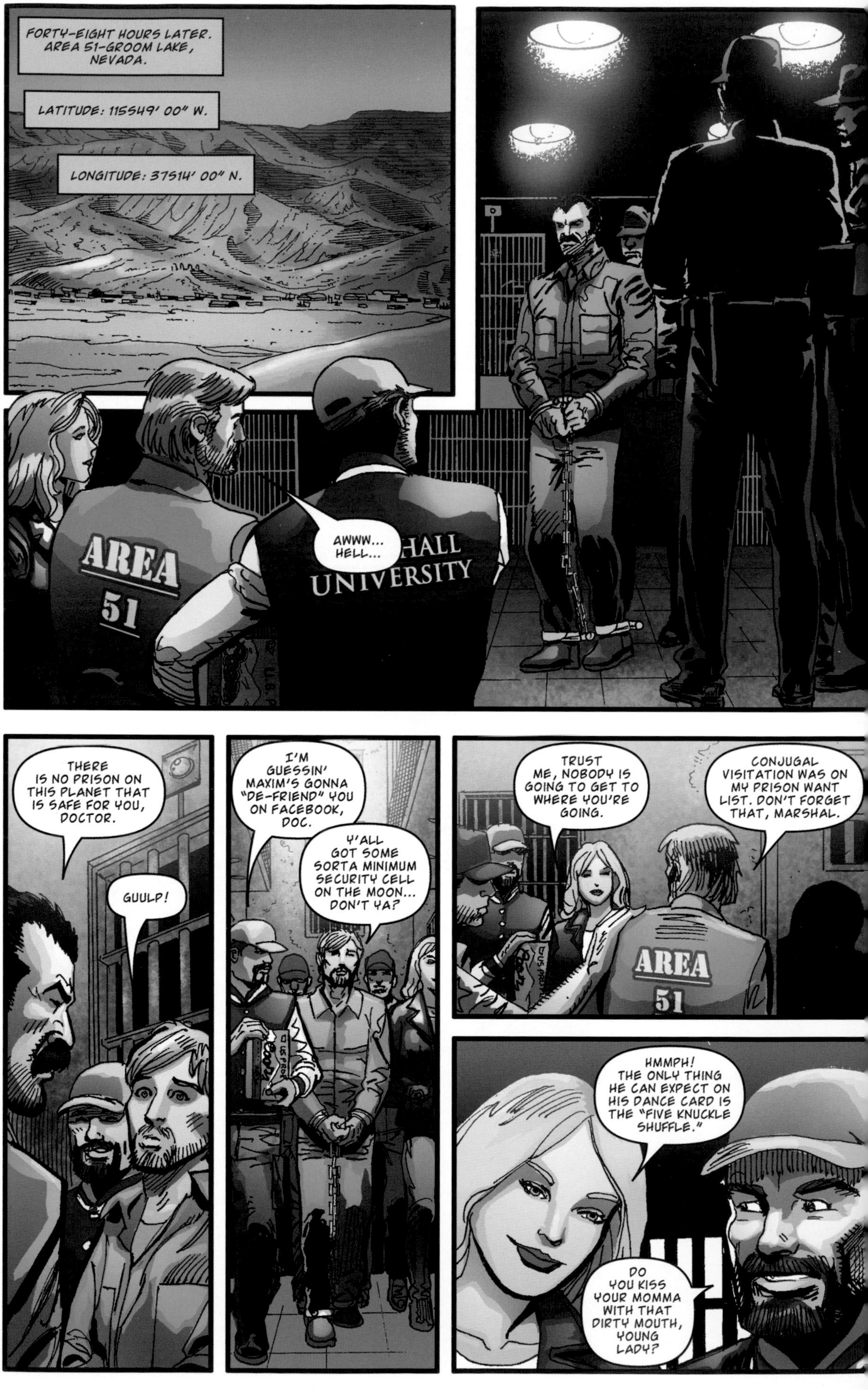

FORTY-EIGHT HOURS LATER. AREA 51-GROOM LAKE, NEVADA.
LATITUDE: 115549' 00" W.
LONGITUDE: 37514' 00" N.
AWWW... HELL...
AREA 51
HALL UNIVERSITY
THERE IS NO PRISON ON THIS PLANET THAT IS SAFE FOR YOU, DOCTOR.
GUULP!
I'M GUESSIN' MAXIM'S GONNA "DE-FRIEND" YOU ON FACEBOOK, DOC.
Y'ALL GOT SOME SORTA MINIMUM SECURITY CELL ON THE MOON... DON'T YA?
TRUST ME, NOBODY IS GOING TO GET TO WHERE YOU'RE GOING.
CONJUGAL VISITATION WAS ON MY PRISON WANT LIST. DON'T FORGET THAT, MARSHAL.
AREA 51
HMMPH! THE ONLY THING HE CAN EXPECT ON HIS DANCE CARD IS THE "FIVE KNUCKLE SHUFFLE."
DO YOU KISS YOUR MOMMA WITH THAT DIRTY MOUTH, YOUNG LADY?

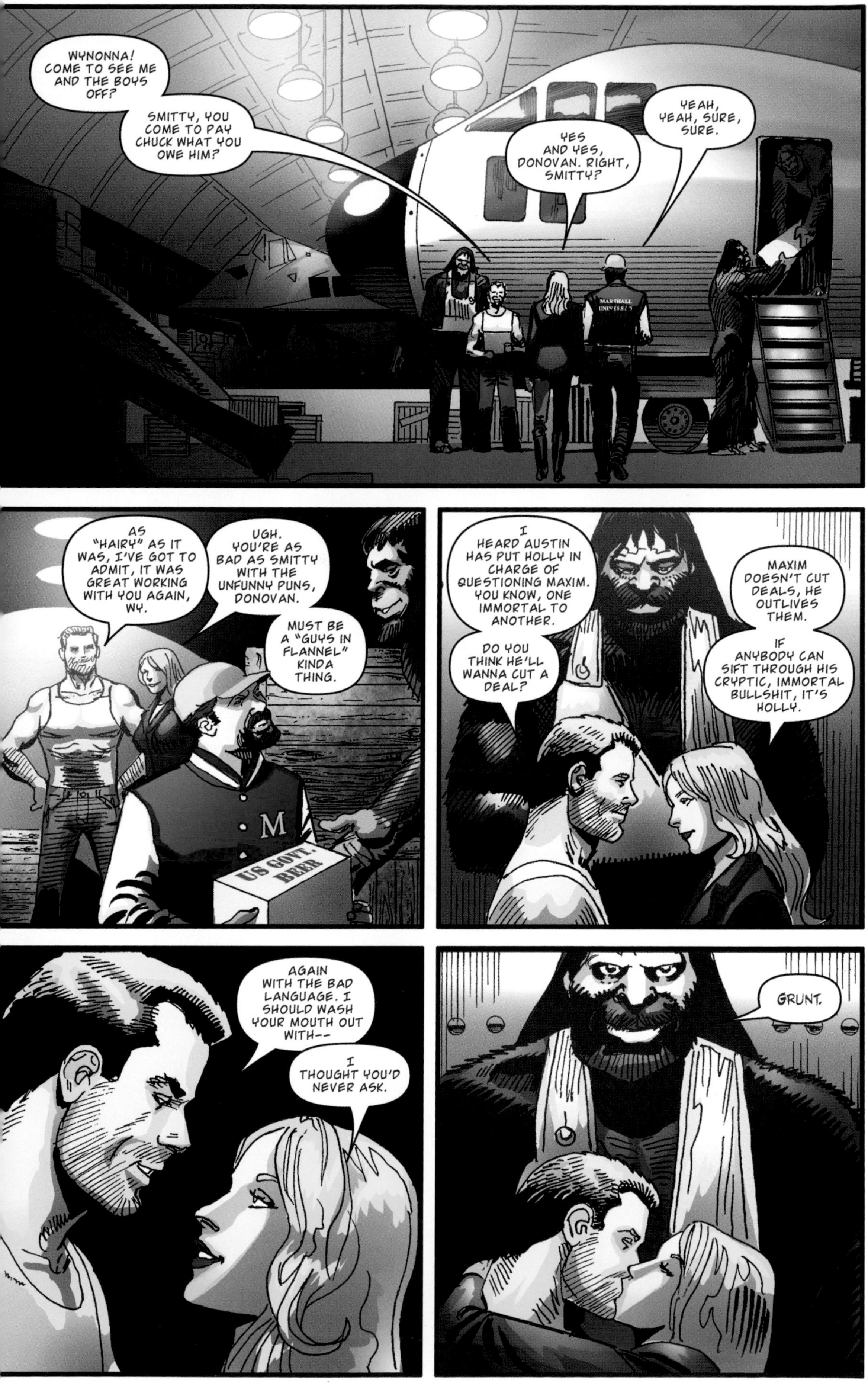
WYNONNA! COME TO SEE ME AND THE BOYS OFF?
SMITTY, YOU COME TO PAY CHUCK WHAT YOU OWE HIM?
YES AND YES, DONOVAN. RIGHT, SMITTY?
YEAH, YEAH, SURE, SURE.
MARSHALL
AS "HAIRY" AS IT WAS, I'VE GOT TO ADMIT, IT WAS GREAT WORKING WITH YOU AGAIN, WY.
UGH. YOU'RE AS BAD AS SMITTY WITH THE UNFUNNY PUNS, DONOVAN.
MUST BE A "GUYS IN FLANNEL" KINDA THING.
US GOVT. BEER
I HEARD AUSTIN HAS PUT HOLLY IN CHARGE OF QUESTIONING MAXIM. YOU KNOW, ONE IMMORTAL TO ANOTHER.
DO YOU THINK HE'LL WANNA CUT A DEAL?
MAXIM DOESN'T CUT DEALS, HE OUTLIVES THEM.
IF ANYBODY CAN SIFT THROUGH HIS CRYPTIC, IMMORTAL BULLSHIT, IT'S HOLLY.
AGAIN WITH THE BAD LANGUAGE. I SHOULD WASH YOUR MOUTH OUT WITH--
I THOUGHT YOU'D NEVER ASK.
GRUNT.

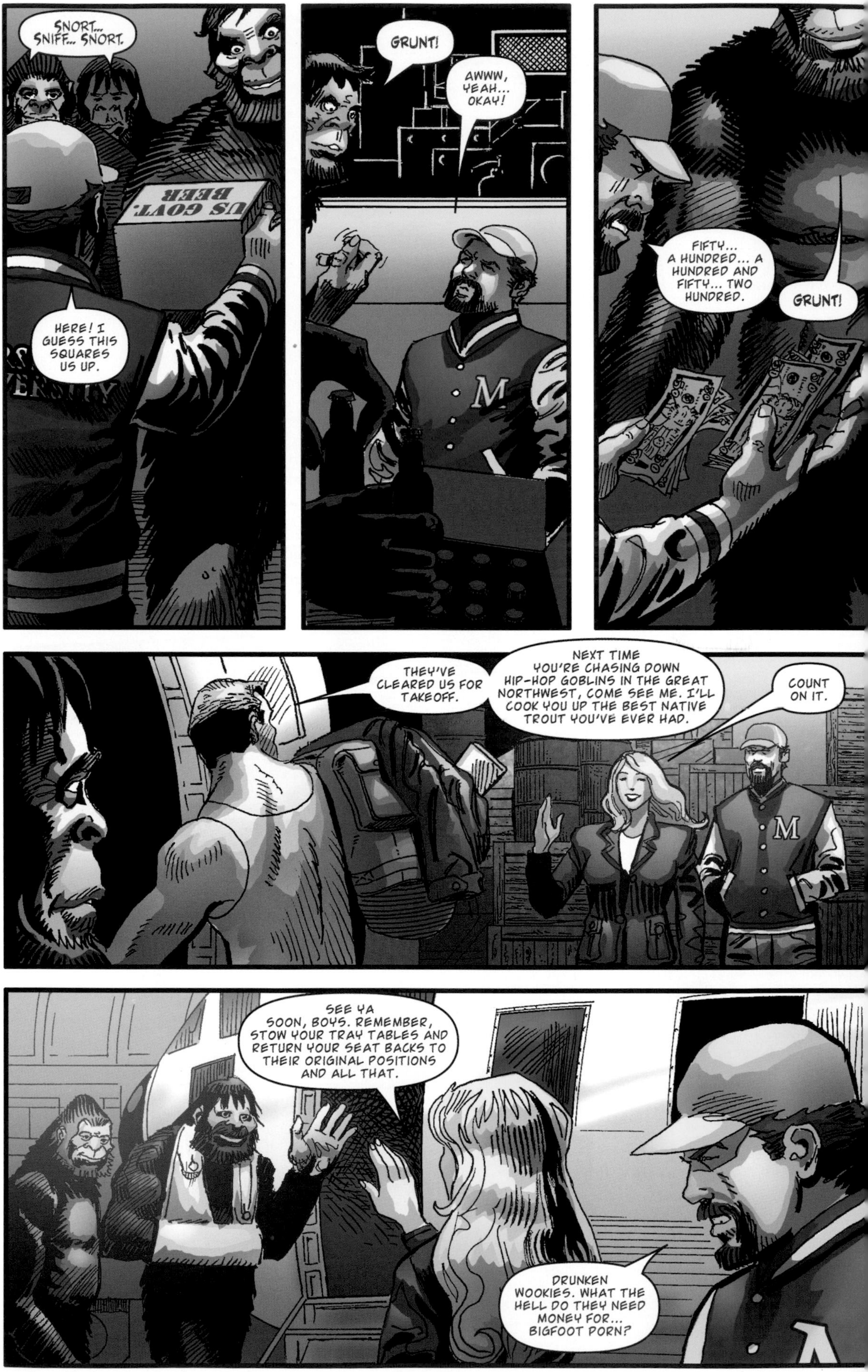
SNORT... SNIFF... SNORT.
US GOVT. BEER
HERE! I GUESS THIS SQUARES US UP.
GRUNT!
AWWW, YEAH... OKAY!
FIFTY... A HUNDRED... A HUNDRED AND FIFTY... TWO HUNDRED.
GRUNT!
THEY'VE CLEARED US FOR TAKEOFF.
NEXT TIME YOU'RE CHASING DOWN HIP-HOP GOBLINS IN THE GREAT NORTHWEST, COME SEE ME. I'LL COOK YOU UP THE BEST NATIVE TROUT YOU'VE EVER HAD.
COUNT ON IT.
SEE YA SOON, BOYS. REMEMBER, STOW YOUR TRAY TABLES AND RETURN YOUR SEAT BACKS TO THEIR ORIGINAL POSITIONS AND ALL THAT.
DRUNKEN WOOKIES. WHAT THE HELL DO THEY NEED MONEY FOR... BIGFOOT PORN?

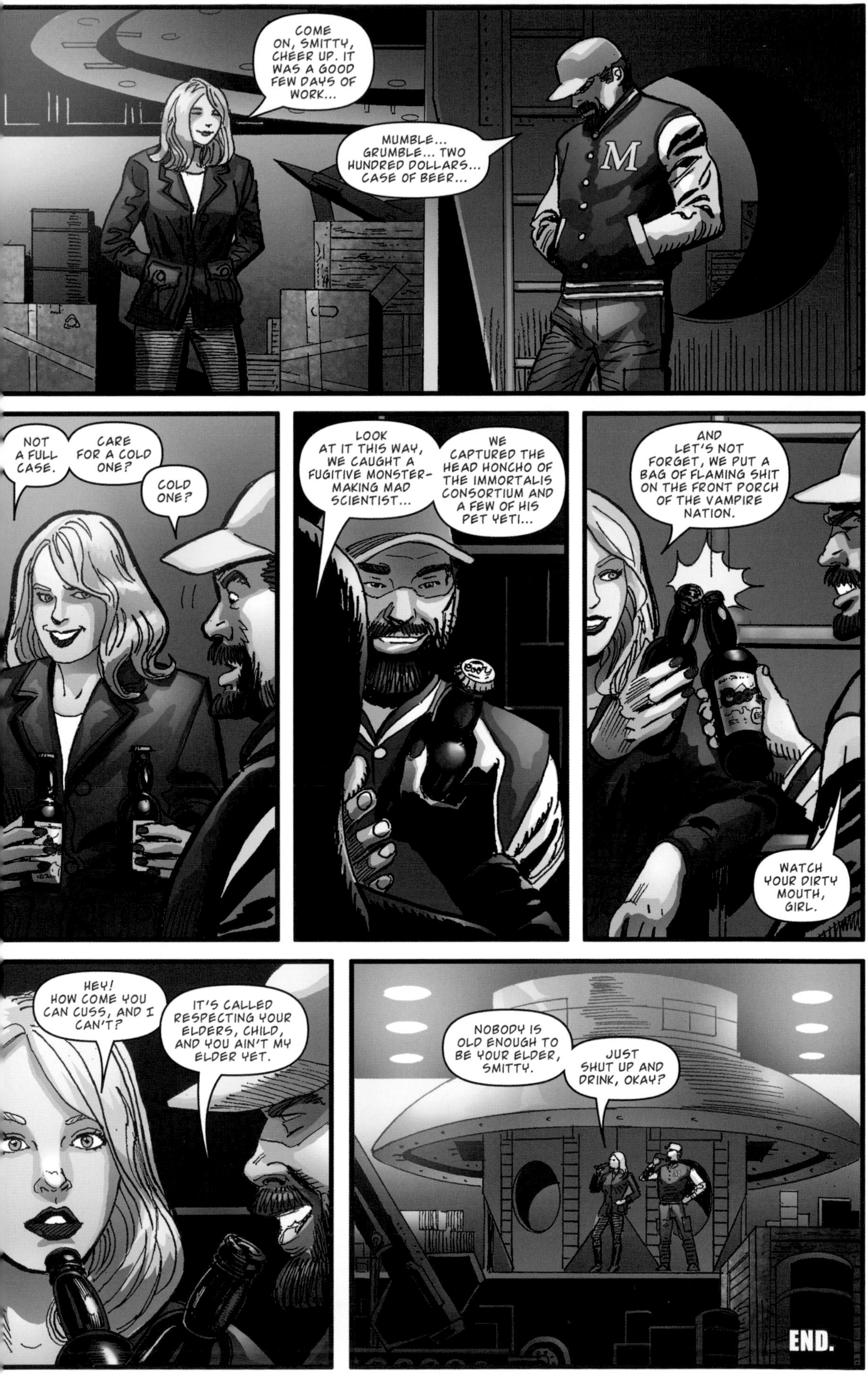
COME ON, SMITTY, CHEER UP. IT WAS A GOOD FEW DAYS OF WORK...
MUMBLE... GRUMBLE... TWO HUNDRED DOLLARS... CASE OF BEER...
NOT A FULL CASE.
CARE FOR A COLD ONE?
COLD ONE?
LOOK AT IT THIS WAY, WE CAUGHT A FUGITIVE MONSTER-MAKING MAD SCIENTIST...
WE CAPTURED THE HEAD HONCHO OF THE IMMORTALIS CONSORTIUM AND A FEW OF HIS PET YETI...
AND LET'S NOT FORGET, WE PUT A BAG OF FLAMING SHIT ON THE FRONT PORCH OF THE VAMPIRE NATION.
WATCH YOUR DIRTY MOUTH, GIRL.
HEY! HOW COME YOU CAN CUSS, AND I CAN'T?
IT'S CALLED RESPECTING YOUR ELDERS, CHILD, AND YOU AIN'T MY ELDER YET.
NOBODY IS OLD ENOUGH TO BE YOUR ELDER, SMITTY.
JUST SHUT UP AND DRINK, OKAY?
END.

WYNONNA EARP BACKGROUND NOTES
BY BEAU SMITH

In the paranormal world there are warring tribes/factions/organizations always fighting for more of the paranormal turf. Some fight for a traditional caste system among the paranormal. Others fight because they're just THAT cranky. It's a paranormal fact that werewolves and others were once used as slaves and minions of vampires. In the early 1800s there was a worldwide revolt that restarted a centuries-old war. Vampires have always seen themselves as the highest of the paranormal pecking order. They are the snobs, the entitled, the elite.

They've always looked down at not only humans, but all other forms of the paranormal as well. To them, all the rest are to be used as food, drink, or sex. Under the Vampire Nation if you're not of personal use, then you're as good as dead. The kind you don't come back from. They only "turn" the humans they feel may be of a semi-eternal use for them.

They find zombies the lowest form of paranormal. They're dirty, they have serious hygiene issues, they're slow, they aren't very smart, and they don't follow orders well.

Witches and warlocks think of themselves as better than the vampires, but their numbers aren't as many. They also have to deal with so many of the uneducated amateurs trying to join their ranks because of fads and trends such as the success of *Harry Potter* novels and TV shows such as *Charmed*. Like everyone else, they blame the news media and *Entertainment Tonight*. True witches and warlocks believe in tradition and classical education in the dark arts is what's most pure. The traditionalists also find the current users of Internet witchery disgusting.

Much of the unrest in the paranormal world comes from the racism and bigotry between the groups. Sometimes this hate and distrust of each other spills over into the human world out of nothing more than frustration. They know that if they commit an overt act of violence against another tribe, it could bring a huge war that where there would be no winner, so they take a lot of it out on the non-enhanced human world.

There's also the crime element. Just because you're a vampire, mummy, immortal, ghoul, or Sudan Snake Devil, doesn't mean you don't want lots of cash, a trophy mate of some shape or form, a really big home, and fancy cars. The crime rate in the paranormal world has increased in the last 100 years, and the Clan Of Immortals has been the heavy-hitter in this area. They figure they're going to be around for a long time, and they want to make sure they have everything they want.

Not everything in the paranormal world is black-and-white. There are good vampires, werewolves, ghosts, and gremlins. (Not zombies. They're never any good.) There are some that just want to be left alone and live their paranormal lives. They pay their taxes, obey the law, and make sure their lawn is cut once a week. There are even some that work hand-in-hand with law enforcement. Wynonna Earp and the Black Badge Division of the U.S. Marshals have no problem with them. It's the ones bent on breaking the law and in pursuit of world domination that they have a serious problem with. Those are the ones they're after.

Break the law, you go to jail.

Break the supernatural law, you face Wynonna Earp.

—Beau Smith
The Flying Fist Ranch

WYNONNA EARP SOURCE FILES

Name: Wynonna Earp

Height: 5 feet, 7 inches

Weight: 135 pounds

Age: 33

Occupation: United States Marshal, Covert Black Badge Division, Level 13.

Base Of Operations: Los Angeles. Mobile United States.

Family: Father (dead); Mother (dead); Sisters—Virginia Earp and Morgana Earp, whereabouts unknown.

Wynonna Earp is the great-great-granddaughter of famous lawman Wyatt Earp. Her great-great-grandmother was Shirley Ann Greene, an actress in Hollywood in the 1920s. Greene had an affair with Earp while he was a consultant on a Tom Mix film she starred in.

Wynonna possesses almost all of her famous ancestor's traits, including his cool composure in dire situations. She's quite proficient with most all weaponry. She's been highly trained in military-style hand-to-hand combat and mixed martial arts, but her greatest physical abilities lie in her boxing skills. She was taught old school from her father and grandfather, both boxers.

Wynonna has incorporated a favorite move of Wyatt Earp in her defensive skills, the art of "buffaloing" a possible enemy before that enemy can commit an act of violence. "Buffaloing" an opponent is done by taking your handgun and bringing it down on their head, rendering them stunned or unconscious. It saves time, trouble, back talk, and bullets.

Wynonna Earp, much like her ancestor, has never been one to suffer fools. She finds herself most at home on the job. While working a case, she is more relaxed and comfortable. She has more of a sense of humor and calm when others tend to panic and get amped up. She's more at home in a room full of paranormals than at a social party or night on the town. She enjoys the camaraderie of her peers, and misses it when in civilian situations. Growing up, she was always the prettiest girl NOT at the dance.

Her personal relationships have been hard at times. She tries hard to overcome her protective instincts when she's seeing a "civilian." She knows what's out there and they don't, causing her to be a bit more controlling in a relationship. Her mentor, Smitty, says what Wynonna calls dating, others call "intimidating."

She's dated within the work environment, but nothing has really had enough grit to stick long-term. She had a semi-serious relationship with Nick Vincent, a former U.S. Marshal washout who returned to his "family" business when his father died. His family business was the Mafia, and his father was the don of that family, killed by the rival Egyptian Mafia. They run into each other now and then. Sparks always fly, but their work gets in the way. They do share the intense goal to bring down paranormal crime. Wynonna does it for justice, and Nick for revenge.

She was also involved with Donovan Jones, special agent for the Department of Fish & Wildlife Covert Operations. Donovan is a Bigfoot handler out of Washington state.

Name: Smitty

Height: 5 feet, 10 inches

Weight: 190 pounds

Age: 53

Born: Huntington, West Virginia

Occupation: Senior U.S. Marshal, Covert Black Badge Division, Level 13. Covert Operations. Gunsmith and Grade-1 Weapons Master.

Smitty is one of the last old-school U.S. Marshals. He's a throwback to the U.S. Marshals of the Old West. He comes from a long line of West Virginia State Troopers. After his service in the military, he joined the U.S. Marshals and set a record for capturing fugitives which still stands today.

After a serious run-in with The Gila Cult in New Mexico, Smitty was recruited to join the Black Badge Division. He has an incredible knack for mechanics and weapons technology that makes him one of the premier weapons inventors in the world today. Smitty uses his "West Virgina-dumb-ol'-country-boy-shucks-and-shuffle" act to mask the fact that he was one of the best inventive brains to ever come out of M.I.T.

He is a relentless brawler and rule bender. He is a dead shot with most any weapon. It was Smitty that took a young Wynonna Earp under his wing when she was recruited by Black Badge. He has been her trainer, mentor, and father figure. He knows Wynonna better than anyone else, in both her skills and faults.

With some of the leftover finds from the 1947 Roswell Crash, Smitty has created some very useful and odd weapons for Wynonna. Smitty has top clearance for Area 51. Smitty is responsible for mounting a pair of bullhorns on the front of a stealth bomber that he has used on a few covert missions.

He's an expert on most all forms of the paranormal. Within the ranks of the Black Badge Division it's said he's tussled with the Skunk Ape in the Florida Everglades and rode the back of the Lake Champlain Monster like it was a rodeo bull.

Smitty favors lost cases of Grizzly Beer and women twenty years younger than himself.

Name: Holly Day

Height: 5 feet, 5 inches

Weight: 115 pounds

Age: Classified (Physically 25 years old)

Born: Classified

Holly Day is one of the cases of the paranormal world siding with the normal world. Holly Day is an immortal. Her past is one of the most classified files in the country and perhaps the world. Rumors abound of her being around since the days of cave people to her being the Princess of Atlantis. She has an exotic look about her that almost seems to be a mix of all cultures, making it hard to pinpoint any direct origin.

It is known that she was off the grid possibly for centuries, then in the early 1900s she was discovered by the first Black Badge agents in an underground vault where Area 51 now stands. She is hated, respected, and feared by other members of the Immortals Consortium. It's suspected that she may indeed be royalty from the first Atlantis family or even the "Eve" of all immortals. Even Holly doesn't know for sure. Her memory is still hazy on certain parts of her past from being in the vault. She does know how she affects other immortals, and is always ready to use that fear to get the job done.

Holly is quite happy to be a U.S. Marshal for the Black Badge Division, and they are more than happy to have her knowledge, power, and special abilities for tracking down paranormal fugitives. It's common knowledge within the division that Holly and Smitty have had on-and-off-again flings. She also enjoys teasing Smitty that he's "so much older" than she is when in reality they both know that is quite the opposite.

Holly is also Wynonna's closest friend in a world where she doesn't have many outside the job. Holly's special abilities include amplified strength and speed and understanding of the world since she has been in it so very long. There is no language she doesn't speak or understand and no culture that she can't blend into. Even today, Holly is still learning of some of her abilities and memories.

WYNONNA EARP SOURCE FILES

The Black Badge Division:

The Black Badge Unit is a division of the U.S. Marshal Covert Operations. The Black Badge Unit was created by President Theodore Roosevelt. He was the first president and government official to recognize the existence of the paranormal world and the rise in organized criminal activity within that underground society.

As the former police commissioner of New York City, Roosevelt first became aware of organized paranormal crime and began recruiting and building a division to combat this rising threat. Only then did he discover that the roots of organized paranormal crime had been embedded in the spine of America since the landing of the Pilgrims.

He also found out that not all in the paranormal world are criminals. He made it a point to find and recruit those in the paranormal society that shared his distaste for crime and corruption. He realized that there were Immortals, werewolves, vampires, warlocks, witches, and other paranormals that wanted to live law-biding lives and didn't crave the spotlight.

For every paranormal that wanted to lead a quiet life there were 10 that wanted it all. Money, items of material wealth, and—of course—power. Fighting paranormal crime is done on all levels: from robbery, drugs, alcohol, weapons, prostitution, rape, and murder to corporate and political corruption. Today in this modern world, paranormal crime has gone international, including the takeover of countries by terrorism.

In recent years it's been the goal of the Immortals to unite the nations and tribes of the paranormal into a more cohesive organization of crime and political power known as The Consortium. The Immortals are here for the long haul since they live forever (unless they have their head cut off and destroyed), and they are trying to get other paranormals to invest in the big picture, not only for themselves, but for their future generations.

The biggest problem for the Immortals is The Vampire Nation. The Vampire Nation hasn't warmed up to the idea of peace treaties, truces, division of power, and the "Can't we all just get along?" slogan of the Immortals. Their hatred of the Immortals runs too deep. The Vampire Nation has been using technology to try and discover a medical breakthrough by using the DNA and blood of Immortals to give vampires true immortality. To achieve this goal there has been many layers of deception and espionage between the two warring parties.

The Immortals are the "blue bloods" of the paranormal world, and have been for as long as anyone can remember. It is believed that the Immortals are descendants of Atlantis, the colony made up of extraterrestrials. It is believed that the Earth's atmosphere is what enabled the human-like extraterrestrials to live forever. The Vampire Nation has always resented the Immortals for having everything given to them on a silver platter. The Immortals have always looked down on the vampires as "back-door immortals" because of their distasteful drinking of blood to remain immortal.

In the paranormal world of crime, the drug Hemo is the most lucrative product. It's a plasma-based drug that can be consumed in liquid, pills, snorted, smoked, and injected. Each of the paranormal factions has their own designs of it based upon the key ingredient of non-paranormal human blood. Making humans not only targets, but also a commodity.

Wynonna Earp and The Black Badge Division have found that where you find Hemo, you find paranormals. The war on drugs just got really scary.

The rise of Hemo has surged greatly along the Mexican border with the savage Chupacabra faction importing Hemo at an alarming rate into the United States. With the import of Hemo rising, it also has increased the export of humans to Mexico as a source of blood in the Hemo labs known as "Pharms." Those working the Pharms are known as "Pharmers." The Chupacabra faction has also been dealing with the import of firearms from the United States to Mexico.

Closing down Pharms is another one of the main objectives of The Black Badge Division.

ART BY **SCOT EATON**

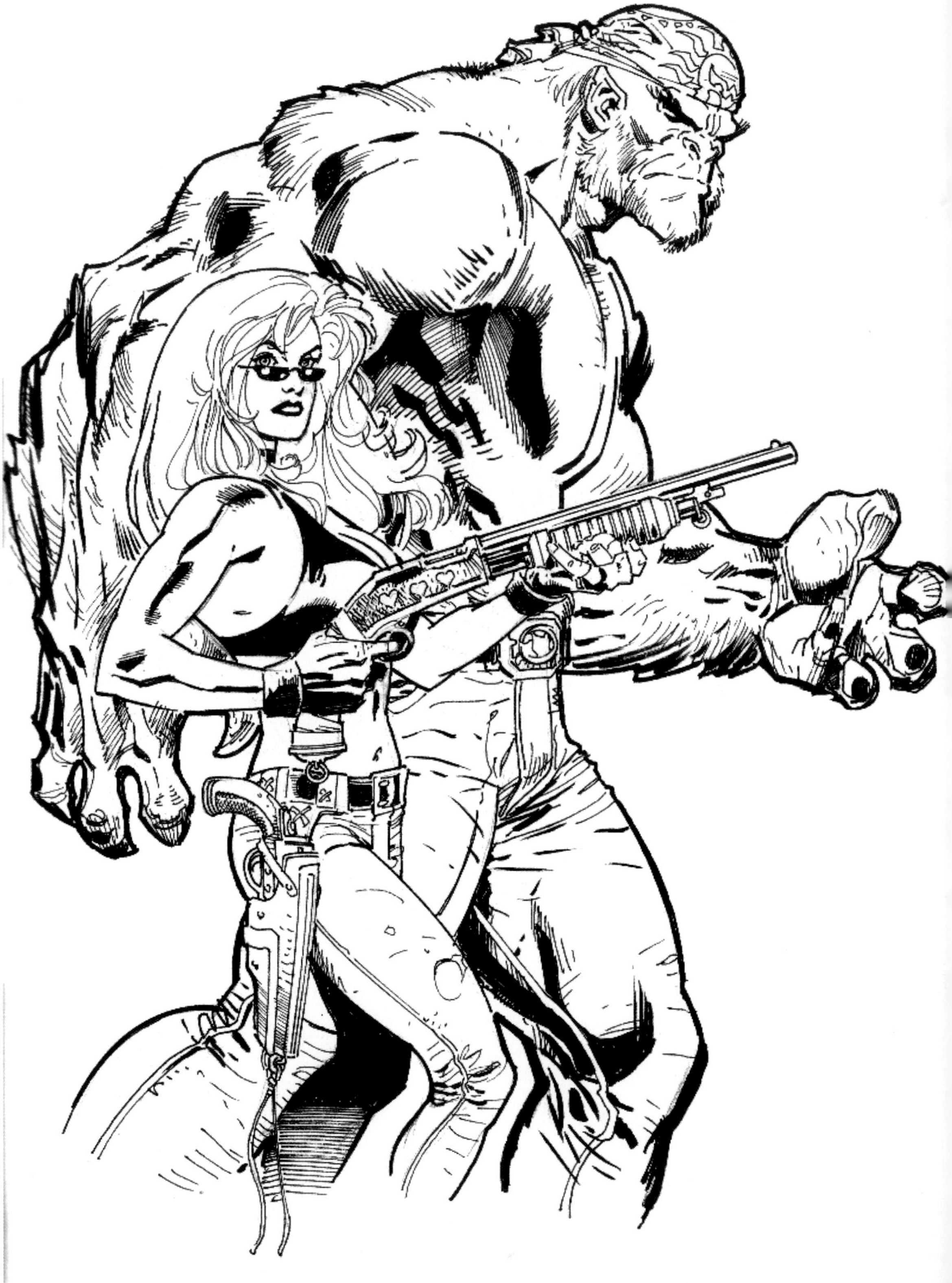

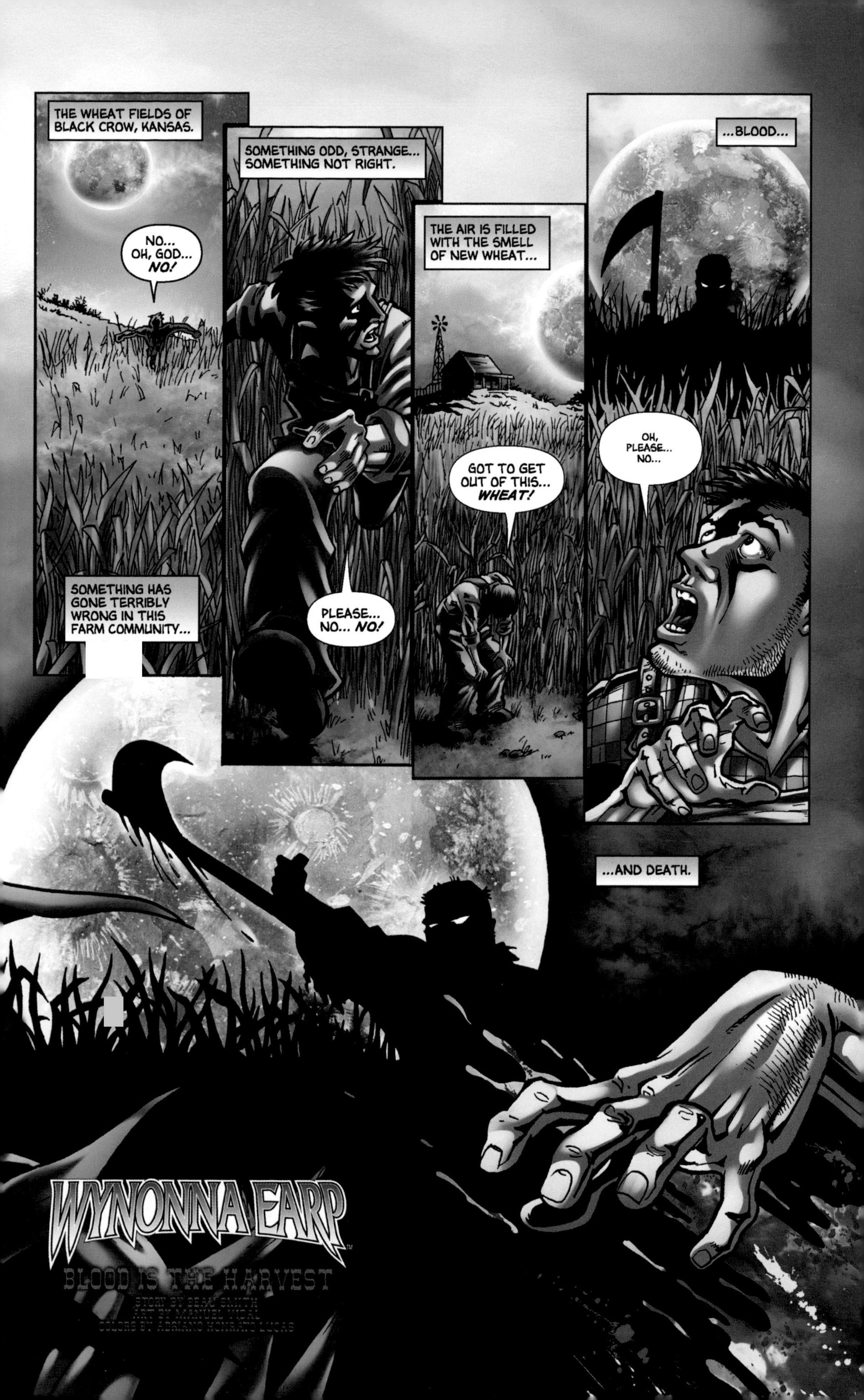
THE WHEAT FIELDS OF BLACK CROW, KANSAS.
NO... OH, GOD... NO!
SOMETHING HAS GONE TERRIBLY WRONG IN THIS FARM COMMUNITY...
SOMETHING ODD, STRANGE... SOMETHING NOT RIGHT.
PLEASE... NO... NO!
THE AIR IS FILLED WITH THE SMELL OF NEW WHEAT...
GOT TO GET OUT OF THIS... WHEAT!
...BLOOD...
OH, PLEASE... NO...
...AND DEATH.
WYNONNA EARP™
BLOOD IS THE HARVEST
STORY BY BEAU SMITH
ART BY MANUEL VIDAL
COLORS BY ADRIANO HONRATO LUCAS

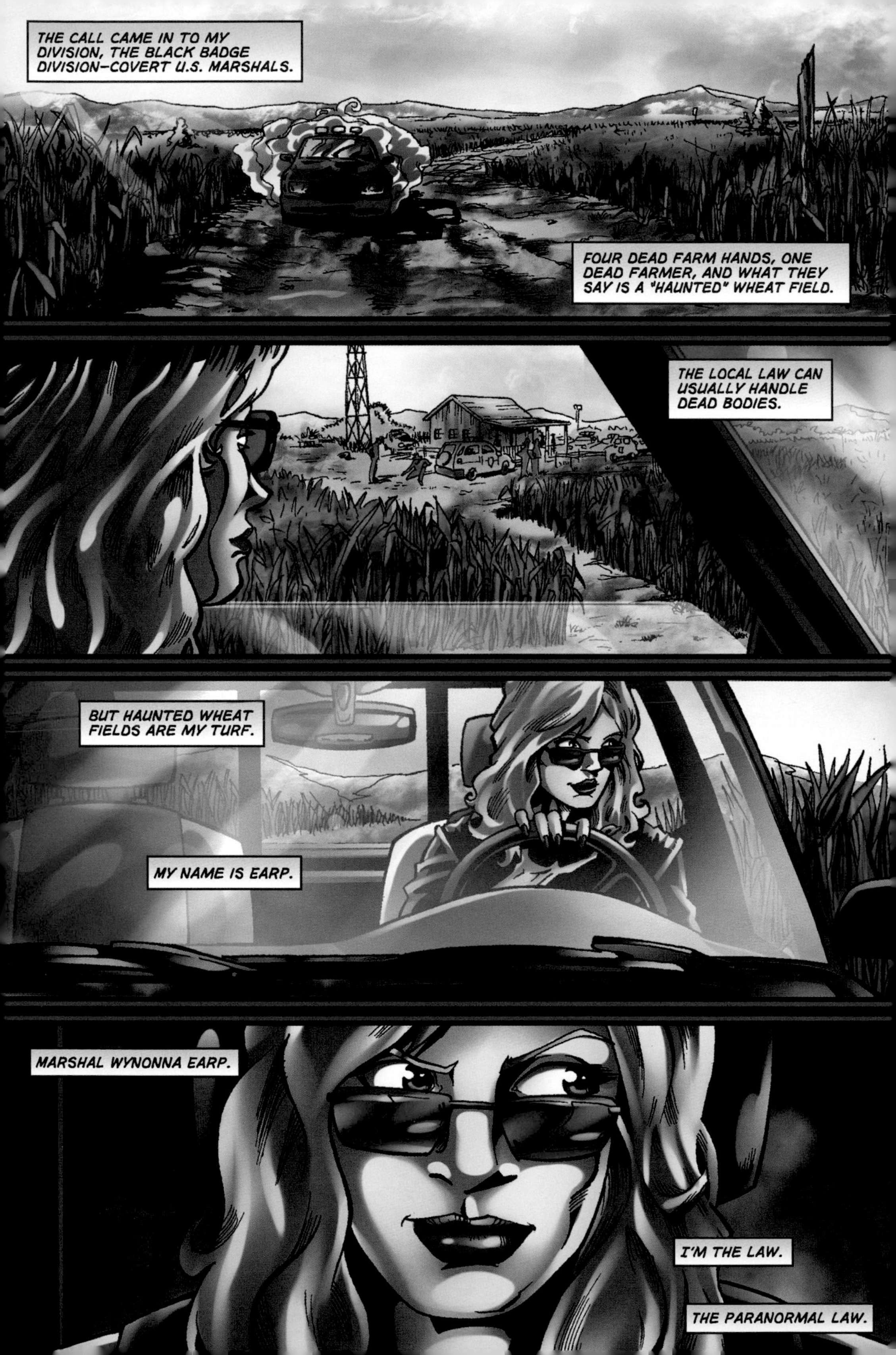
THE CALL CAME IN TO MY DIVISION, THE BLACK BADGE DIVISION–COVERT U.S. MARSHALS.
FOUR DEAD FARM HANDS, ONE DEAD FARMER, AND WHAT THEY SAY IS A "HAUNTED" WHEAT FIELD.
THE LOCAL LAW CAN USUALLY HANDLE DEAD BODIES.
BUT HAUNTED WHEAT FIELDS ARE MY TURF.
MY NAME IS EARP.
MARSHAL WYNONNA EARP.
I'M THE LAW.
THE PARANORMAL LAW.

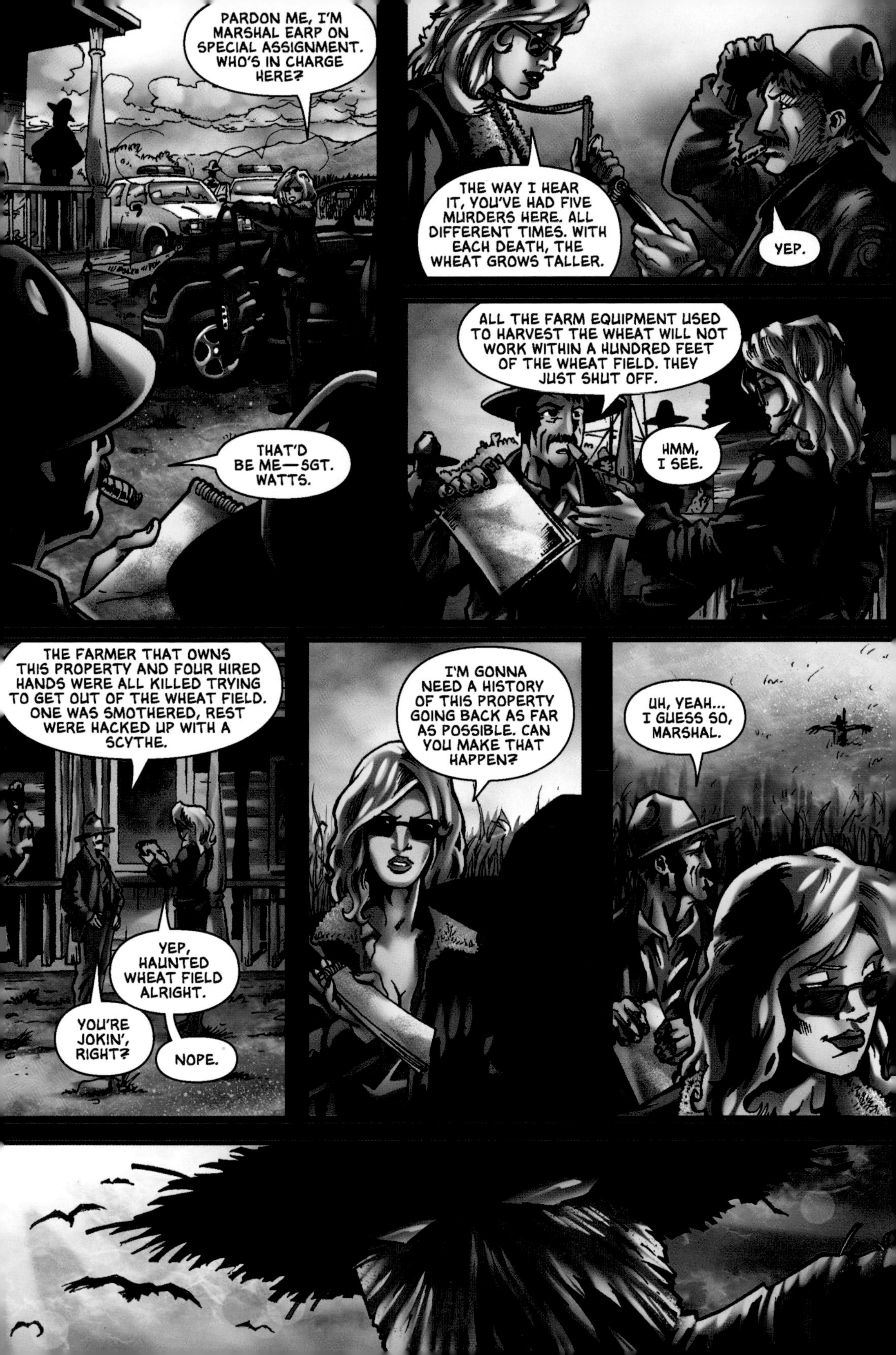
PARDON ME, I'M MARSHAL EARP ON SPECIAL ASSIGNMENT. WHO'S IN CHARGE HERE?
THAT'D BE ME—SGT. WATTS.
THE WAY I HEAR IT, YOU'VE HAD FIVE MURDERS HERE. ALL DIFFERENT TIMES. WITH EACH DEATH, THE WHEAT GROWS TALLER.
YEP.
ALL THE FARM EQUIPMENT USED TO HARVEST THE WHEAT WILL NOT WORK WITHIN A HUNDRED FEET OF THE WHEAT FIELD. THEY JUST SHUT OFF.
HMM, I SEE.
THE FARMER THAT OWNS THIS PROPERTY AND FOUR HIRED HANDS WERE ALL KILLED TRYING TO GET OUT OF THE WHEAT FIELD. ONE WAS SMOTHERED, REST WERE HACKED UP WITH A SCYTHE.
YEP, HAUNTED WHEAT FIELD ALRIGHT.
YOU'RE JOKIN', RIGHT?
NOPE.
I'M GONNA NEED A HISTORY OF THIS PROPERTY GOING BACK AS FAR AS POSSIBLE. CAN YOU MAKE THAT HAPPEN?
UH, YEAH... I GUESS SO, MARSHAL.

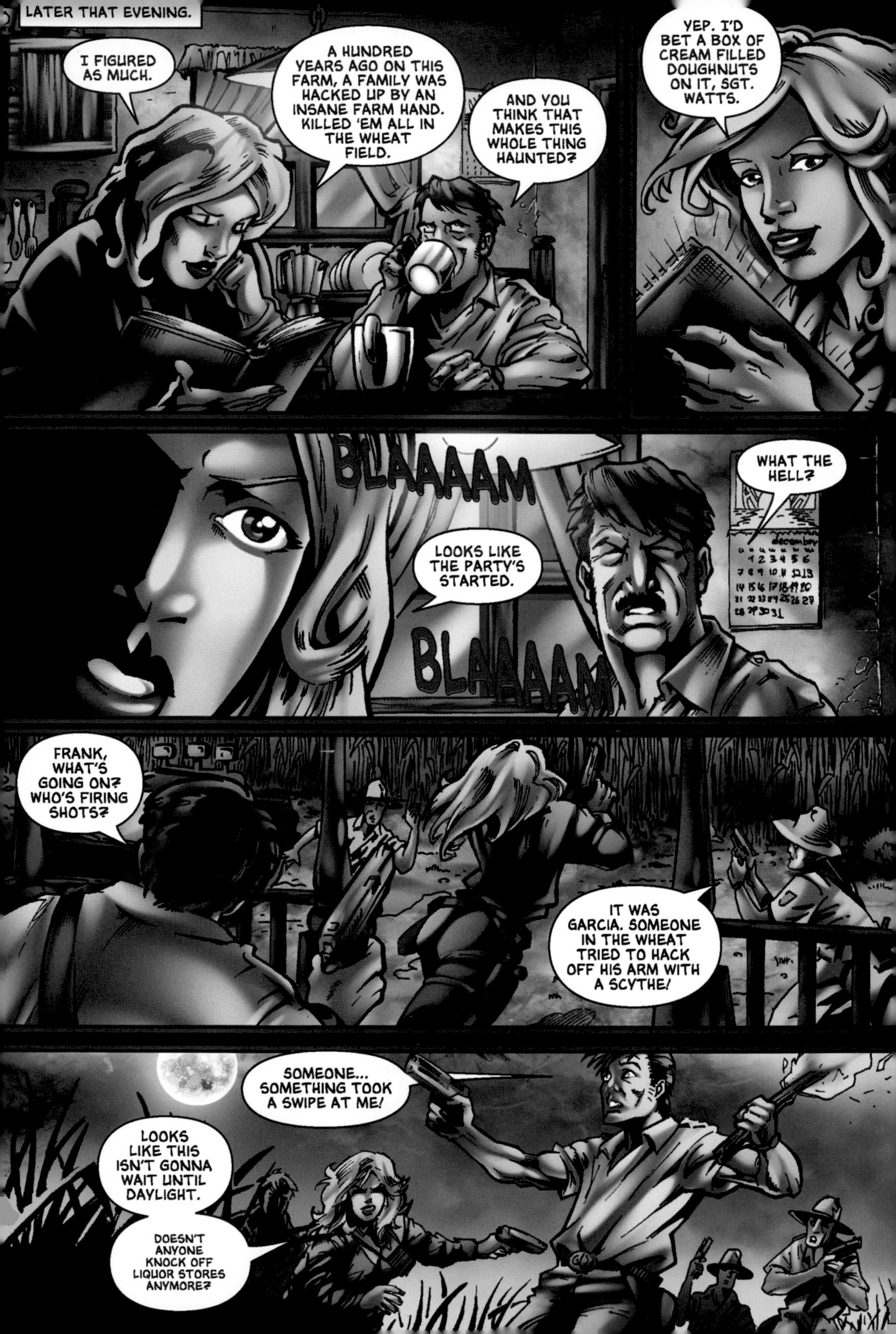
LATER THAT EVENING.
I FIGURED AS MUCH.
A HUNDRED YEARS AGO ON THIS FARM, A FAMILY WAS HACKED UP BY AN INSANE FARM HAND. KILLED 'EM ALL IN THE WHEAT FIELD.
AND YOU THINK THAT MAKES THIS WHOLE THING HAUNTED?
YEP. I'D BET A BOX OF CREAM FILLED DOUGHNUTS ON IT, SGT. WATTS.
BLAAAAM
WHAT THE HELL?
LOOKS LIKE THE PARTY'S STARTED.
BLAAAAM
FRANK, WHAT'S GOING ON? WHO'S FIRING SHOTS?
IT WAS GARCIA. SOMEONE IN THE WHEAT TRIED TO HACK OFF HIS ARM WITH A SCYTHE!
SOMEONE... SOMETHING TOOK A SWIPE AT ME!
LOOKS LIKE THIS ISN'T GONNA WAIT UNTIL DAYLIGHT.
DOESN'T ANYONE KNOCK OFF LIQUOR STORES ANYMORE?

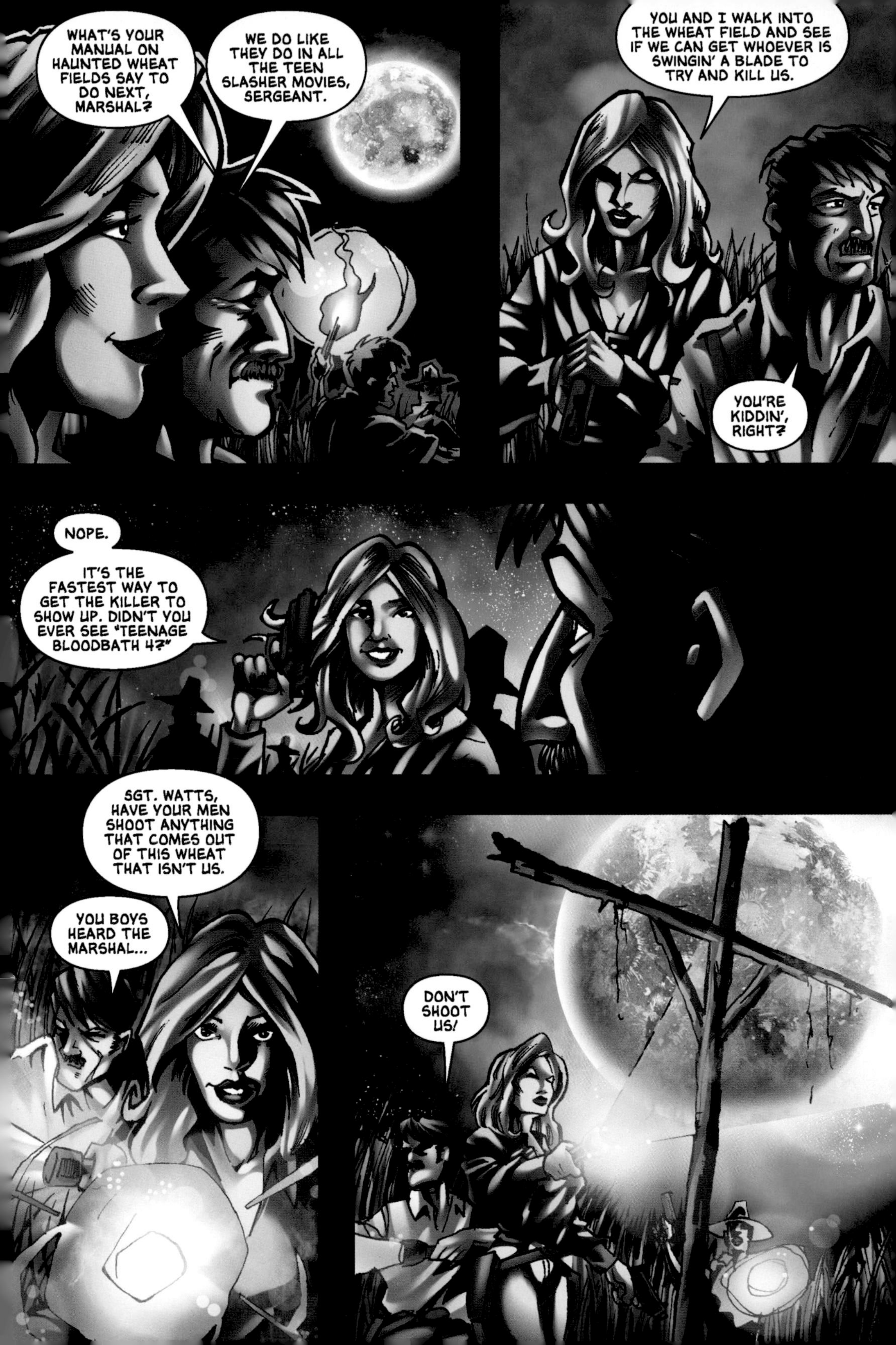
WHAT'S YOUR MANUAL ON HAUNTED WHEAT FIELDS SAY TO DO NEXT, MARSHAL?
WE DO LIKE THEY DO IN ALL THE TEEN SLASHER MOVIES, SERGEANT.
YOU AND I WALK INTO THE WHEAT FIELD AND SEE IF WE CAN GET WHOEVER IS SWINGIN' A BLADE TO TRY AND KILL US.
YOU'RE KIDDIN', RIGHT?
NOPE.
IT'S THE FASTEST WAY TO GET THE KILLER TO SHOW UP. DIDN'T YOU EVER SEE "TEENAGE BLOODBATH 4?"
SGT. WATTS, HAVE YOUR MEN SHOOT ANYTHING THAT COMES OUT OF THIS WHEAT THAT ISN'T US.
YOU BOYS HEARD THE MARSHAL...
DON'T SHOOT US!

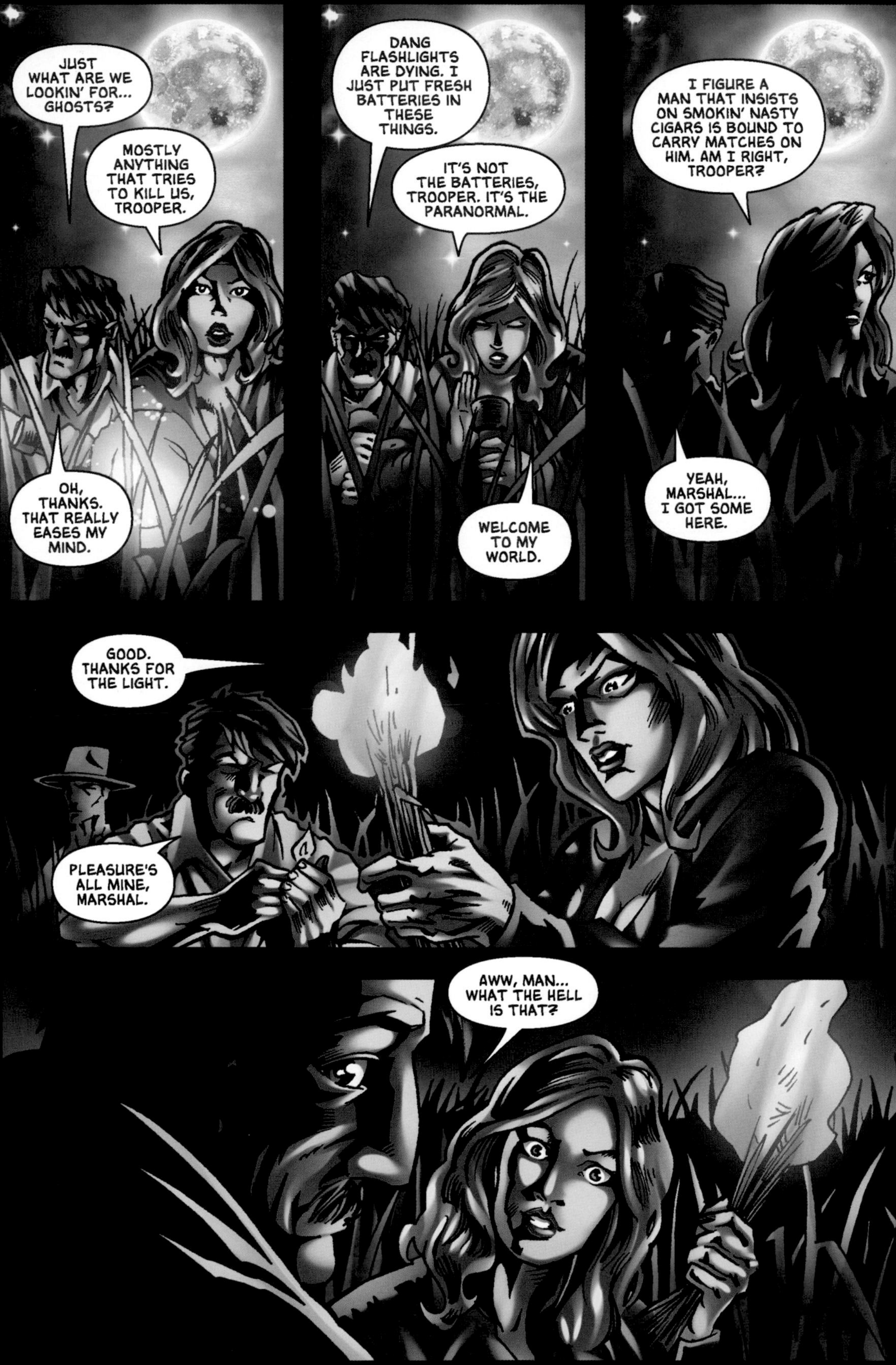
JUST WHAT ARE WE LOOKIN' FOR... GHOSTS?
MOSTLY ANYTHING THAT TRIES TO KILL US, TROOPER.
OH, THANKS. THAT REALLY EASES MY MIND.
DANG FLASHLIGHTS ARE DYING. I JUST PUT FRESH BATTERIES IN THESE THINGS.
IT'S NOT THE BATTERIES, TROOPER. IT'S THE PARANORMAL.
WELCOME TO MY WORLD.
I FIGURE A MAN THAT INSISTS ON SMOKIN' NASTY CIGARS IS BOUND TO CARRY MATCHES ON HIM. AM I RIGHT, TROOPER?
YEAH, MARSHAL... I GOT SOME HERE.
GOOD. THANKS FOR THE LIGHT.
PLEASURE'S ALL MINE, MARSHAL.
AWW, MAN... WHAT THE HELL IS THAT?

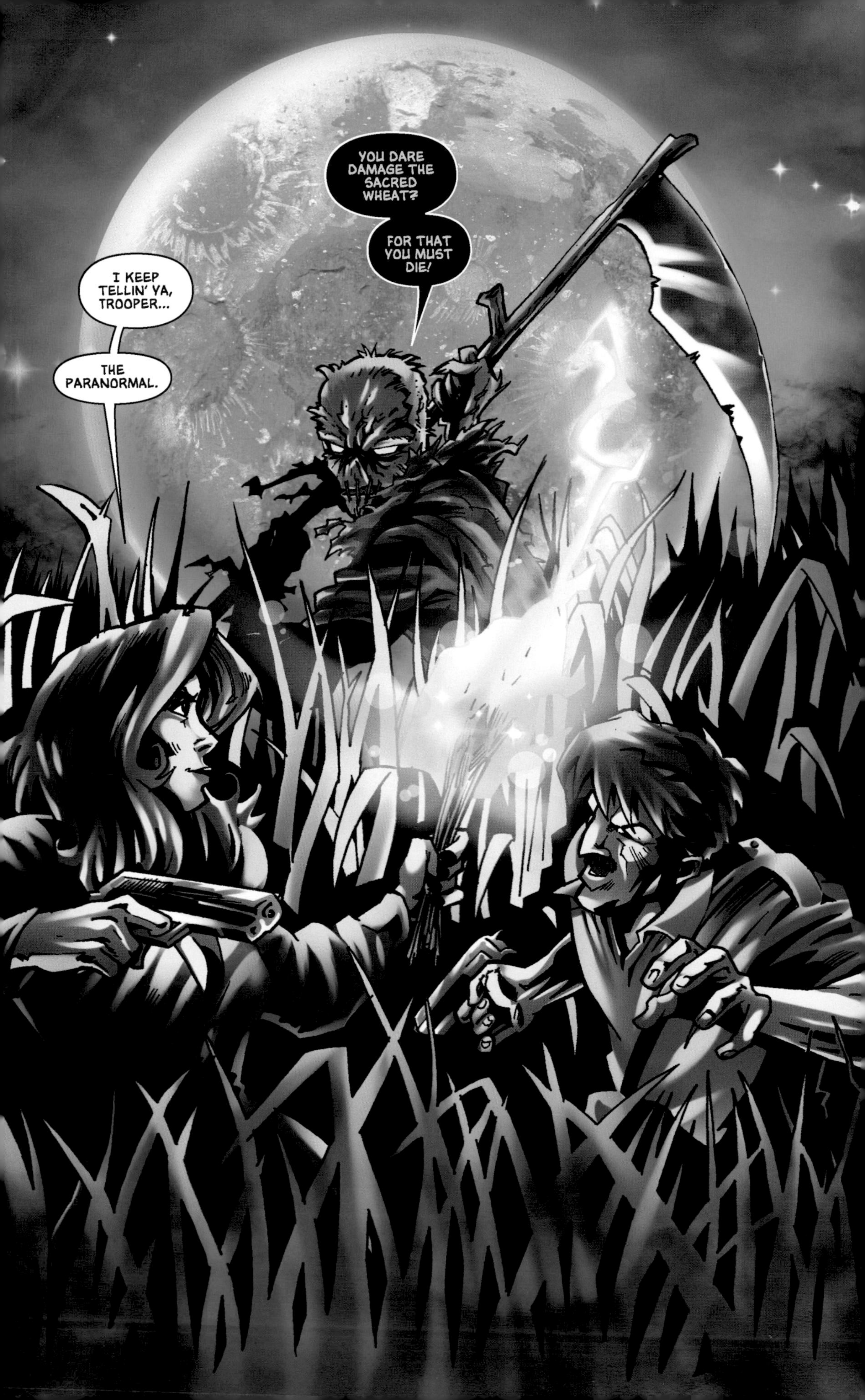
I KEEP TELLIN' YA, TROOPER...
THE PARANORMAL.
YOU DARE DAMAGE THE SACRED WHEAT?
FOR THAT YOU MUST DIE!

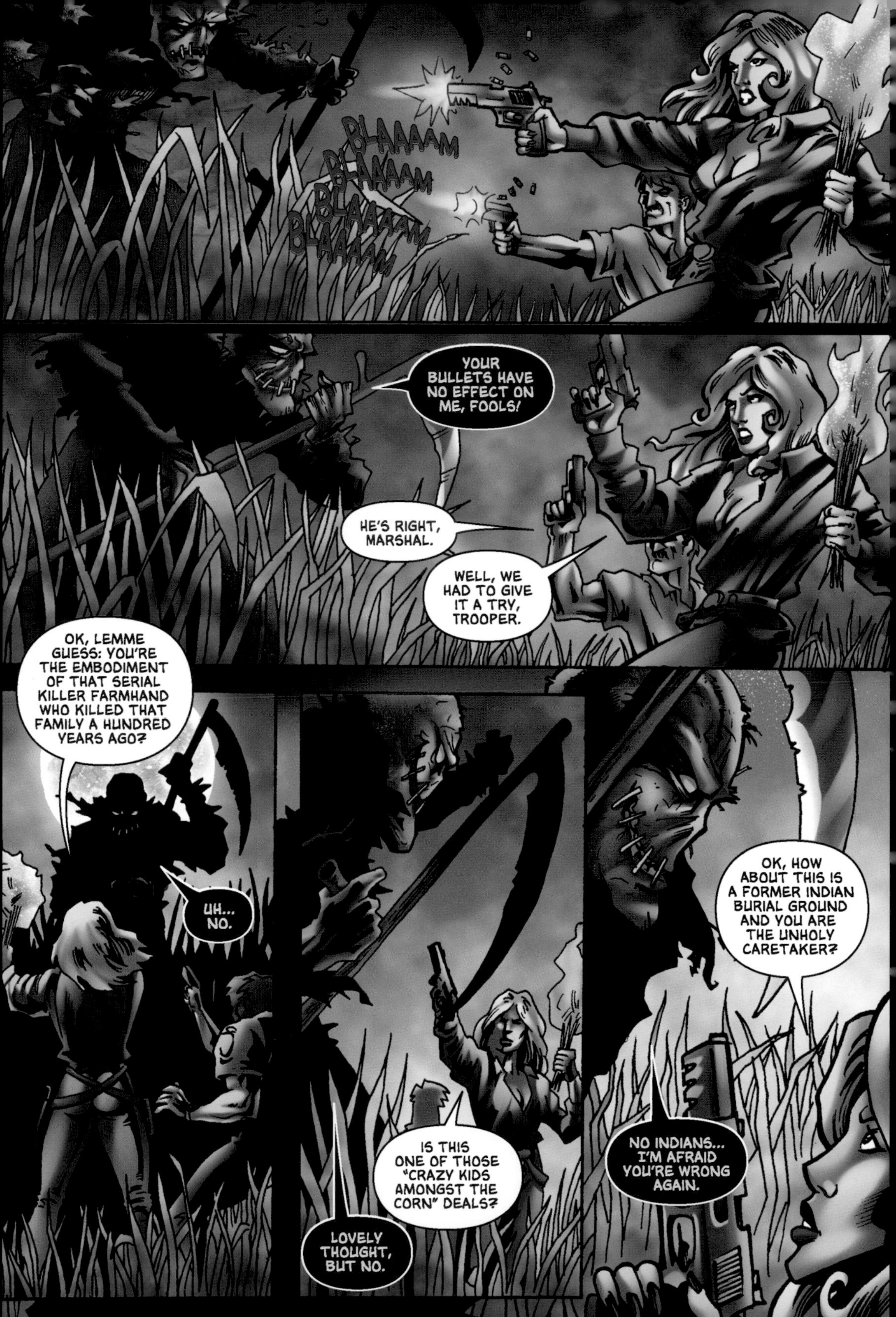
BLAAAAM
BLAAAAM
BLAAAAM
BLAAAAM
YOUR BULLETS HAVE NO EFFECT ON ME, FOOLS!
HE'S RIGHT, MARSHAL.
WELL, WE HAD TO GIVE IT A TRY, TROOPER.
OK, LEMME GUESS: YOU'RE THE EMBODIMENT OF THAT SERIAL KILLER FARMHAND WHO KILLED THAT FAMILY A HUNDRED YEARS AGO?
UH... NO.
IS THIS ONE OF THOSE "CRAZY KIDS AMONGST THE CORN" DEALS?
LOVELY THOUGHT, BUT NO.
OK, HOW ABOUT THIS IS A FORMER INDIAN BURIAL GROUND AND YOU ARE THE UNHOLY CARETAKER?
NO INDIANS... I'M AFRAID YOU'RE WRONG AGAIN.

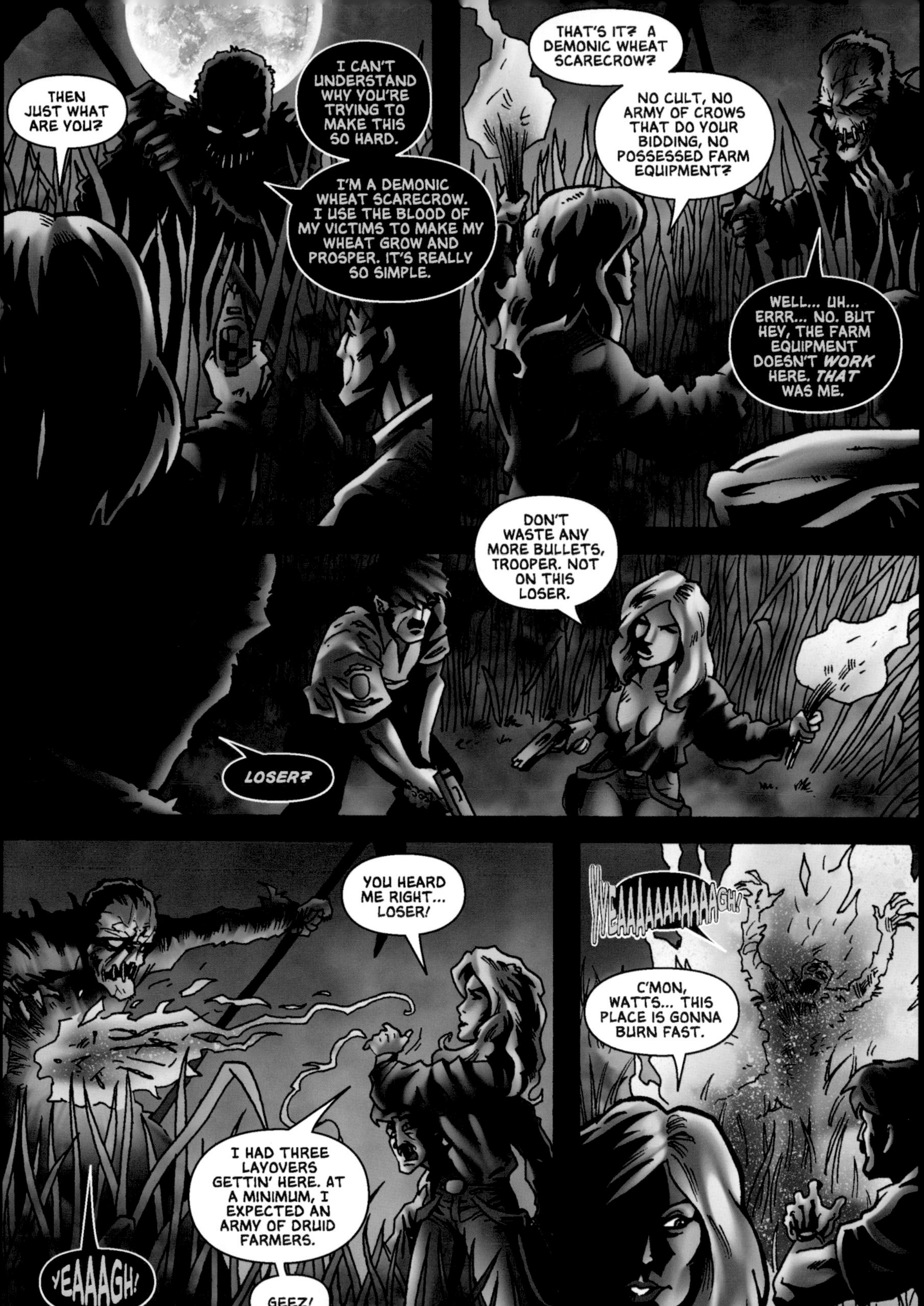
THEN JUST WHAT ARE YOU?
I CAN'T UNDERSTAND WHY YOU'RE TRYING TO MAKE THIS SO HARD.
I'M A DEMONIC WHEAT SCARECROW. I USE THE BLOOD OF MY VICTIMS TO MAKE MY WHEAT GROW AND PROSPER. IT'S REALLY SO SIMPLE.
THAT'S IT? A DEMONIC WHEAT SCARECROW?
NO CULT, NO ARMY OF CROWS THAT DO YOUR BIDDING, NO POSSESSED FARM EQUIPMENT?
WELL... UH... ERRR... NO. BUT HEY, THE FARM EQUIPMENT DOESN'T *WORK* HERE. *THAT* WAS ME.
DON'T WASTE ANY MORE BULLETS, TROOPER. NOT ON THIS LOSER.
LOSER?
YOU HEARD ME RIGHT... LOSER!
I HAD THREE LAYOVERS GETTIN' HERE. AT A MINIMUM, I EXPECTED AN ARMY OF DRUID FARMERS.
GEEZ!
YEAAAGH!
C'MON, WATTS... THIS PLACE IS GONNA BURN FAST.

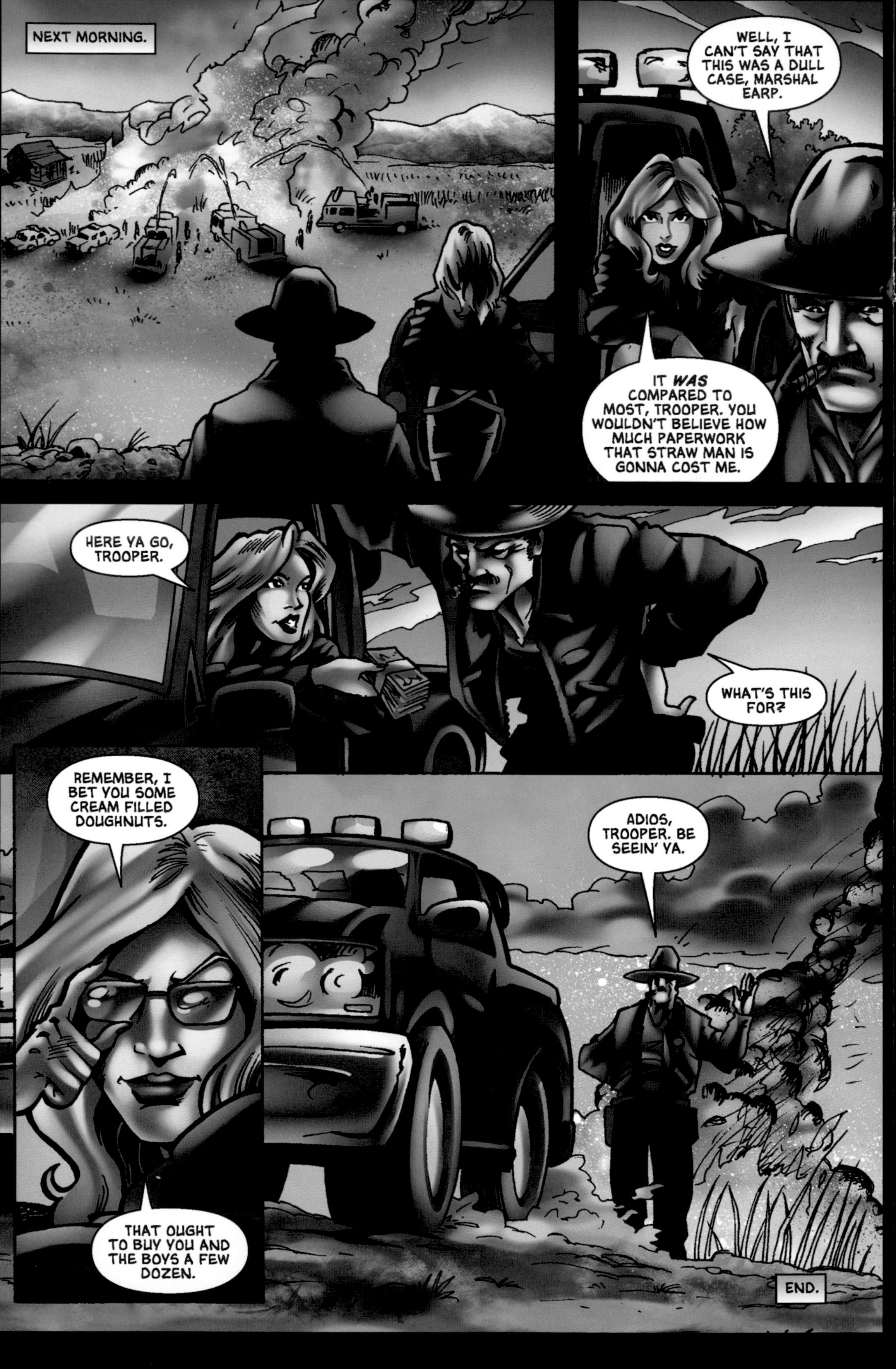
NEXT MORNING.
WELL, I CAN'T SAY THAT THIS WAS A DULL CASE, MARSHAL EARP.
IT *WAS* COMPARED TO MOST, TROOPER. YOU WOULDN'T BELIEVE HOW MUCH PAPERWORK THAT STRAW MAN IS GONNA COST ME.
HERE YA GO, TROOPER.
WHAT'S THIS FOR?
REMEMBER, I BET YOU SOME CREAM FILLED DOUGHNUTS.
THAT OUGHT TO BUY YOU AND THE BOYS A FEW DOZEN.
ADIOS, TROOPER. BE SEEIN' YA.
END.

ART BY **ENRIQUE VILLAGRAN**

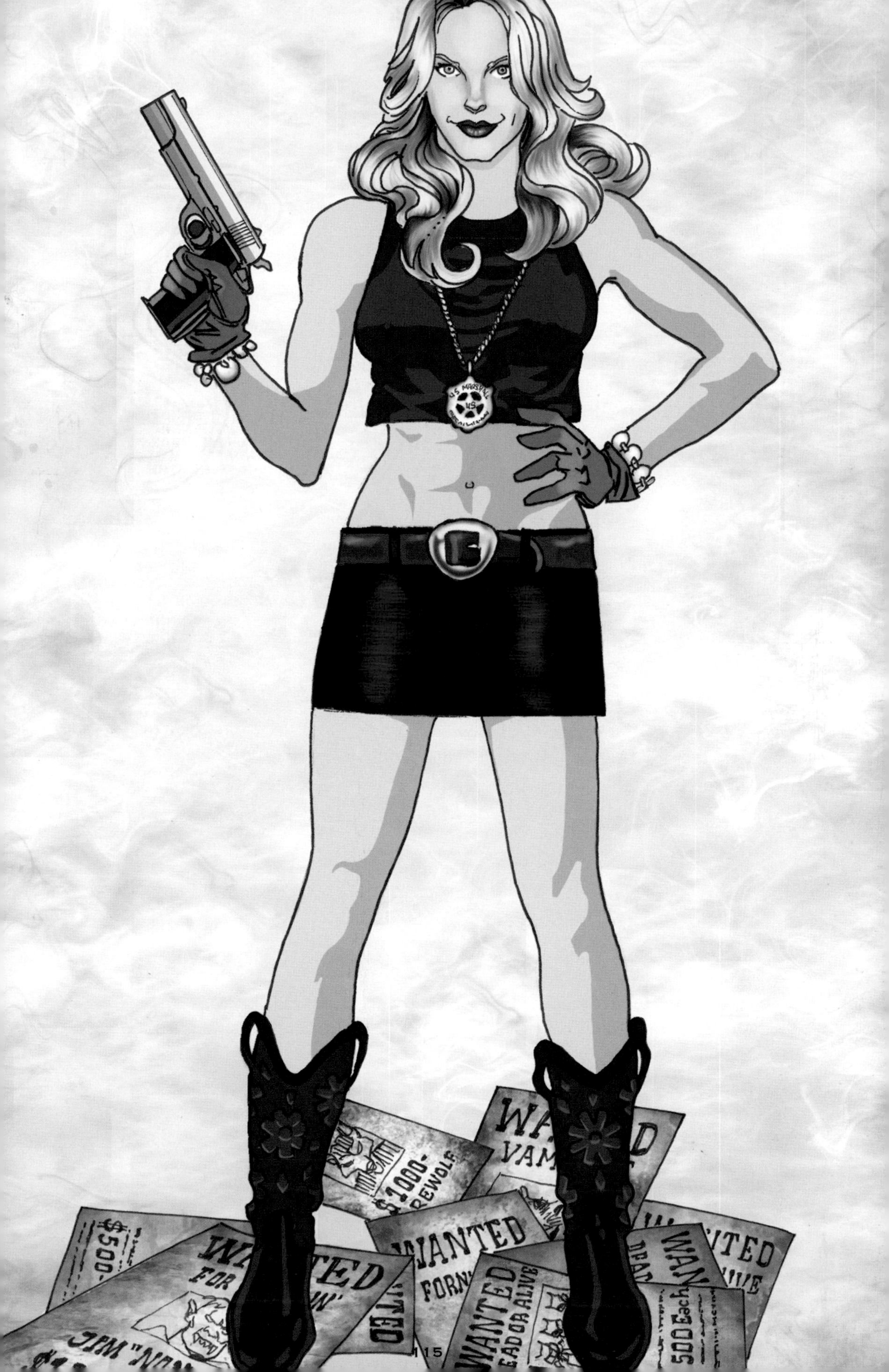
WANTED
$1000-
$500-
WANTED
DEAD OR ALIVE
500 Each

Beau Smith

WYNONNA EARP

THE YETI WARS

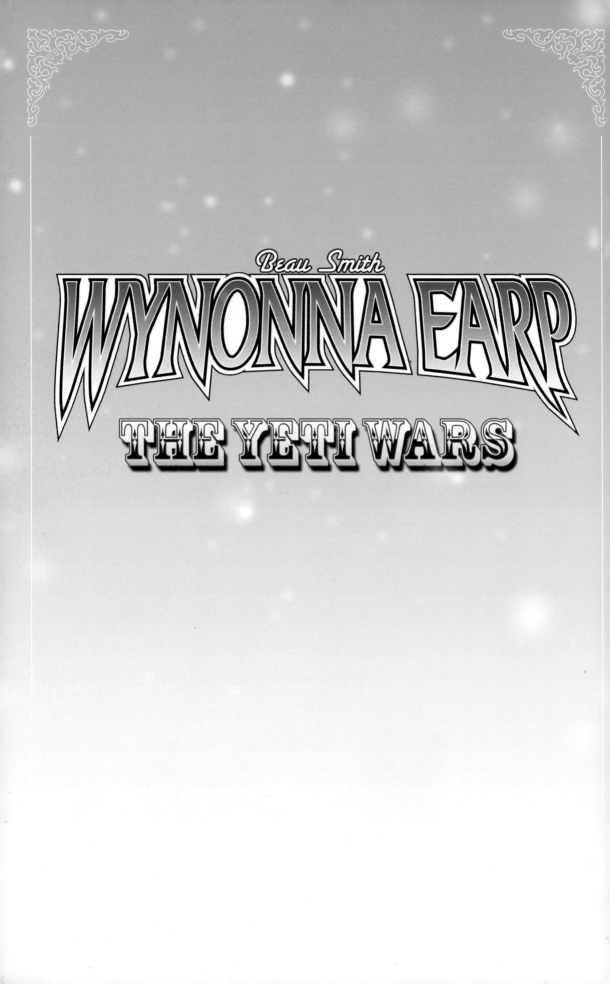